THE MULTICULTURAL PRISON

CLARENDON STUDIES IN CRIMINOLOGY

Published under the auspices of the Institute of Criminology, University of Cambridge; the Mannheim Centre, London School of Economics; and the Centre for Criminological Research, University of Oxford.

General Editor: Lucia Zedner
(University of Oxford)

EDITORS: MANUEL EISNER, ALISON LIEBLING, AND PER-OLOF WIKSTRÖM
(University of Cambridge)

ROBERT REINER, JILL PEAY, AND TIM NEWBURN
(London School of Economics)

IAN LOADER AND JULIAN ROBERTS
(University of Oxford)

RECENT TITLES IN THIS SERIES:

The Multicultural Prison

Ethnicity, Masculinity, and Social
Relations among Prisoners

CORETTA PHILLIPS

OXFORD
UNIVERSITY PRESS

OXFORD

UNIVERSITY PRESS

Great Clarendon Street, Oxford, OX2 6DP,
United Kingdom

Oxford University Press is a department of the University of Oxford.
It furthers the University's objective of excellence in research, scholarship,
and education by publishing worldwide. Oxford is a registered trade mark of
Oxford University Press in the UK and in certain other countries

First Edition published in 2012

Impression: 1

British Library Cataloguing in Publication Data

Data available

ISBN 978-0-19-969722-9

Printed in Great Britain by
CPI Group (UK) Ltd, Croydon, CR0 4YY

General Editor's Introduction

Clarendon Studies in Criminology aims to provide a forum for outstanding empirical and theoretical work in all aspects of criminology and criminal justice, broadly understood. The Editors welcome submissions from established scholars, as well as excellent PhD work. The *Series* was inaugurated in 1994, with Roger Hood as its first General Editor, following discussions between Oxford University Press and three criminology centres. It is edited under the auspices of these three centres: the Cambridge Institute of Criminology, the Mannheim Centre for Criminology at the London School of Economics, and the Centre for Criminology at the University of Oxford. Each supplies members of the Editorial Board and, in turn, the *Series* General Editor.

The Multicultural Prison revisits the theoretical models developed in classic writings on the sociology of prisons in the USA in the light of major changes in the life of the prison and transformations in racial politics. It opens with a fascinating analysis that draws together the influence of globalization, migration, and racial politics on the political economy of modern punishment. It then builds on the best traditions of prison ethnography to address the daily negotiation of race, culture, and masculinity in prison. *The Multicultural Prison* answers challenging questions about the interior life of the prison. Its major contribution is to explore and expose the racial and political dynamics of prison life.

A fine, disarmingly honest, and highly revealing methodological chapter—which should be compulsory reading for all those contemplating doing research in prisons—precedes three chapters that describe and analyse the resulting data. These explore the internal dynamics of prisoner society and address, in particular, the role of racial identities in social relations within prison. The findings derive from detailed observation and extended interviews with prisoners in two selected prisons undertaken by Coretta Phillips and researcher Rod Earle. The material presented in these chapters is rich, informative, and thought-provoking. It throws new light on prisoner identity, faith, and cultural practices, on inmate relations within prison, on the exercise of power, and the ways in which inmates evolve adaptive strategies. In so doing it makes a substantial contribution to our understanding of inmates' experiences of prison life and the ways in which ethnicity, culture, religion, and masculinity inform and affect inmates' interactions with one another and their ability to cope with the pains of imprisonment. The ever present menaces of violence and racism, vividly evidenced in the interview material and researcher observations, paints an upsetting picture of social relations that stands in tension with the vibrant multiculturalism, which is also shown to be a feature of prison life.

Coretta Phillips has a well-established and well-deserved reputation for her work in the field. She has published widely, especially in the field of ethnicity, race, and criminal justice. In addition to her extensive research and publications, she has long experience working within the Home Office as a researcher. She has also acted as consultant to the United Nations, the Home Office, Her Majesty's Prison Service, and as a member of the National Offender Management Service (NOMS) Independent Equalities Advisory Group. Her first-hand knowledge and practical experience combines with an evident talent for ethnography that has resulted in a sensitive and genuinely illuminating analysis.

This welcome addition to the *Clarendon Studies in Criminology Series* fills a significant gap in ethnographic studies of prison life and, as such, it is an important contribution to criminological knowledge. It will be of interest to criminology, law, and social policy students at undergraduate and postgraduate level, to prisons scholars and to those working within the prison service or on issues of race and ethnicity in the criminal justice system more generally.

The Editors welcome this new addition to the *Series*, not least because it exemplifies the ambitious mix of theoretical and empirical work for which the *Series* was originally founded.

Lucia Zedner
University of Oxford
September 2012

Preface

The topics researchers choose to study are almost always a 'combination of personal factors, disciplinary culture, and external forces in the broader political, social and economic climate' (Davies 1999: 27; Reiner 1998). This was certainly true in my case and explains well the genesis of the study on which this book is based. I had long been interested in understanding how the contemporary complexities of multiculture play out. Intellectually, my engagement with the discipline of social policy has always been more than a flirtation and I have remained wedded to the discipline's principal concerns of inequality and social justice, particularly with regard to race and class. Yet my professional interests have been dominated by criminological concerns in the field of ethnicity, race, and criminal justice. This study represents a coalescing of these interests in an examination of race, multiculture, and inequality in the social world of the prison.

Political debates have skirted the issues of race for many years but the prevailing political climate in England and Wales in the first decade of the 21st century has been far more attuned to questions of race and racism than any other in my lifetime. The political watershed was, of course, the Macpherson Report (1999) following the public inquiry into the Metropolitan Police Service's failed investigation of the racist murder of black teenager Stephen Lawrence in 1993. This brought a receptiveness to hearing about and challenging racism and religious discrimination in British society. In the prison the shocking racist murder of Zahid Mubarek by his white cell-mate Robert Stewart in Feltham Young Offenders' Institution in 2000 marked a fundamental shift towards mainstreaming race equality. The ensuing years have seen a self-critical inspection of the dynamics of race (and less so, faith) in prisons and other criminal justice institutions. The progressive changes in legislation through the Race Relations Amendment Act 2000 and later the Equalities Act 2010 cemented a range of protections in prisons as well as other public bodies, providing mechanisms for ensuring action against discrimination, victimization, and harassment.

At the same time there has been a faltering in the progress towards equality, as Britain has faced the implications of the racialized disturbances in several Northern towns in 2001, the horrific 9/11 and 7/7 bombings, and most recently the summer riots in England in summer 2011. These events have prompted a familiar yet unresolved colloquy about minority ethnic criminality, police-minority ethnic relations, and racism in the criminal justice system, but also, particularly with regard to the terrorist attacks by British Muslims, the meaning and nature of Britishness. Under the spotlight are issues of culture, heritage, national belonging, and community cohesion, coupled with fears of disunity, segregation, and exclusion. The nature of integration, or lack thereof, and the challenges of multiculture also rear their heads in a variety of cultural domains from celebrity TV shows[1] to national sporting events. At the time of writing, two incidents involving alleged racism in football have raised some interesting questions about the limits of multiculture in British society, amidst a perceptible climate of fear about the terms of racism in the 21st century. This is not without irony given that this is the year of the Olympic Games in London, and Britain's successful bid to host the games was at least partly on the back of 'an image of vibrancy based on harmonious multicultural diversity' (Falcous and Silk 2010: 170). Whether we look to England player and Chelsea football club captain, John Terry, who has been charged with the racist abuse of a black footballer, Anton Ferdinand, under section 28 of the Crime and Disorder Act 1998, or to the angry reaction of the Scottish Football Association to claims of racist abuse by Brazilian soccer striker Neymar in March 2011, it is abundantly clear that the stakes of race are high indeed.[2] Both Terry, who has vowed to clear his name, and the reaction of the Scottish FA Chairman to being wrongly accused of having racist fans, highlights how being identified as a racist is something to be staunchly defended against; it no longer holds any positive purchase in British social life.

[1] The BBC, for example, received complaints after press reports that *Strictly Come Dancing's* professional dancer Anton Du Beke had called his celebrity dance partner Laila Rouass a 'Paki' in an off-air exchange. The show's compère and national treasure, Bruce Forsyth, contributed to the furore by rejecting such complaints as humourless.

[2] Terry stands accused of calling opponent Anton Ferdinand, a 'fucking black cunt' in October 2011. Neymar cited a banana being thrown onto the pitch amidst racial chants from Scottish fans during a match with Brazil; a Metropolitan Police investigation found a German student to blame for the banana-throwing.

Collectively such issues strike at the heart of what it means to be a multicultural society in Britain in the 21st century. Fortuitously, I was able to explore these cross-disciplinary issues through the Economic and Social Research Council (ESRC)-funded *Identities and Social Action* research programme (2004–9) with an exclusive focus on a peculiar multicultural society—the late modern prison. As such, the book provides a lens through which to say something about the 'country's racial temperature' (Gilroy 2004: ix), in the context of the continued overrepresentation of minority ethnic individuals in the prison populations of England and Wales.

Elsewhere Rod Earle and I have argued that race, class, and gender always matter in prison (Phillips and Earle 2010), but this, of course, does not mean it is the most pressing issue facing prisons in the second decade of the 21st century. Other scholars have brilliantly illuminated critical concerns such as legitimacy, the old and new pains of imprisonment, overcrowding, and issues of human rights in prison. Perhaps disappointingly for some readers, that is not what this book is about and it only touches on these issues at the periphery.

Instead, the book begins in Chapter 1 by exploring the political economy of punishment and its racialized dimensions, historically and in the contemporary period. It establishes the context of disproportionality in prison populations based on class, gender, and race. The role of globalizing forces of production, consumption, and migration, on the nationality profile of Western prisons and the symbolic politics of racialized incarceration are also discussed. Moving from the macro level to the meso level, this chapter ends with an examination of the institutional environment of the prison. This dissects and ultimately rejects the tendency to extrapolate from the racial dystopia of US imprisonment but holds on to an engagement with the sociological models of prisoner identities and social relations originally formulated there. It situates this discussion within a sociological literature (with a hint of cultural studies) analysing the complex and shifting dynamics of race and ethnicity from modernity to late modernity in Europe. Chapter 2 also charts the development of 'race relations' policies in the prisons of England and Wales from the 1980s to their reconstitution as race equality and diversity policies in the 2000s. The backdrop to these changes has been the political and civic recognition of, and the claims-making by, minority ethnic groups. Chapter 3 outlines the mechanics of how the study was conducted in HM Rochester Young Offenders'

Institution and HMP Maidstone, including the study's epistemological foundations and its methodological approach.

Chapters 4, 5, and 6, are the book's empirical chapters, which draw heavily on the stories told by prisoners in interview, informally in conversations around the prison, or in actions directly observed. Collectively they help to delineate the significance of prisoners' ethnic, religious, and national identities for how prison life is lived. All capture a moment in time, beginning with Chapter 4 which explores these dimensions of prisoners' identities, informed by their biographies, the constraints of incarceration, and together their role in configuring social relations in these two male prisons. Chapter 5 continues this theme but with a more explicit look at masculinity inside, and how this is shaped and moulded by the hegemonic characteristics of being a man and being a prisoner, but also how this is mediated by class and spatial identities, race, ethnicity, age, faith, sexuality, and parental status. Chapter 6 engages with what we might call the underbelly of race equality, considering different configurations of racism, inequality, and discrimination from the standpoint of both minority ethnic and white prisoners. This entails exploring different manifestations of racial discrimination, including its covert forms, but also considering its absence in relationships between prisoners and prison officers. This chapter reviews the politics of white resentment and the displacement of whiteness in prisoner hierarchies, an issue increasingly coming to political attention outside the prison, because of fears about the electoral popularity of the British National Party. Chapter 7 provides a careful review of the book's major empirical findings, reconnecting the macro, meso, and micro levels of life in the multicultural prison. The chapter also reflects on the implication of the findings for the development of academic knowledge and understanding, particularly in the field of prison sociology. It emphasizes the value of looking outside criminology for some answers, as well as engaging with their policy relevance in the current era of coalition politics and austerity.

The final note sounded must be an optimistic one. The concluding chapter was written in January 2012, shortly after the belated conviction and imprisonment of two of Stephen Lawrence's racist murderers. The time between his death in April 1993 and January 2012 reminds us that racism is no longer silenced in the way it once was, and as the chapters of this book unfold, it will be evident that this transformation has been keenly felt within the confines of the multicultural prison.

Acknowledgements

This book is based on a study, *Ethnicity, Identity, and Social Relations in Prison* (RES-148-25-005), funded by the ESRC under its *Identities and Social Action* research programme. I am grateful for the support provided by the programme's director, Professor Margie Wetherell, and to other researchers on the programme, from whom I learned a lot. Much of the fieldwork for this study was carried out by Rod Earle, and he has been the most fantastic colleague to work with. My thinking has been enormously enriched by the data he produced and the reflections on it that we have discussed.

I owe a further debt of gratitude to the men whose stories feature in this book. Their willingness to talk, often at painful times in their lives, was humbling. I would like to thank John Wilson (Governor of HM Young Offenders' Institution Rochester) and Stephen O'Connell (Governor HMP Maidstone) for so generously facilitating access, office space, and being so open to research scrutiny. Dave Baker, Yolande Marcussen, Shafiq Ud Din, Mark Long, and Bob Shewan provided copious information and resources on the ground, and Chris Barnett-Page and Claire Cooper from the National Offender Management Service were extremely helpful in providing national data and policy information.

A huge thanks to Ben Bowling whose generosity and kindness, as an intellectual colleague and friend, knows no bounds. Alongside Ben, Rod, and Alison Liebling, I have received considerable support, guidance, and encouragement from the following people who have all helpfully and carefully commented on draft chapters: Claire Alexander, Mary Bosworth, Steve Garner, Loraine Gelsthorpe, and Colin Webster.

Tim Newburn, Niki Lacey, and Paul Rock offered invaluable advice when I was seeking funding for this project and when approaching Oxford University Press to publish this book. Together with other colleagues at the London School of Economics, I have learned the true meaning of collegiality. I would also like to thank Anne Brunton, Stan Cohen, David Downes, Frances Heidensohn, Robert Reiner, and Michael Shiner. As a prison novice, Ben Crewe and Alison Liebling were very kind in helping with my induction into the prison field, and I am indebted to them. Thanks also to Ernestina Coast, Alexandra Cox, Davinia Darch, Ivan Darch, Deb Drake, Kimmett Edgar, Alpa Parmar, Neena Samota, and Jo Staples.

My children Yasmin, Isaac, and Joseph have been very patient and understanding of my need to work at times when I should have been with them, although I think they enjoyed the extra time they got watching TV and playing on the Xbox! They have made me lots of cups of tea to chivvy me along, and despite being rather exasperated by just how long it took me to write Chapter 5, they have been enormously supportive! And, of course, I owe enduring thanks to my husband Jem.

Permissions

Chapter 4 includes material previously published in 'Negotiating Identities: Ethnicity and Social Relations in a Young Offenders' Institution', *Theoretical Criminology* 12(3): 313–31, as permitted by Sage Publications. Parts of Chapter 5 are reproduced also by permission of Sage Publications, from '"It Ain't Nothing Like America with the Blood and the Crips": Gang Presence in English Prisons' *Punishment and Society* 14(1): 51–68. Permission has been granted to include in Chapters 1 and 2 some material which appears in Bowling, Phillips, and Sheptycki, '"Race", Political Economy and the Coercive State', in Tim Newburn and Jill Peay (eds), *Policing: Politics, Culture and Control* (Oxford: Hart Publishing, 2012).

Contents

List of Abbreviations

BME   Black and Minority Ethnic
CRE   Commission for Racial Equality
EHRC   Equality and Human Rights Commission
HMIP   Her Majesty's Inspectorate of Prisons
HMP   Her Majesty's Prison
IEP   Incentive and Earned Privileges
MQPL   Measuring the Quality of Prison Life
MOJ   Ministry of Justice
NOMS   National Offender Management Service
ONS   Office for National Statistics
PSO   Prison Service Order
PSI   Prison Service Instruction
VPU   Vulnerable Prisoners Unit
YOI   Young Offenders' Institution

Profile of Interviewed Prisoners' Identities

HMYOI Rochester

Pseudonym	Ethnic Origin	Nationality	Religion
Abbott	White	British	Christian
Abdullah	Black African	Foreign—East African	Muslim
Ainsley	Black Caribbean	British	Christian
Alan	White	British	Christian
Alex	Black African	British	Christian
Alfie	White	British	Christian
Amjad	Arab	Foreign—Western Asia	Muslim
Aniq	Bangladeshi	British	Muslim
Ant	White	British	Christian
Anton	Black Caribbean	British	Christian
Arcel	Black African	Foreign—Central African	Christian
Arnold	White	British	Nil
Asad	Bangladeshi	British	Muslim
Austin	White	British	Nil
Bradley	Mixed Race	British	Muslim
Clinton	Black African	British	Christian
Dabir	Pakistani	British	Muslim
Dale	Black African	Foreign—West African	Christian
Darren	White	British	Nil
Daryl	White	British	Nil
Dexter	Black African	British	Christian
Dimitri	White Other	British	Nil
Egon	White	Foreign—Baltic state	Muslim
Frankie	White	British	Christian
Gavin	White	British	Nil
Glen	Mixed Race	British	Christian
Ian	Black African	British	Christian
Ianos	White	Foreign—Eastern European	Christian

Jack	White	British	Christian
Jackson	Black Caribbean	Caribbean Island	Christian
James	White	British	Christian
Jan	Black Caribbean	Foreign—Western European	Christian
Jason	White/Gypsy	British	Christian
Jonathan	White	British	Christian
Lennard	Mixed Race	British	Christian
Leon	White	British	Muslim
Luke	White	British	Nil
Manu	Black African	Foreign—Central African	Christian
Martin	White	British	Christian
Michael	White	British	Christian
Micky	White	British	Nil
Nazir	Black African	Foreign—East African	Muslim
Neal	Mixed Race	British	Christian
Pearce	White Traveller	Foreign—Irish	Christian
Philip	White	British	Christian
Preston	White	British	Nil
Rafael	Black African	British	Christian
Robert	White	British	Christian
Sacha	Black African	British	Christian
Sahmir	Asian	British	Muslim
Salif	Pakistani	British	Muslim
Saul	White	British	Christian
Sharif	Black Caribbean	British	Muslim
Simon	White	British	Christian
Stefan	White	Foreign—Baltic State	Christian
Stuart	White	British	Nil
Tony	Black Caribbean	British	Christian
Umar	Pakistani	Foreign—South Asian	Muslim
Varinder	Indian	British	Other
Yohan	Black African	British	Nil

(*continued*)

HMP Maidstone

Pseudonym	Ethnic Origin	Nationality	Religion
Aaron	Black Caribbean	British	Muslim
Adam	White	British	Christian
Anan	Black African	Foreign—East African	Christian
Andre	Black Caribbean	British	Christian
Andrew	Mixed Race	British	Christian
Anthony	White	British	Christian
Arthur	White	British	Christian
Barry	White	British	Nil
Bernard	White	British	Nil
Colin	White	British	Nil
Conor	White	Foreign—Irish	Christian
Daniel	Mixed Race	British	Christian
Dean	White	British	Nil
Dominic	Black Caribbean	British	Christian
Don	White	British	Christian
Douglas	White	British	Muslim
Gamal	White	Foreign—North African	Muslim
Gareth	White	British	Christian
Gary	Black African	Foreign—Southern African	Muslim
Jasper	White	British	Christian
Jed	White	British	Nil
Jimmy	White Romany	British	Christian
John	White	British	Nil
Larry	White	British	Nil
Lawrence	Black Caribbean	British	Christian
Lloyd	Black Caribbean	British	Christian
Mark	White Other	Foreign—Oceanian	Nil
Martel	White	Foreign—Western European	Christian
Matthew	White	British	Christian
Max	White	British	Nil
Melvin	Black African	British	Muslim
Monifa	Black African	Foreign—West African	Christian
Nathan	White	British	Nil
Paul	Black African	British	Muslim
Pete	White	British	Christian

Piers	White	British	Nil
Ralph	White	British	Nil
Ramiz	Bangladeshi	British	Muslim
Regan	Black Caribbean	British	Christian
Richard	Black Caribbean	British	Christian
Rufus	Black Caribbean	British	Muslim
Ruhi	Bangladeshi	British	Muslim
Sami	Arab	Foreign—Western Asia	Muslim
Samson	Black African	British	Other
Sandy	White	British	Christian
Shane	White	British	Christian
Tarun	Bangladeshi	British	Hindu
Tommy	White	Foreign—Irish	Christian
Vanni	White	Foreign—Southern European	Nil
Xavier	White	Foreign—Baltic state	Muslim

1
Enduring Trialities, Globalization, and Prison Populations

In the introduction to *Urban Outcasts*, Wacquant (2008) underlines the importance of historical and spatial specificity in analysing the interaction of class and state which produce each society's 'wretched of the city'. This echoes Fanon's (1963) *The Wretched of the Earth* in which he captures the powerful psychological effects of individual and collective humiliation and degradation wrought by the imperialist domination of Algeria by France. It is 'the wretched', of course, who are also most likely to be found in penal populations as Wacquant (2009a, 2009b) considers more fully in *Punishing the Poor* and *Prisons of Poverty*, about which more later. In the post-colonial moment, constituents of the late modern prison also typically include those who are marked by their subordinate race position. In this chapter and Chapter 2, I elucidate the structural mechanisms through which penal populations are formed and in the book's later chapters consider the implications of these broader social forces for social interaction among prisoners in Her Majesty's Young Offenders' Institution Rochester (hereafter 'Rochester') and Her Majesty's Prison Maidstone (hereafter 'Maidstone') in South East England.

Alongside the need for specificity, there is an attempt in this chapter and Chapter 2 to move between the macro-level social structure and the micro-level experience via the meso-level institutional frame. In essence, this means ensuring that the determinism of macro-level theorizing is challenged and its substance enriched by the voices of the 'wretched' while also incorporating the situating and contextualizing features of institutional structures and processes (Bosworth 1999; Lacey 2010; Phillips, C. 2011). Macro-level analyses of penality and crime control commonly address processes of social change in the move from modernity to late modernity. Recognizing the valuable insights of scholars such as

Garland, Simon, and Wacquant, this chapter emphasizes transformation and stasis in Western societies, noting that the well-trodden path from road[1] to prison is most often taken by those in socially and economically disadvantaged positions in the social structure based on their class, gender, and race. These enduring trialities are mapped out as defining features of today's 'society of captives' (Sykes 1958). A new feature is the late modern prison's ethnic, religious, and cultural diversity, created by the influx of marginalized migrants who are also vulnerable to incarceration.

The Well-trodden Path from Road to Prison: The Political Economy of Punishment

The historical work of Rusche and Kirchheimer (1939) situates punishment within societies' existing economic and social structures, decoupled from patterns of crime, and inextricably linked to patterns of labour. In times of labour shortage, as in the mercantile period, we see a scaling back of punishment and social support for the labouring classes. Conversely, when labour is abundant, as in the 19th century, prisoners were held in conditions of extreme overcrowding, with poor diets, and employed in torturous and pointless labour. This principle of lesser eligibility ensured a work ethic of compliance so that prison life was never favoured over life outside.

The substantive limitations identified by Garland (1990) in his critique of Rusche and Kirchheimer (1939) have been followed up in subsequent work which has more fully incorporated an ideological and political motive for punishment. Melossi, Parvarini, and Cousin (1977), for instance, claim that the prison produces docile proletarians for industrial society when labour supply is scarce, but when plentiful, the prison provides low levels of subsistence and reduces labour supply through rehabilitative imprisonment. Western and Beckett (1999) have demonstrated that this can

---

[1] This is the term used by prisoners to refer to outside society (see also Crewe 2009). Hallsworth and Silverstone (2009) suggest that it represents a liminal space in which young men can feel free from societal constraints (see also Young, T. 2009). For Earle (2011a), it has a wider symbolism linked to youthful transitions to adulthood, and a rather romanticized vision of adventure and freedom, but it also pertains to the harsh realities of urban life from which prison may ironically be a refuge.

disguise the political problem of unemployment as prisons contain the short-run effects of reducing labour supply by shaving 2 per cent off the unemployment figures in the United States (but nearer 8 per cent from the black unemployment figures), and there is an additional long-run effect as ex-prisoners struggle to re-enter the labour market with a criminal record.

De Giorgi's (2006) account of political economy and punishment is concerned with the recent transformation of the relations of production in the post-Fordist economy following the demise of manufacturing production. The effects of these macro-levels changes were felt by prisoners in this study. Nathan,[2] a prisoner at Maidstone, recalled the devastating impact of the economic and social dislocations wrought by the coal mine closures of the 1980s. He described dual-earner families losing two incomes (from pit work and administrative jobs in the industry) with little assistance to find alternative employment. Aside from the loss of individual and community identity that was part of 'pit life', Nathan talked of the area he lived being 'turned into a shit hole' where crime became an attractive alternative to unemployment. Adam,[3] also at Maidstone, told a similar story of the loss of shipbuilding in his home town, which, because of its coastal location, later became a major drug importation hub. In advanced post-industrial capitalist economies production is diffused, decentralized, and flexibly organized to produce a fragmented, feminized, and exploited labour force often made up of immigrants or those on the margins of society.

The 'new excluded' precariously positioned within the informal economy are subject to new strategies of social control[4]—CCTV surveillance, exclusion from gated communities, and mass containment. This incarceration of the poor, for De Giorgi (2006), has historically been, and continues to be, the leitmotiv of the prison. Importantly—and this reflects the key theme of stasis in this chapter—there is nothing new in this. Immigration centres represent a further spread of state incarceration where actuarial assessments help to manage and incapacitate the 'risk producers' in society, those artificially constructed as dangerous, deviant, or

---

[2] Of white British origin, no religion.
[3] Of white British, Christian origin.
[4] There is, of course, also the high-income workforce, engaged in virtual, 'immaterial' labour, which produces communication, social networks, and symbols which are commodified and marketized for consumption.

undeserving by the media, politicians, and the public (Fekete 2009). There is little solidarity between these groups and the next strata up of the labour force because of the former's depiction as deeply threatening. Fear-making justifies casting the carceral net around the poor, socially excluded, welfare-dependent, or those excluded because of their ethnicity or nationality.

The idea of the prison as a tool in the governance of social marginality can also, of course, be found in the work of Garland and Simon. Garland's (2001: 14) seminal work, *The Culture of Control*, notes the re-emergence of the prison as a 'seemingly indispensable pillar of contemporary social order', in the context of broad social, cultural, economic, and political changes. Yet the racialized nature of this ordering process is not central to his account, despite the pronounced 'blackening' of the prison populations in both the United States and the United Kingdom. Simon (2007) too suggests that the incapacitative zeal of the US state has the prison, divested of its correctional function, acting only as a social waste management facility containing the criminal's toxic behaviour (see also Mendieta 2007). But for Simon, mass imprisonment is a policy solution to the politics of middle-class insecurity which supports governance through crime, and not primarily a mechanism of racial domination, which has been at the heart of another body of scholarly work.

Racialized Incarceration

The political economy of punishment *through* race in the United States has its origins in the work of African American scholars such as W.E.B. Du Bois, whose contribution to criminology has only recently been acknowledged (Gabbidon, Greene, and Young 2001). Du Bois' (1901/2007) attention centred on the economic advantages to the state of the convict leasing system. An abusive and brutalizing form of labour supply in which black convicts did building, mining, logging, and agricultural labour produced a profitable US income of $48,000 in 1890. The state who 'deliberately multiplied' the Negro criminal population through the excessive punishment of black convicts was referred to by Du Bois (1901/2007: 120) as a 'dealer in crime'.

Angela Davis' (2003: 25; 2005) contemporary account similarly talks of the US prison-industrial complex as concealing 'congealed forms of anti-black racism' as punishment is meted out, obscured by the mask of a colour-blind justice system. The mass incarceration of African Americans constitutes state-ritualized violence, legitimized by a normative racial contract which unquestioningly accepts domination of, and harm against, racial minorities. The 'imprisonment binge' results from a failure of state welfare policies to address entrenched social problems linked to poor housing, education, and health, and it upholds private profit through prison expansion and supports black disenfranchisement.

The themes of a neoliberal shrinking of welfare entrenching disadvantage and criminality at a time of labour surplus, a criminal justice system systematically excluding racial minorities through mass incarceration, and legitimized by a punitive 'law and order' rhetoric, are present in the work of many scholars. Goldberg (2000: 218), for example, refers to the 'late-modern racially fashioned regimes' of residential segregation and prison containment, while M. Alexander (2010) talks of 'racial caste-making' as African Americans are controlled through mass incarceration, and on release are often denied the right to vote, excluded from juries, and denied employment, housing, and welfare assistance, as part of a permanently inferior undercaste, trapped in a 'closed circuit of perpetual marginality' (Alexander, M. 2010: 191).[5]

The work of Loïc Wacquant

Sidestepping the narrow confines of the 'race and crime' debate,[6] Wacquant's (2001) argument is that the prison, like its peculiar institutional predecessors (slavery, the Jim Crow socio-legal regime,[7] and the pre-civil rights ghetto) has been enlarged to physically, socially, and symbolically exclude the unskilled male African American population not engaged in the secondary labour market. Many of these prisoners, Wacquant notes, grew up in disrupted families, living in social housing, where family criminality, violence,

[5] Facing little resistance from the African American civil rights community and political leadership who have been surprisingly quiet about the 'disappearance' of black men from their communities.

[6] This centrally examines whether the over-representation of minority ethnic groups in prison is the result of their elevated rates of offending or discrimination in the criminal justice process.

[7] Jim Crow refers to a system of formal laws post-slavery and pre-civil rights which maintained effective racial segregation and the inferior treatment of African Americans in public and social life.

and abuse occurred. Similar biographical histories were recorded among Rochester and Maidstone prisoners of all ethnicities illustrating their anguished, dislocated pre-prison lives, in which severe educational and economic disadvantage was experienced, as well as poor physical and mental health (Social Exclusion Unit 2002; Stewart 2008). Simon,[8] a young prisoner at Rochester, described his placement in foster care and his regular absconding as he sought to redevelop a relationship with his disinterested father and mother who abandoned him when they started new relationships. Dean,[9] a Maidstone prisoner, talked of a father and brother who had been in prison. Lawrence's[10] account was of a 'being broughten up with a belt' by his dad, a belt which hung in the front room of his house, used against him and his brothers unless his mother intervened and took the lashes for them. Other prisoners portrayed their neighbourhoods as being rife with crime—drug dealing, robbery, burglary, and gang violence; these were the areas into which they were socialized, felt trapped by, and often wanted to avoid on completion of their sentences. As Bradley, a Rochester prisoner, put it:

… I shouldn't have been on road I should have just been to college … like I've come from [urban area in East London], you know what I'm saying, I've known what drugs were from the age of like five, six … that's what got me into selling it.…(Bradley, mixed race British, Muslim)

Wacquant (2001) identifies a 'deadly symbiosis' between the prison and the new 'hyperghetto' which function in similar ways, an idea that resonates with Wyclef Jean's (2002) song *Message to the Streets*, in which a radio DJ tells his audience 'you can do the time or let the time do you, doesn't matter where you bunk, the jail or the projects, they're all vertical prisons'. The racialized underclass found in penal populations comes from the 'hyperghetto', which, unlike its pre-civil rights predecessor, has lost its middle-class, African American social and institutional buffer to public sector professions and political office (Wilson, W. J. 1987).

Reflecting post-Fordist economics of deindustrialization, labour informalization, and service industry suburbanization, the Chicago hyperghetto operates as a dumping ground for the economically surplus and deeply poor (Wacquant 2008). Shorn of its infrastruc-

---

[8]   Of white British, Christian origin.
[9]   Of white British origin, no religion.
[10]   Of black Caribbean British, Christian origin, at Maidstone.

ture of business, religious, political, and leisure institutions, it is characterized by rigid racial segregation and grinding poverty. Moreover, the hyperghetto's institutions (schools, welfare offices, housing projects) bear the hallmarks of custodial institutions with militarized security measures and checks part of their social architecture (Wacquant 2001); what Davis (2003: 41) calls 'prep schools for prison'. Social housing is in a state of chronic disrepair, and other health and public services have been severely depleted as the charitable state has been rolled back. For poor women, welfare benefit levels have dropped, and eligibility criteria have been tightened with bureaucratic administration and greater surveillance of recipients, many of whom must now submit to coercive workfare. It is noteworthy that Wacquant's (2009a: 70) latest work also recognizes that prison containment of the 'human rejects of the market' include many who are white.

The climate of the hyperghetto is one of economic insecurity as residents try odd-jobbing or hustling to maintain a marginal but precarious escape from absolute poverty. Predatory crime, drug dealing, and male violence which often proves fatal is common (Wacquant 2009a). The experience of the character Bubbles in HBO's *The Wire* exemplifies the limited range of degraded economic options available in the hyperghetto. Homeless, walking the West Baltimore streets during the day with his belongings in a shopping trolley, he hustles, scams, and steals drugs and needles from an ambulance, whilst living out drug-hazed nights in abandoned houses.

The neoliberal state controls economically marginalized and racialized men through penal supervision and incarceration. This disciplining of the poor facilitates their movement into inferior, peripheral jobs in the secondary labour market, operating as a mechanism of statecraft, reinforcing state authority and extricating the state from responsibility for poverty wrought by neoliberal economics and politics. Wacquant's work suggests that the state does not just have materialist ambitions, however. The exclusionary nature of incarceration allows for the confinement of racialized aliens—forever inassimilable to the nation's sense of itself as the state engages in what Wacquant (2001: 98) refers to as 'social and moral excommunication'. Echoing Goldberg's (2002) claims for modern racial state configurations which position the 'not white' population as 'anxiety-promoting threat or surplus', Wacquant sees the carceral institution and the associated hyperghetto as a means to separate the inferior, racialized underclass from white society. The structural-functional equivalence of the hyperghetto and the prison operates as race-making 'caste containment' as both offer a logic of depoliticized, racialized control which is furthered by publicly acceptable, repressive law and order policies.

That the prison serves a disciplinary as well as a political function is, of course, not a new idea. Foucault's (1975) genealogy incorporates elements of a traditional structuralist analysis when he suggests that the prison's failure in terms of recidivism and harm is actually its covert success. The prisoner is effectively primed to reoffend when he leaves prison, having engaged in economically meaningless work inside and lived within a criminal milieu which, together with the stigma and exclusionary nature of an ex-convict status and continued police surveillance, ensures continued delinquency. The success of the prison, despite its objective failings, is to fabricate delinquency of a kind which is not politically or economically problematic (or only among its socially subordinate, lower-strata victims) but which can fuel continued state surveillance and the exercise of disciplinary power through the police initially and later statisticians and sociologists. In this way the law-abiding seek state protection from law-breakers, encouraging penal solutions in which the prison is centre stage.

There is much insight in Wacquant's work. He provides a powerful, eloquent, and damning exposition of the structural forces that bear on the 'wretched' in the Chicago hyperghetto, and which, as ever, reproduce the trialities of class, gender, and race which define penal populations in the United States and elsewhere. However, Wacquant's (2009a: 197) claim that 'carceral affirmative action' was the 'main impetus' for penal expansion is the most profound and also the most controversial. Surprisingly, this argument has rarely surfaced in the critiques of Wacquant's work (but see Daems 2008). Possibly this is because Wacquant himself also effectively underplays this by laying the blame of hyperincarceration at the door of neoliberalism rather than racial domination per se. For the latter explanation to be convincing, there is a need to explain the varying black–white state incarceration ratios documented by Mauer and King (2007). These range from a high of 14:1 in Iowa and 13:1 in Vermont to 2:1 in Hawaii and 3:1 in Georgia, with the leading ratios highest in the states of the Northeast and Midwest (see also Newburn 2010). Such data do not sit easily within the penal logic of racialized hyperincarceration when the lowest rates of racial disproportionality can be found in some Southern states (such as Georgia, Mississippi, and Alabama) where ideologies of white racial supremacy were at their apogee well into the last century.

It is here that Wacquant's analysis would be enriched by a meso-level institutional account linking the macro- and micro-level propositions, a point also raised in Lacey's (2010) critique of Wacquant's ideas in *Punishing the Poor* and *Prisons of Poverty* (see also Jones 2010). The institutional dimensions of how state agents directly and indirectly contribute in their everyday practices to the massive over-representation of black men in prison (see Walker, Spohn, and DeLone 2004) needs to be brought together with macro-level insights of the role of neoliberal discourses, to uncover the precise causal mechanisms and mediating processes which explicate the expulsion of the black body from the state's care. This is critical to knowing whether racial minorities are the deliberate, targeted victims of the new penal hegemony or whether they are neoliberal collateral damage, there simply as socially marginal 'urban outcasts'. Wacquant, like Davis and Alexander, largely suggests the former, but the mechanism of statecraft which leads to this new structural formulation of *racialized* containment is not as well delineated as it could be.

Some indication of this is implicit in Wacquant's (2008) comparative study of France's Red Belt. Resembling the American hyperghetto, but geographically smaller, the French banlieues, Wacquant maintains, are economically impoverished, youthful, stigmatized, and whilst depopulating, still including diverse populations of migrants and minorities. Significantly they are still supported by welfare, educational, and cultural institutions, and do not exhibit the unparalleled physical depletion and political abandonment of the US hyperghetto. The banlieues are not ethnically homogenous as in Chicago. Nor do they experience the levels of homicidal violence that is found in the violent street world of Chicago's South Side.

For Wacquant (2008) in these French 'pluri-ethnic zones' marginality is produced first and foremost through class, but at least in the case of migrants, marginality does not appear to be a fixed structural position. Wacquant suggests that social mobility can occur when economic integration is under way—the essence of the spatial assimilation model of ethnic settlement (Massey 1985). He also identifies a series of occupational and educational indicators which are suggestive of progression, which extend to cultural

integration, interracial intimate relationships, and an urban conviviality not dissimilar from that described by Gilroy (2004) in
Britain, and which are a central focus of this book.

Applying the multiple strands of the Wacquantian thesis to the
specific context of England is challenging and may even seem inappropriate. Yet Wacquant (2009a) rightly identifies some similarities
in the liberal market states of the United Kingdom and the United
States which are seen as key ingredients in the social marginality–
extreme penality nexus. Post-Fordist economics, welfare state
retrenchment, and widening inequalities in income and wealth are
powerful determinants of social marginality, and their presence in
the United Kingdom has been clearly observed (Hills et al. 2010),
although a careful analysis of the interweaving impact of such
processes in a racialized political economy remains to be written[11]
(but see Reiner, 2007). Even applying Wacquant's French case study
to Britain, it is still easy to quibble with some of Wacquant's claims.
There is ample European evidence, for example, that stratifying
processes mediated through race and class continue to maintain
significant housing disadvantage (Harrison, Law, and Phillips, D.
2005) but also affect the white poor. In the present study, most
white, black, and Asian prisoners' narratives were similar in their
depiction of life in their often economically deprived neighbourhoods. Almost all had lived in social housing, often throughout
their childhood and into adulthood. Prisoners variously described
their home areas as a 'shithole', 'harsh', 'not a very nice place', 'the
ghetto', 'gangland', 'kind of rough', 'deprived', 'a jungle', and 'a war
zone'.[12] Arcel[13] reflected on his North London neighbourhood as 'a

---

[11]   Hall et al.'s (1978) *Policing the Crisis* looks at some of the arguments regarding the role of black lumpenproletariat or subproletariat labour and its relationship
with the police as state agents. In *The Empire Strikes Back*, Solomos et al. (1982)
express similar sentiments to Wacquant in an attempt to articulate a political economy of race which recognizes the emergence of British state authoritarianism and
popular racism, but its timing precludes a full post-Fordist analysis which takes
account of the now well-documented effects of neoliberalism.

[12]   These often fatalistic dismissals of neighbourhood environments coexisted
with sentiments of intense pride (see Chapter 5). Notwithstanding, the mark of
stigma associated with living on housing estates which have a poor reputation
locally should not be underestimated either for its psychological impact on individual residents or for the difficulties it presents in accessing education and employment opportunities (Howarth 2002; Rogaly and Taylor 2009).

[13]   Of black Central African, Christian origin at Rochester.

dumping ground' where there were high levels of teenage preg-
nancy, single parent households, and therefore a high proportion of
young people. Whilst this made the area 'fun' for Arcel, the conflu-
ence of youthful populations and economic disadvantage spelt high
crime areas.[14]

Yet it would be wrong to represent Rochester and Maidstone
prisoners as only propelled along by the structural forces of post-
industrial Britain where the toxic waste of neoliberal policies show
state authority and abandonment of the poor to the vagaries of the
market. This neglects individual agency and excludes the emotive
appeal of transgression which has been a central motif of cultural
criminology. Melvin,[15] a Maidstone prisoner, had been working in
retail when he was arrested for robbery. His path to crime was after
a realization that his parents could not provide the money and
high-end consumer items that he wanted; crime was an easy option,
a Mertonian 'way out' of relative poverty and disadvantage (see
Young 1999; also Hallsworth 2005). For Tony[16] too, the pull of
making money 'the fast way instead of trying to get a job' which
paid meagre earnings was too strong to resist. The buzz of offending, the danger, often proved too attractive, as Varinder describes
here what attracted him to crime:

Well, when I first found out about town I would go there like to meet girls
or go to the cinema or just like chill, like go around town. Later on I started
coming out later at night so seen another new side to it like, people selling
drugs and obviously people doing their thing, like always your criminals,
everyone was criminal if you're out after 10 o'clock you're doing some
criminal activity....And to tell you truth like it excited me, I wanted to be
part of this world like. I knew it was wrong. (Varinder, Indian British)

Notwithstanding, the degree and depth of racialized residential
segregation along US lines is consistently denied by most geography scholars, at least in the United Kingdom (see, for example,
Finney and Simpson 2009). The evidence on ethnic penalties in the
labour market, indicative of racialized discrimination, also suggests a less rosy picture for minority ethnic groups in accessing

---

[14] Conspiratorially, when asked about why his friendship group was predominantly black, he suggested this was 'a question for the government...Is it a
coincidence or did they dump us in a ghetto?'

[15] Of black African British, Muslim origin.

[16] Of black Caribbean British, Christian origin.

employment, occupational attainment, and earnings (Heath and Cheung 2006). And although it is certainly true that homicide levels are far lower in the United Kingdom than the United States, black homicide rates in England and Wales are disproportionately high compared with those of white people (Phillips and Bowling 2012).

At first sight, the spectre of black hyperincarceration is more faintly observed in England and Wales. In June 2010, 14 per cent of the prison population comprised those of black origin. This included those of foreign nationality, but when limited to only British nationals, the figure is reduced to 11 per cent, with a further 6 per cent of Asian origin, 4 per cent mixed, and less than 1 per cent of Chinese/other and unknown ethnic origins. Unsurprisingly, 80 per cent of the prison population of England and Wales is of majority white origin (MOJ 2011a). The significance of these figures lies in the fact that black people comprise 11 per cent of the prison population but only 3 per cent of the general population. This can be contrasted with the staggering numerical dominance of African Americans and Hispanic Americans in the federal, state, and local prison populations despite their minority representation in the US population (Wacquant 2001). This has led Comfort (2008a) to refer to incarceration as a 'modal event, something which often follows from high school as an alternative to college' in the lives of African American men. In 2008, of the 1.54 million imprisoned for over a year in federal and state prisons, 34 per cent were white, 38 per cent were black, and 20 per cent were Hispanic (Sabol, West, and Cooper 2009). The estimated US population in 2004 was 80 per cent white, 13 per cent black, 4 per cent Asian, with the remainder made up of other minority ethnic groups (US Census Bureau 2005).

Yet the sheer scale of black (or any other minority ethnic) incarceration in England and Wales pales against the situation in the United States only because incarceration rates for *all ethnic groups are higher in the United States* (see also Daems 2008). Globally, the United States accounts for around a half of the world's prison population, with a rate of 748 per 100,000 of the national population in 2009 (Berman 2010). This compares with the much lower rate of 151 per 100,000 in England and Wales. However, as Tonry (1994) observed long before Wacquant's (2006) initial foray into this field, racial disproportionality in England and Wales is not behind but actually ahead of the United States. Tonry's analysis, using data from 1990, found racial disproportionality in prisons in England and Wales at 7.1:1 compared with 6.44:1 in the United States. The most recent available comparison from 2000 shows a black:white (male and female) incarceration ratio of 8.5:1 in England and Wales compared to 7.7:1 for men and 6:1 for women in the United States (Home Office 2000; Becker and Harrison 2001).

These comparative patterns present problems for Wacquant's (2009a, b) analysis. His contention that Europe is beginning to witness the transfer of American penal hypertrophy in a veritable law and order 'pornography' as a neoliberal response to advanced social marginality has been the subject of recent journal symposia and trenchant critique.[17] Wacquant (2009b) stresses that in European countries, penal solutions have not (yet) simply depended on the prison. They have included net-widening and uptariffing, and an increase in supervision and surveillance in welfare and penal contexts—part of a new social panopticism. Wacquant stops short of arguing that the dystopia of *black* hyperghettoization and penal segmentation in the United States has been fully transposed onto the European penal scene.[18] As Daems (2008) notes, there is an unresolved tension in that America is, on the one hand, deemed to be unexceptional, an exporter of punitive penal policies which also leads to the incarceration of 'Europe's blacks' (minority ethnic groups and recent migrants). On the other hand, America is simultaneously regarded as racially exceptional in its hyperincarceration of African Americans. This contradiction underlines the lack of clarity in Wacquant's assertion that penal expansion in the United

[17] Critiques of Wacquant's work point to the conflation of penal expansion or punitiveness with neoliberalism (Daems 2008), with both examples of punitiveness in countries not heavily invested in neoliberalism such as Greece (Cheliotis and Xenakis 2010), or where counter-trends of decarceration can also be found, as in Italy (Nelken 2010), but also neoliberal states or countries which have largely resisted the punitive turn, such as parts of Australia (Lacey 2008). Newburn (2010) has challenged the assumption that the new penal logic has been exported wholesale into policies of the UK, instead emphasizing their symbolic and rhetorical content over their precise formulation and implementation.

[18] Nonetheless, questions remain as to how far the hyperghetto experience can be extrapolated even within the US. Small (2007), for example, argues that poor black and poor non-black neighbourhoods differ significantly from Chicago's South Side, and the ethnic heterogeneity of many urban and marginal neighbourhoods in the US is also missed by Wacquant's black–white duality. Abu-Lughod (2008) also cautions that Wacquant's ethnographic fieldwork is less extensive in France than it is in the US.

States is primarily about racialized expulsion and containment but also about social marginality in Europe's urban centres, despite his recognition that racial disproportionality in European prisons has often exceeded that of the United States (Wacquant 2006). Thus, if penal hyperinflation in America has ultimately been fuelled by the state's desire to maintain ethno-racial division, how and why is it just neoliberalism in European countries which is responsible for the punitive turn despite similar patterns of racial disproportionality there?

It is not the intention of this chapter to attempt an alternative formulation, interesting and valuable as that might be. Nor will the presentation of the empirical findings in later chapters of the book shed light on the state's intentions, although it will consider prisoners' own reflections on state practices through the prison regime and the actions of individual prison officers. In any case, by Wacquant's (2008) own standards, a detailed exposition would require an historical and spatially specific account in which the precise contours of the economic, social, political, and material conditions of 'the wretched' are laid out, together with a specification of the symbolic and materialist elements of neoliberal penality. And while Daems (2008) wonders whether comparing penal experiences in a country with a legacy of slavery with those in Europe is too 'farfetched', it should be remembered that the hallmarks of colonialism and its patterning of ethno-racial hierarchy are not entirely dissimilar. Suffice to say here, it is clear that class and race are etched into the names on prison rolls in many Western nations, but that the well-trodden path from road to prison for an increasing number of prisoners has first involved travel across national borders (Tonry 1997; Wacquant 2006).

Global Diversity

In his critique of Wacquant's thesis, Daems (2008) has observed that European prisons also differ from their American counterparts because they are characterized by ethnic and national diversity. Certainly this is true in England and Wales, where 13 per cent were foreign nationals in 2010, originatng from 166 countries, with the largest number from countries with former colonial connections (Ireland, Jamaica, Nigeria, Pakistan, and India), where there has been recent civil or political conflict (Somalia, Zimbabwe, China, Vietnam, Iran, and Iraq) or considerable EU emigration (Poland,

Portugal, Romania) (Berman 2010). This is consistent with the globalizing tendencies of migration with population movements
spurred by ethnic and nationalist strife, socio-economic and demo-
graphic pressures, and ecological crises (Castles and Miller 2003).
These reactive forces have initiated population movements from
developing and transitional nations to the developed world, with
proactive movements prompted for the purposes of family reunifi-
cation and the opening up of employment opportunities, and these
factors had also influenced foreign national prisoners in this study.
Xavier,[19] a Maidstone prisoner, had left one of the Baltic States to
enjoy the possibilities of 'an easy life' of gainful employment rather
than having 'to go bins and find food' or experience starvation in
the war-torn country of his birth. Jackson,[20] a Rochester prisoner,
had been working illegally doing a night shift in a hospital; previous jobs had him working 16 hours a day in contrast to life in the
Caribbean which meant 'getting up and doing nothing' with jobs
hard to come by and requiring contacts. The personal risk of ordinary and political violence had cemented his decision to enter Britain
illegally and join other members of his family. Echoing C. Wright
Mills, it is precisely these kinds of accounts which resonate with
Back's (2007: 11) call to develop a 'global sociological imagination
subtle enough to open the public issues in these private troubles'.

Politically, migration has often been accompanied by national
agonizing over perceived threats to national identity and cohesion,
with some indication of a rise in right-wing nationalist political
parties or sentiment (Gibson 2002). A further feature of Western
immigration has been the restriction of social citizenship rights
which preclude inclusion through labour market participation and,
in many cases, access to welfare benefits (Dwyer 2005; Sainsbury
2006). For migrants excluded from effective inclusion, engaging in
crime is often a rational response to meeting material needs. Anan,
a black migrant from a Central African country, was tortured during his time in military detention and then was homeless on his
arrival in the United Kingdom, having been literally abandoned in
the street by his travel facilitator. His struggle to claim asylum
whilst experiencing post-traumatic stress, alleviated by alcohol
misuse, was what, in his words, 'pushed him off the limit'. His fear

---

[19] Of white, Muslim origin, from a Baltic state.
[20] Of black Caribbean, Christian, origin.

of being forcibly returned had led to a suicide attempt two weeks before he committed the crime which resulted in a medium-term sentence.

Some scholars have maintained that race-making is inscribed in globalizing processes, particularly in relation to the use of migrant labour (Bhattacharyya, Gabriel, and Small 2002). Goldberg (2002), for instance, regards the racial state of the 21st century as acting as traffic cop, simultaneously upgrading the privileged labour elite and downgrading the disprivileged through economic and cultural consumption, capital accumulation, and labour exchange. Both circulate in the new global racial order but the diasporic and migrant flows are regulated by the state through mechanisms of containment in the case of the disprivileged who perform labour tasks rejected by the local citizenry. As De Giorgi (2006) has observed, the denial of full citizenship rights in the case of illegal immigrants ensures a ready labour supply of workers who will accept any work conditions, supporting post-Fordist, neoliberal economic imperatives. As well as being constructed as undeserving of welfare assistance (employing the concept of 'lesser eligibility' like the prisons of old), this category of workers have been criminalized as the causes of economic insecurity ('they take our jobs') and linked to criminality and terrorism, producing for the public a 'social legitimacy' justifying a punitive response by the state (Weber and Bowling 2004; Wacquant 2006). This containment catches migrants who are criminalized either through being punished more harshly for offences than when those same offences were committed by citizens, or through the punishment of immigration offences. These are each nation state's internal 'suitable enemies' (Wacquant 1999), or as Bosworth and Guil (2008) note, the 'darker skinned' who are subject to cultures of control. These operate either through deterrent, punitive, and incapacitative measures, or through arbitrary bureaucracy in immigration law which implicitly supports an exclusionary white British identity and the impossibility of non-citizens belonging to the nation.

Wacquant (2006: 95) sees this 'penal spectacle' of migrant containment and expulsion as a ritualized method of reasserting state authority, reinforcing a collective resentment against the groups assumed to disrupt the national order, and obscuring state responsibility for immigrant integration. As Bohrman and Murakawa (2005: 109) have observed, this is facilitated by a 'pernicious cross-fertilization' of personnel, tactics, and strategies between agencies of social security, criminal justice, and immigration within the disciplinary state (see also Bosworth 2011).

Internal Dynamics of the Prisoner Society

This cross-fertilization is enacted at the meso level of state institutional practices, which include the prison. It is arguably rather a stretch to use the metaphor of 'peculiar institution' to refer to the prison unless it is being used in the context of slavery from which the term originates[21] (see Wacquant 2001). However, the late modern prison is more literally a peculiar institution in that, unlike most societal institutions, it mostly houses only men. Men's micro-level experiences of prisoner societies are inextricably linked to, and to some degree determined by, the macro-level structural forces discussed earlier, as well as meso-level institutional practices. Yet the role of masculinity in offending, punishment, and the experience of imprisonment has, until relatively recently, received little criminological attention (Sim 1994; Collier 1998). If it is accepted that the gender order is situated within particular social practices, structures, and institutions, it is axiomatic that masculinity has relevance for the prison as an institutional environment in which 'doing gender' must be accomplished.

The persistent patterning of penal populations by class, gender, and race have been alternatively constructed as peripheral or central to the social dimensions and organizational culture of the prison environment. The rich tradition of US prison ethnography and qualitative research has provided the foundational texts of the sociology of prisons literature. The classic study of the prison as a social organization begins with a recognition of the effects of socioeconomic and political factors on the composition of the prison community. Echoing a Mertonian analysis, Clemmer (1958/1940: 6) talked of a type of man destined for the prison, someone who is a 'residue of our individualistic society', and whose life is affected by poverty and destitution, long working hours, and poor pay, but who sees success, affluence, and corruption all around him. Moving on to the prison environment, Clemmer (1958/1940) identified core features of prisonization which socialized and assimilated the individual man into prison culture—its customs, mores, codes, and

---

[21] The term was used by Southerners in the United States (Stampp 1956).

rules. It was accepted that there were individual degrees of adaptation to this experience, but also universalistic features such as accepting the stigma of the prisoner identity, learning about the way prison life was organized—with new practices of eating, drinking, sleeping, and working. Whilst prisoners were ultimately concerned with their freedom, their actions were guided by an antipathy towards prison officials. This formed part of the unwritten code in which loyalty towards other prisoners was espoused if not always realized in practice.

These ideas informed Gresham Sykes' (1958) *indigenous model* of prison social relations developed from his qualitative research in Trenton maximum security prison in the United States. He describes in some detail the common inner social structure of the prison which renders the prisoner in a dependent state. The 'pains of imprisonment' are multiple and various—including the deprivations of liberty, emotional and sexual relationships, status and a positive self-image, autonomy, and personal possessions. The prison is an environment where movement is restricted and there are authoritarian rule systems. According to Sykes, these features are inherent to the carceral experience, determining prison subcultures and social relations inside. It is the prison which foregrounds prisoner identities rather than their classed, gendered, and racialized subjectivities.

Likewise, for Goffman (1961), total institutions, which included jails and penitentiaries, were characterized by continual surveillance, the control of information, and a hostile relationship between inmates and institutional staff. On entry, the inmate experiences a profound 'series of abasements, degradations, humiliations, and profanations of self' which has mortifying and violating effects on the individual but meets the organizational exigencies of the prison to maintain order and conformity with high staff–inmate ratios (Goffman 1961: 23). The individual must abandon the social roles he adopted outside, he is dehumanized, objectified, subjected to tests of compliance through extreme daily regimentation, and contaminated by the enforced proximity of others. These institutional practices strip the individual of his identity, producing a different self which does not fit with the individual's previous self-conception, and creates immense psychological stress and anxiety. In this extreme environment, inmate fraternalization provides mutual support, perhaps even friendship, although close ties may be undermined by a lack of trust. Indeed, as Sykes observed in Trenton prison, the ever-present threat of masculine contests, exploitation, and violence further enhance feelings of vulnerability and insecurity.

It is these features of the prison, Sykes (1958) asserts, to which prisoners must adapt and which shape the vertical (prisoner–guard) and horizontal (prisoner–prisoner) relationships in prisoner society. An inmate social system develops according to individual prisoners' reactions to the essential and unique psychological and physical deprivations they must endure in custody. A code of values functions to guide social relations in prison, the central tenets of which are not ratting or interfering with other prisoners, 'playing it cool' and 'doing your own time', not exploiting other prisoners, showing personal strength, courage, and integrity, and not being hoodwinked by prison officers. Whilst not always strictly adhered to, a variety of social roles for prisoners exist in reference to the inmate code. Prisoners' adaptations to best alleviate the pains of imprisonment can be individualistic and purely instrumental as characterized by the roles of 'rat', 'gorilla', 'merchant, 'tough', and so on, adopted by some Trenton prisoners observed by Sykes, or more collectivistic and idealized, facilitating prisoner solidarity where 'right guys or 'real men' emerge who respond to the pains of imprisonment by demonstrating loyalty and the mutual aid of other prisoners (Sykes and Messinger 1960). The normative system of behaviour extols group cohesion in opposition to the 'enemy out-group' (prison staff), which ultimately serves to partially mitigate the pains of imprisonment by providing material and psychological support, personal security, desired goods, and preserves the dignity and self-respect of the prisoner.

We see an alternative model developed in the work of Irwin and Cressey (1962), who claimed that prisoner subcultures and social relations inside were determined by criminal behaviour outside. Rather than resulting from the internal conditions of imprisonment, the social world of the prison is structured around the identities of prisoners imported from criminal subcultures. The inmate code proscribes behaviour such as 'ratting' but so too do most criminal and legitimate subcultures. Irwin and Cressey do not dispute individual adaptations to the experience of imprisonment, but in this *importation model* they stress external behaviours as structuring these responses. The thief subculture upholds the importance of being solid, cool-headed, and trustworthy, inside and outside prison, while the convict subculture extols the virtues of exploiting goods and resources in the prison which provides an advantaged position in the prison hierarchy. Finally, according to Irwin and Cressey, the legitimate subculture consists of prisoners who are goal-oriented and conform lawfully. In *The Felon*, Irwin (1970) collapsed the criminal identities of prisoners further into thieves, dope fiends, heads (frequent recreational drug users), hustlers (mainly 'Negro'), violent state-raised youth, disorganized criminals, lower-class criminals driven by machismo and fatalism, and conventional square johns.

Jacobs' (1977) institutional analysis of Stateville Penitentiary in Illinois, self-consciously presented in the Chicago School tradition, argues that the organizational and cultural dynamics of prison in the 1970s was more centrally dictated by mass society, or put another way, by broader societal claims for equal citizenship and political rights. The tumultuous 1960s saw a challenging of traditional institutional authority in the United States and a determined politicization of the citizenry which particularly affected racial minorities but also coincided with an acceptance of prison reform and a belief in rehabilitation as the mission of the prison. The opening up of the prison to outside society, particularly through various information and media channels, meant that the prison institution was no longer as isolated and separate from mainstream society as it had once been. Jacobs carefully traces how these broader social and political forces impacted on the prison administration of Stateville. In particular, Jacobs describes the influence of black politicized street gangs who mitigated the pains of imprisonment for members and structured prison social relations. This occurred within the context of racial minorities assuming a majority in American prisons (Jacobs 1979).

In a subsequent piece, Jacobs (1979) extends his account to highlight the scholarly neglect of the effects of racial identities and discrimination on prisoner subcultures in direct support of the importation thesis. There is much more to be said about Jacobs' and others' work (including Wacquant) on the contours of race and ethnicity in prison relations, and this is returned to in Chapter 2. An important final point here is that scholars of the prison had promoted a synthesis position or integration model. This recognized elements of prisoner experience being structured by both the intrinsic conditions of imprisonment (Sykes' *indigenous model*) and biographical histories and social identities formed outside prison (Irwin and Cressey's *importation model*), with the relative influences depending on the conditions of control and deprivation experienced (Thomas, Petersen, and Zingraff 1978; Grapendaal 1990).

The more recent absence of prison ethnographies or qualitative research in US prisons has fortunately not been matched in the United Kingdom where it has thrived with some important contributions to penology and the sociology of imprisonment. Sparks et al.'s (1996) research in Albany and Long Lartin prisons, for example, was concerned with how social order is maintained in prison, drawing on the concept of legitimacy, and recognizing the moral elements of imprisonment. It usefully illustrates the multiple ways in which power is negotiated in prison, with prisoners themselves centrally involved as agents in the exercise of power used to control them, despite the unequal power relations they experience. While criticized by Bosworth (1999) for not considering prisoners' identities fully enough, including subjectivities of race and gender, recent policy-oriented research is beginning to engage with ideas of legitimacy within the frame of procedural justice in prisoner–staff interactions which can be affected by race (Jackson et al. 2010).

The issue of the moral integrity and performance of the prison has been the subject of a monumental study by Liebling (2004) in which she judiciously examines the complex climates in which prisoners and staff interact which determines the material, moral, and emotional quality of life in prison. This is set against the context of punitive expressiveness, managerialist imperatives, and the move towards developing decency in prison relationships. Liebling's analysis devotes much of its attention to attempting to operationalize concepts such as respect, trust, and fairness, which can jar with macro-level analyses of the political economy of punishment. In those accounts there has been somewhat of a tendency to downplay micro-realities, with prisoners' material, physical, psychological, and emotional needs regarded as subordinate to the needs of state and capital. Liebling's work is a reminder of how much is owed to the sociology of Erving Goffman and other sociologists of the prison, that such meso- and micro-level analyses must remain part of the contemporary picture. In Liebling's work there is also an important message for research to avoid the binaries of characterizing prison regimes as either dysfunctionally brutal (or indeed racist) or managerially high-performing, instead recognizing that fair and just interactions may occur alongside abuses of power and institutional indifference.

Examining the interaction of institutional processes and individual experiences, framed by broad social and economic changes, is achieved in Crewe's (2009) *The Prisoner Society*, which beautifully captures the deployment and operation of penal power, how individual prisoners adapt agentially to its variegated forms, and the development of prisoner cultures in an ethnography of Wellingborough prison. Tackling head-on the indigenous versus importation debate empirically, Crewe provides an insightful account of the multiple ways in which prisoners negotiate institutional power which is at least partially determined by the external realities of life before prison, but which is also shaped by the intrinsic conditions and pains of imprisonment in the late modern context. Whilst living standards have improved and the inhumane and authoritarian treatment of prisoners was not part of the staff–prisoner picture at Wellingborough as it was in earlier US and UK studies of prison life, power, according to Crewe, operated in more diffuse and neo-paternalistic ways. Managers, observing central targets, maintained control, but front-line prison officers could still determine life on the wings through the exercise of 'soft power' to grant requests, ignore a misdemeanour, provide incentives and privileges, but also ostensibly to promote compliance and self-governance. The boundaries were thus blurred for many prisoners. How power was experienced and adapted to was influenced by imported biographical histories, individual personalities, and values relating to crime and criminality, as well as experiences inherent in late modern modes of penal power which largely undermined any oppositional prisoner solidarity.

Conclusion

There is a permanence about penal populations which is encapsulated in the political economy of punishment. Prisons largely contain 'the wretched' who are positioned in the lower echelons of the social structure subject to punishment by the state and deprived of their liberty in the company of others like them. The precise mechanism which produces these effects has been linked directly to economic imperatives, particularly capitalist profit, to the symbolic control and disciplining of the surplus labour force, and even to caste segregation in the case of the economically wretched and politically expendable descendants of slaves. For these groups, their pre-prison lives have often been marked by family disruption, economic disadvantage, and social and political marginalization. To these experiences are then added the pains of imprisonment. The extent to which institutional constraints structure the social experience of the prisoner and the culture of prisoner society has been the subject of dispute. Decades after the indigenous–importation dualism first emerged, it still remains a starting point for analyses concerned with the interior social world of the prison. However, there is wide agreement that elements of both are important for understanding prisoner identities and social relations. In Chapter 2, I turn to consider more fully the dynamics of race and how they are manifested in interactions between prisoners and staff, and between diverse groups of prisoners. Central to debates in the United States, undoubtedly because of the large numerical presence of minority ethnic prisoners in penal populations and the hyperinflation of the prison population, such issues have been rather downplayed in the United Kingdom, despite, as it turns out, similar patterns of racial disproportionality.

2

Racial Identities, Social Relations, and Prison Policies

> Prisons are, to put it simply, woefully understudied locales, and the lack of attention to the construction of 'race' inside carceral facilities is a prime example. Goodman (2008: 740)

In *White Law*, Gordon (1983) describes the racist taunting of black prisoners by white prison officers who were members of the National Front, an ultra-right-wing nationalist political party. A decade later, the Director General of Her Majesty's Prison Service (HMPS) issued a public apology to the family of Zahid Mubarek, a British Pakistani Muslim prisoner who was subject to a savage and fatal beating by his racist cell-mate in Feltham Young Offenders' Institution. Nearly another ten years on, the National Offender Management Service (NOMS) (2008: Foreword) published its review of implementing race equality policies in prisons. In that report the then Director General noted that whilst 'actions taken over the last five years have generated substantial improvements…the experience of BME [black and minority ethnic] prisoners and staff has not been transformed'.

This is the backdrop for understanding the shaping of the institutional frame of the prison as it pertains to race, ethnicity, and social relations, the key theme of this book. This chapter explores prison race relations as revealed in sociological studies of the prison, influenced by Irwin and Cressey's (1962) importation model of prisoner identities. It traces the development of policy, set against wider, changing understandings of race in modernity and late modernity, and considers how these have impacted on the social world of the prison.

Prison Subcultures and Social Relations in US Prisons

In the opening article of the first ever edition of the respected series *Crime and Justice*, James Jacobs (1979: 2) castigated the sociology of prisons for failing to acknowledge the racialized dimensions of

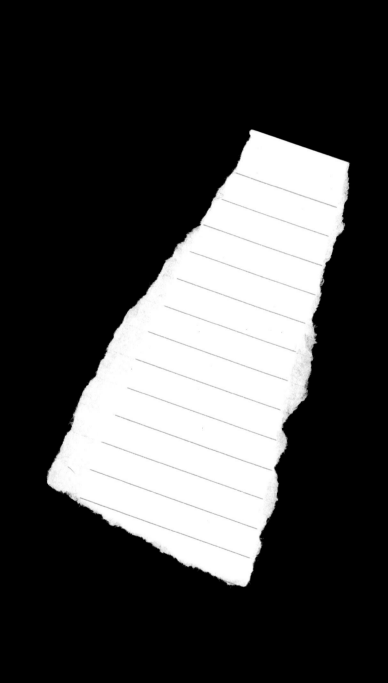

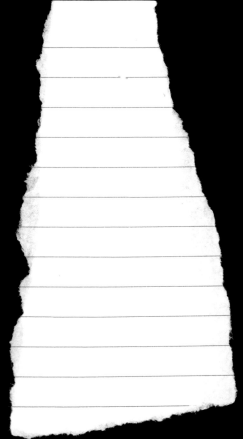

prison life. Absent from empirical research which outlined the social organization and culture of prisons, including the classic works of Clemmer (1958/1940) and Sykes (1958), was an account of what Jacobs called 'racial etiquette and norms' and its influence on prisoner leadership, hierarchies, or the inmate code used to survive the pains of imprisonment.[1] This is extraordinary given the unique history of race relations in American society which has been marked by racial segregation and discrimination in most spheres of life. Indeed, Carroll (1974: 220) recognized the possibilities of racial prejudice and mutually antagonistic relations in prisons even within the therapeutic institutions founded on cooperation and equal status. This was because 'institutional race relations are nothing more or less than particular manifestations of race relations in the surrounding society'.

This was borne out by Jacobs' (1977) research in Stateville Penitentiary and Irwin's (1980) study of prison life in California which revealed political turmoil in the prison system through the 1950s, 1960s, and 1970s. The emergence of a defiant and oppositional racial consciousness among Black Muslim prisoners preached black racial superiority and urged collective challenges to the traditional authoritarianism and racism of the prison system. Importantly this claims-making was aligned with societal demands for the increased civil rights of both black people *and* prisoners. In *Soul on Ice*, Eldrige Cleaver (1968: 58) described how black prisoners regarded themselves as prisoners of war rather than criminals, 'the victims of a vicious, dog-eat-dog social system that is so heinous as to cancel out their own malefactions', with imprisonment a continuation of societal oppression black people had known all their lives (see also Jacobs 1975; Gottschalk 2006[2]). Black Muslim prisoners called for the right to practise their Islamic faith inside; demands were made to honour prayer times, supply the Quran, provide Imams to take services, serve 'kosher' food', and for prison officers to cease the demonization of Muslim prisoners. Some of these demands were met following high-profile litigation which forced fundamental changes in prison organization

---

[1] Incidentally, Sykes also carelessly assumes equality brought about by the near-equivalence of numbers of 'Negro' and white prisoners.

[2] Gottschalk notes how the demise of the Black Nationalist movement in prisons in the mid-1970s created a vacuum easily filled by the 'siren call of law-and-order politics' (Gottschalk 2011: 487).

and administration, while others were accepted as part of the wider drive for political equality (Jacobs 1977). Diaz-Cotto (1996) similarly documented Latina(o) political challenges to the custodial hegemony of the 1960s in New York state between 1970 and 1987. Using oral histories of ex-prisoners and political activists, she described the ways in which political consciousness grew with solidarity between Latina(o) prisoners' cliques including (sometimes fictive) kin networks and homeboy/homegirl (neighbourhood-based) networks which assisted prisoners in their day-to-day survival inside, particularly in the provision of material, psychological, and emotional support.

Carroll's (1974) study of the Eastern Correctional Institution was among the first to examine how race was inflected in horizontal (prisoner–prisoner interactions) and vertical (staff–prisoner) relationships inside prison. The prison population he studied was 78 per cent white and 22 per cent black. Social rules adopted in the prison originated both in the conditions of incarceration and in outside subcultures, but for black prisoners racial identification was the key axis of life inside. There was a shared fate which encompassed all 'brothers' who had experienced white oppression inside and outside prison. Sharing prison resources was better facilitated among black than white prisoners; for example, dues and fines paid to the Afro-American Society were used to buy musical equipment, provide loans, or supply essential supplies to new inmates, and black prisoners were expected to back each other in a 'beef' (dispute). This communal orientation rivalled Sykes' (1958) claim that prisoners did their time individually. It also begged questions of the universality of the inmate code; as Carroll (1982: 183) observed, '[i]t is hard to imagine a convict code of solidarity spanning the social distance that prisoners of different races place between themselves' (see also Diaz-Cotto 1996; cf. Kruttschnitt's (1983) study of a female prison in Minnesota where there was considerable informal racial integration). While some black inmates had developed a future-oriented Black Nationalist consciousness, most were 'half-steppers': committed to the expressive spiritual 'soul' perspective of the present which united black people in their cultural behaviour, dress, music, and language. Carroll found little normative solidarity among white prisoners who operated in cliques of three to five, although these were often in conflictual or exploitative relationships.

Black prisoners' collective orientation was the object of fear and envy among white prisoners. Conversely, black prisoners viewed white prisoners as weak, racist, and lacking political consciousness. Although interracial contact was inevitable, where prisoners could opt for segregated activities, for example in recreation or goods trading, they did. One exception was drugs, where 'biracial' interaction was more common as dealers used 'runners' from other races to ensure quick sales. Rape was also frequently interracial with more commonly black perpetrators and white victims. Carroll speculated that this represented an aggressive 'black rage' in response to white racism, encouraged by the black collectivity as a demonstration of black masculinity. Serious violence between groups of white and black prisoners in the Eastern Correctional Institution had erupted on occasion in the late 1960s, but at the time of Carroll's study, cooperative agreement had been reached between the powerful white Mafia and the black revolutionaries to contain racialized conflict at the individual level so that it did not lead to 'race wars' which both groups believed only benefited prison staff.

Carroll's (1974) study was among the first to find that black prisoners were more often surveilled and disciplined than white prisoners although they did not experience more severe penalties on average. White prison officers held stereotypical views of black prisoners (often referring to them as 'niggers'), resented their political activities, and tended negatively to assume that black prisoners were behaving illegitimately. As a result prison officers more often exercised their discretion in favour of white than black prisoners, although the latter could mediate this by virtue of a threat of collective action against staff.

In his review of race relations in prison, Jacobs (1977, 1979: 8) referred to the collective orientation of black prisoners as resulting in the 'balkanisation' of prisoner society as black and white prisoners occupied their 'separate conflict-ridden social worlds'. Jacobs found white prisoners complaining that they were the victims of racist talk and behaviour by black prisoners. Understanding their racial identity to be a key determinant of their prison experience, in a way that it had not been on the outside, led some prisoners to form coalitions with prison officers in seeking protection from harassment by black prisoners. Irwin (1970) appreciated the significance of these divisions for relations in Californian prisons. Prisoners there were informally segregated in the cells during TV watching and whilst eating, and protected each other in any kind of disputes. Both Irwin (1970: v) and Jacobs (1979: 15) saw race as the overriding identity marker and feature of prison social relations, which by the 1970s, meant that racialized friction was the norm in state and federal prisons (see also Minton's 1971 description of 'race wars' in Soledad prison).

Like Jacobs (1975), Bartollas et al. (1976) reported black assertiveness in an Ohio juvenile institution with white prisoners situated at the bottom of the prison pecking order. This subordination left white prisoners bewildered and resentful of black prisoners' perceived superior position. In order to fit in, there was an imitation of black cultural patterns of behaviour, such as the eating of 'soul food' or the use of the black 'ghetto dialect' by some white prisoners. Black supremacy in the prisoner hierarchy allowed them to control the supply of cigarettes, food, clothes, and sex, and to maintain control of the pool and table tennis tables, and even decide the music played in the prison. Bartollas et al. (1976) argued that these patterns of behaviour were determined by a normative code for black prisoners which exhorted the exploitation of white prisoners, prohibited the sexual victimization of other black prisoners, and required mutual defence in interracial disputes. Like adult prisoners, the deprivations of imprisonment for black juveniles were amplified by prison officers' discriminatory treatment in punishment and the giving of privileges.

In Stateville, black prisoners' solidarity was bolstered by gang allegiance, as gangs migrated from the street to the prison. These gangs were of African American and Latino origins, providing collective solutions to the deprivations of imprisonment, staving off poverty, providing information, distributing goods in the illicit economy, and, most importantly, providing psychological support and belonging (Jacobs 1974; see also Moore 1978). For Irwin (1980), the development of these deep ties between prisoners aligned to often opposing Chicano gangs in the Californian prison system, together with the rise of violent macho lowriders, who were exploitative of other prisoners and strikingly racist; and the move to rehabilitation by prison administrations undermined the previously admired universal convict loyalty.

The raft of studies conducted in the 1970s were centrally preoccupied with racial dynamics in horizontal and vertical relations, but such studies have largely disappeared in the intervening period (Simon 2000; Wacquant 2002). In their place have come quantitative analyses, primarily concerned with prisoner misconduct and violence rates. Variations in methodology frustrate comparisons[3] and these studies lack the rich contextualization of prison ethnographies and qualitative research which have analysed the meaning of inter- and intra-racial solidarity, conflict, and violence.

Wacquant's (2001) work on the meshing of the prison and the hyperghetto has revived the importation model of prisoner subcultures with a racialized twist. Like Robertson (2008: 799), who refers to the prison as 'the nation's most racialised type of real estate', Wacquant (2001), drawing on qualitative research from the 1980s and 1990s, paints a picture of the shape and texture of prison social life as being supremely characterized by racial division. At the same time as America's prisons have been transformed into overcrowded, violent warehouses, prison interiors have come to resemble ghetto exteriors.[4] They are both ethnically divided through gang affiliation and a heavy investment in drug use and dealing, and marked by an oppositional street culture. Gone are the unified and stabilizing features of yesteryear's captive society; exclusive racial affiliation, and segregation within the activities and facilities of the prison predominate. It is now also accompanied by the hyper-masculinist behaviour of the streets where brutality and violence are easily precipitated by personal slights and perceived disrespect, and the informal economy of the prison is orchestrated through organized gangs. Together, these elements create a chaotic and dangerous social world for prisoners which is analogous to life in the hyperghetto. Cultural symbols of the ghetto and the prison are also fused—graffiti, tattoos, language, dress (the ubiquitous baggy pants with low crotch), and interaction patterns are imported and exported between the two institutions, and even into mainstream adolescent culture. The intertwining of prison and hyperghetto, according to Wacquant, promotes and sustains black socio-economic marginality and cements in the public imaginary an inherent black criminality which is politically unchallenged in the ratcheting up of law-and-order rhetoric. For Wacquant, the classic contrasting

---

[3] Some have reported higher levels of (mostly intra-racial) assaults by black prisoners (Fuller and Orsagh 1977; Huebner 2003) and others have revealed no race or mixed race effects depending on the type of prisoner (Ellis, Grasmick, and Gilman 1974; Wright 1989; Camp et al. 2003; Berg and DeLisi 2006) and the data used to measure disciplinary infractions (Poole and Regoli 1980).

[4] See also Shabazz's (2009) discussion of the carceral power of apartheid mining compounds and prisons in the South African context.

positions of the 'indigenous' and 'importation' models of prisoner identities and social relations have been rendered obsolete in this racialized characterization of prison life.

Apart from Wacquant's (2001) vivid account, there is little recent qualitative work on race and social relations in US prisons. Goodman's (2008) observational study of two reception centres provides a rare glimpse into the racialized conditions of prison experience in California in the 2000s. He describes separate boxes holding barbers' tools for each racial group (marked Black, White, Hispanic Barber); a prison officer casually remarks that prisoners would refuse a haircut using tools that had cut the hair of another racial group.[5] Goodman argues that this informal segregation is underscored by institutional practices.[6] On entry, the reception speech which prisoners receive from prison officers alerts and initiates them into the racial and gang-based divisions in prison. Prisoners are exhorted to check with 'your peoples' to learn the ropes and the lay of the land of the prison, and ethnic monitoring forms privilege singular racial categories and racialized gang affiliations above other relevant information, including offence sentenced. Unfortunately, there is no further indication of whether racial identities are further collapsed, distorted, mediated, or reformed in prison social relations beyond the reception process.

In his later work, with prisons operating as warehouse storage facilities in the punitive political environment, Irwin (2005) claimed that criminal identities were reasserting themselves. In Solano, a Californian prison, Irwin found little intense inter-group conflict, except between rival Mexican Norteños and Soreños. The reduc-

---

[5] The Commission for Racial Equality (CRE) (2004a) investigation of Feltham prison similarly reported white prisoners' complaints about having to use hair clippers used by black prisoners.

[6] The question of official segregation policies in US prisons has recently been revisited by the US Supreme Court, acknowledging that despite previous judgments by state courts, prison officials have resisted desegregation arguing that it presented an unreasonable security risk given the nature of prison race relations (but see Henderson, Cullen, and Carroll 2000). In 2005 in the *Johnson v California* ruling, the court decided that the standard of strict scrutiny had to be applied which meant that segregation could only be used if prisoner safety could not be ensured through other means (Trulson et al. 2008). Research by Trulson et al. (2008) found that white prisoners are most opposed to desegregation. Significantly, Trulson and Marquart (2002a, 2002b) indicated that only 10 per cent of interracial cell incidents in Texas prisons were racially motivated and there was a reduction in racially motivated incidents as cell integration increased.

tion of violence, according to Irwin, had resulted from improvements in prison architectural design and planning which facilitated surveillance, rapid response by prison officers to incidents, plus the use of supermax prisons with segregated housing units to take the more violent prisoners from the lower prisons. Despite the reduced racial hostility, prisoners' friendships were still determined by ethnicity, with only some mingling by Mexican American prisoners and white and black prisoners. Within-group friendships were based on home town, criminal identities, gangs, religion, age, or in-prison interests.

The nature of vertical and horizontal relations in US prisons has undoubtedly been shaped by the very particular historical legacy of slavery, institutionalized discrimination, and black political activism which has been a significant part of the picture there. England similarly has a unique set of historical, legal, and political dynamics which have created and conditioned the nature of prison social relations in circumstances of racial disproportionality, and ethnic, cultural, and national diversity. In turning to these now, it is worth remembering that scholars outside the United States have pondered many of the same issues which captivated the US scholars so far discussed, in exploring the relevance of race in the social world of the prison—the nature of prisoner friendships and hierarchy, conflict and violence, the underground economy, and, particularly, the use of discretion in treatment by prison officers with respect to discipline and punishment.

Race Relations in UK Prisons

Evidence of black disproportionality in the prisons of England and Wales has existed since the mid-1980s (Home Office 1986) with ongoing speculation about whether this reflects their elevated rates of offending or discrimination by the police and courts (Bowling and Phillips 2002). This debate need not detain us here. The first communication between the Prison Service and staff on race relations followed shortly after Lord Scarman's Report (1981) into the Brixton street riots which identified the negative stereotyping of black people by a 'few bad apples' in the police force as igniting the major disturbances. Couched in a similar language, Circular Instruction 28/1981 emphasized the dangers of cultural misunderstanding and ensuring equal and professional treatment of prisoners by prison staff regardless of their race, colour, or creed. Somewhat incongruously, the Circular cautioned that ethnic minorities might misunderstand the nature of authority and use their position to their own advantage, although how precisely is not outlined. Circular Instruction 56/1983 outlined the Prison Service's opposition to any verbal or physical displays of racial prejudice by staff, including the use of derogatory language ('nigger', 'coon', and 'wog') and referring to minority ethnic inmates as 'immigrants' when they may have been born in Britain. Additionally, it stressed the need for vigilance against disproportionality in education and work allocations and ethnic dominance in any prison activity (showers, leisure, eating, and so on). Staff were reminded that overzealousness in pursuing equal treatment could lead to white majority ethnic disadvantage. As we shall see in Chapter 6, the issue of minority ethnic advantage and white majority disadvantage remains live 20 years on.[7]

In spite of these policy efforts, in 1987 a black prisoner, John Alexander, successfully won a case of racial discrimination against the Prison Service. He had been denied a kitchen job at Parkhurst prison in 1983 because of his race. In his initial assessment report, which had been prepared at Wandsworth prison, he had been said to display 'the usual traits associated with his ethnic background, being arrogant, suspicious of staff, anti-authority, devious and possessing a very large chip on his shoulder'. His induction report at Parkhurst used similar language and added that he showed the 'anti-authority arrogance that seems to be common in most coloured inmates'.[8]

Genders' and Player's (1989) seminal study of race relations in British prisons marked the first criminological entrée into this field, and it remains the most comprehensive to date. For this reason it is worth discussing the findings in some depth. Government-funded, Genders' and Player's study was carried out in five prisons with different security ratings, size, function, and proportion of minority ethnic prisoners. Wider in scope than the present study, it examined the implementation of race relations policy as well as examining prisoners' relationships with each other and staff through over 200 interviews (mostly randomly sampled) of prisoners and officers, observational work, and document analysis.

---

[7] Circular Instructions 32/1986 and 39/1990 established various infrastructural and accountability measures through ethnic monitoring.

[8] In response the Prison Service issued a comprehensive *Race Relations Manual* for staff in 1991 (Amendment to Circular Instruction 13/1991).

Genders and Player found none of the political organization of black prisoners shown in the US studies of the 1970s, but reported that 31 per cent of black prisoners were concerned about prisoner–officer relations, while this was true of only 14 per cent of white prisoners. Conversely, 82 per cent of white prisoners were troubled by racial prejudice among prisoners, compared with 63 per cent of black prisoners and 29 per cent of Asian prisoners. This manifested in verbal aggression and avoidance of contact rather than violence. In two youth custody centres, prisoners tended to see a physical dominance of black prisoners in certain activities, or use of services and equipment, but this pattern was less marked in the adult prisons. In one of the prisons studied with a relatively stable prisoner population, Genders and Player observed 'white gangsters' at the top of the prisoner hierarchy, 'terrorists' and 'black prisoners' in the next echelon down, and a fragmented mass still higher in esteem than the 'nonces' at the bottom of the pecking order. The black prisoners were somewhat marginal but occupied positions in the informal economy. Relations between these groups were largely peaceful, but on occasion the white gangsters wielded power, and on others the separate cliques united where there was a common threat from prison officers or the regime. Less clearly identifiable cliques existed in the local prison, which had a more transient population. The power groups in the youth detention centre seemed more fluid, with black predominance at one point in time, but high levels of bullying and exploitation engaged in by both white and black prisoners.

Comments recorded by Genders and Player revealed that black prisoners were negatively stereotyped on physical, intellectual, and moral grounds by staff and were seen as presenting control and management difficulties such that many wanted to control proportions in their prison (see also McDermott 1990 for similar findings in West Midlands prisons). Most wing officers saw black prisoners as a solidary group but individually as arrogant, hostile, resentful of white authority, lazy, noisy, belligerent, unintelligent, and with 'chips on their shoulders'. Meanwhile Asian prisoners were viewed as 'model prisoners'—hardworking, intelligent, polite, unobtrusive, and, unlike black people, not inherently criminal.

In their efforts to downplay race relations issues and resist policy implementation in their prison, officers were reluctant to see racial conflict in any situation including disputes between prisoners which the researchers believed had been motivated by racial hostility

(Genders and Player 1989). More direct racial bias was seen in disciplinary proceedings and in housing and work allocations which favoured white prisoners, as interviews with work supervisors revealed that they often wanted to fill positions with their favoured prisoners.

Almost ten years after Genders' and Player's research, Sparks et al.'s (1996) important study of legitimacy and social order in Albany and Long Lartin prisons maintained that race was not a defining feature of life in prison. Racial conflict between prisoners rarely surfaced; Sparks et al. reported some tensions with older white prisoners resentful of younger, boisterous black prisoners and the perception that black sex offenders were protected, but little more than this. Nor, seemingly, were prisoner–officer relationships marked by racialized discrimination and conflict. In her 1999 study of three women's prisons Bosworth signalled the use of identity as a means of maintaining selfhood, but the influence of prisoners' ethnicities was rather diffuse as class identities were prioritized by prisoners, with some commonalities of experience engendered among white and black prisoners who came from city housing estates or who had formerly been in interracial, intimate relationships outside prison. National identities were more salient; prisoners of Scottish, Irish, and Welsh heritage distinguished themselves from English prisoners, and minority ethnic identities more often came to the fore in the case of foreign national prisoners. For Bosworth, women's feminine identities were deployed in small ways to wrestle some control from prison officers and to resist the universal power of the prison regime. Such acts of transgression may have had personal significance or have been about being heard, even if they were limited in their effects as a mechanism of political dissent (Bosworth and Carrabine 2001). Claims of resisting institutional control were also made by Wilson (2003) in his study of young black men in prison. Sometimes this meant 'keeping quiet', occasionally 'going nuts', but above all, drawing on support and solace from other black prisoners.

Despite Jacobs' (1977) exhortation that we can only understand prison social relations by looking outside the walls to mass society, these studies, with the exception of Bosworth's (1999) theoretical reflections on the politics of identity, have not heeded this message. As this book unfolds, it will be abundantly clear that prisoner subcultures and social relations in Rochester and Maidstone prisons cannot be interpreted without reflecting on the underlying forces of social change with regard to race relations and race equality in the late modern context. But first we need to take an historical detour, to illustrate the wider context in which the studies of race relations in UK prisons should be read.

Race and Ethnicity in Europe: From Modernity to Late Modernity

Just as the legacy of slavery bears an imprint on race relations in US society today, we can turn to Enlightenment thinkers such as Kant and Hegel to learn about Northern European depictions of the 'lower races' who today are represented as national minority ethnic groups or migrants in many Western countries (see, for example, Eze 1997). Assuming distinct anthropological ancestries, for example, de Gobineau's (1853–5) hierarchical order was simple, distinguishing the black, yellow, and white races in ascending order of superiority in relation to intellect, behaviour, morality, personality, and sexuality (de Gobineau in Biddiss 1999). According to Goldberg (2009: 163–4), whilst the Muslim fared somewhat better in the Great Chain of Being to God, s/he was still marked by being 'ordinarily strange in ways, habits and ability to self-govern, aggressive, emotional, and conniving in contrast with the European's urbanity, rationality and spirituality'. Scholars of race have long asserted its central inscription in the global order of European modernity. Goldberg (2002), for example, described how white supremacy and entitlement was etched into the foundational social arrangements of most modern European nation states through racial categorization, the regulation and mediation of relations between white citizens and others, and governance via surveillance and the economic management of racially defined populations. Kymlicka (2007) describes the typical process of nation state-building when the dominant national group (usually but not always the majority) used the state to define its nationhood through the assertion of an official language, domination of political, legal, and judicial power, the teaching of the dominant group's history and literature in schools, and the diffusion of the dominant group's culture through public media and cultural institutions. The dominant group, determined by Enlightenment ideas of racial superiority, was able to infuse institutional structures with its own homogenous national identity precisely because this was seen as part of the natural order. But given the massive social changes we have witnessed in the last few decades, it would be reasonable to assume that modern racial hierarchies have been transformed in the contemporary period.

At a macro level there are claims that (modern) hierarchies of race (and class) have simply expanded to fit the world stage buoyed by globalizing processes. Thus there is now a global division of labour and associated power relations under post-Fordist capitalism in which mythologies of race support economic subjugation of the global South by and within the industrialized economies of the global North (Bhattacharyya et al. 2002). At the same time, there has been a contestation of national homogeneity in the post-colonial period, often by the minority groups who have been the victims of projects of national homogenization (Kymlicka 2007). Minority groups have struggled for equal participation in political life where their minority ethno-racial identities can be maintained rather than assimilated into the majority culture, essentially challenging for a multicultural rather than a monocultural state. Baltej Singh Dhillon's claim to a right to wear a turban rather than a felt hat in the Royal Canadian Mounted Police, agreed by the Canadian Solicitor General in 1990, is an apt illustration of these minority claims for national inclusion and representation.

Yet despite formal equality having been achieved in many countries in which minority ethnic groups have settled (in Britain through the Race Relations Act 1976, for example), debates continue as to why access to societal resources is restricted for some minority ethnic groups. This has led to calls for affirmative or positive action—a group rights differentiation of citizenship to respond to the continued economic or cultural exclusion of minority and historically disadvantaged groups (Young, M. 1990). Yet now we may be witnessing a retreat from such multiculturalism in the academy and in rather surprising quarters of the political sphere. The argument that cultural identities should be pursued privately not publicly, and not accommodated or privileged by state policies (Barry 2001; Joppke 2004), has been echoed by Trevor Phillips, the head of the state body mandated to promote good race relations and race equality (the Commission for Racial Equality (CRE); now the Equality and Human Rights Commission (EHRC)). Following the bombings in London on 7 July 2005 Phillips warned of the separatist and divisive dangers of liberal multiculturalism. The refashioning of 'non-racist', right-wing nationalist parties indicates a further challenge to multicultural states; the suited rather than booted British National Party signals lesions in the traditional political landscape of two-party politics (Copsey 2011).

It therefore seems premature to regard ourselves as in a post-racial state (Goldberg 2009). However, academic opinion is in agreement in recognizing the complexities of race and racism in the contemporary late modern period. 'Race' itself is recognized as a social construction in which phenotypical features are imbued with behavioural and cultural characteristics which act as a sorting mechanism of structural stratification in society, with othered groups typically most disadvantaged socially, economically, and politically; this is the crux of racism. The consensus is that these characteristics are not rooted in biology but in social myth (Mason 2000). They are what St Louis (2009: 563) calls 'more fictive determinations than objectively real entities'. However, while racial classifications are deemed somewhat arbitrary in the academy, Elam and Elam (2010) remind us that the 'fraud of race informs the realities of daily lives, social organizations, religious rituals, and political institutions'. We act in ways which signify a continued understanding of racial difference however problematic the category is as a conceptual tool (Phillips, A. 2007). Some sociologists, such as Fenton (2003), have argued instead for ethnicity as a more valid analytical category which represents a self-ascribed collectivity with origins sharing symbolic attributes relating to culture, ancestry, religion, nationality, territory, and language, and with the potential attraction that ethnicity is divested of the notions of superiority that come with race. However, similar ordering processes operate when considering various minority ethnic and other cultural groups and nowhere is this more evident than in Western notions of 'Muslimness'. As Goldberg (2009: 165–6) suggests, the Muslim has become 'the monster of our times', symbolizing 'fanaticism, fundamentalism, female (women and girls') suppression, subjugation and repression'. Indeed, for Goldberg and others it is the exclusion from privilege and resources which underscore the potential of *racism*, regardless of whether it depends on biological, ethnic, or cultural hierarchies (see also Barker 1981).

Notwithstanding, the picture at the micro level reveals some positive signs of change but also considerable differentiation and complexity. Individual feelings of racial prejudice towards othered groups are one way of examining this issue and appear to have reduced somewhat in the last two decades, although this may reflect socially desirable responses as it is now less acceptable to be blatantly prejudiced. Across the time series available (1983–2006), the British Social Attitudes survey found that self-reported prejudice[9] was at its highest in 1987 at 39 per cent, and at its lowest at 25 per cent in 2000 and 2001, but standing at 30 per cent when it was last measured in 2006 (Heath, Rothon, and Ali 2010; see also Ford 2008).

There are also signs that minority ethnic groups, contrary to the concerns expressed by Trevor Phillips, tend to see themselves as belonging to British society, perhaps surprisingly, even more than their white counterparts. Lloyd's (2010) analysis of the 2008–9 Citizenship Survey found that Pakistani (95 per cent) and Indian (94 per cent) people were slightly more likely than white (92 per cent) people to feel part of British society. Between 74 per cent (other Asian) and 91 per cent (Pakistani) of minority ethnic groups felt that they strongly belonged to Britain compared with 84 per cent of white respondents. Muslim respondents were as likely to express similar views as those from other religious groups (cf. Cantle 2001; McGhee 2003). This does not, of course, mean that these sentiments are reciprocated; in the 2008 Pew Global Attitudes Project, 23 per cent of British respondents held unfavourable views of Muslims, but this was much lower than in Spain, Germany, Poland, and France. Generally speaking, these surveys indicate that older people are less tolerant of minority ethnic groups than young people. In the international league tables of negative attitudes towards immigration and racial integration, Britain seems to be about average (Heath et al. 2010).

Of concern, however, was the finding from the 2008–9 Citizenship Survey which showed that white respondents (53 per cent) were more likely to perceive greater racial prejudice today than five years ago, whereas this was true of 29 per cent of all minority ethnic groups (ranging from 17 per cent of Chinese to 41 per cent of Pakistani respondents). This finding is tricky to interpret as it could mean that white respondents themselves felt more prejudice towards other racial groups, that they believed other whites were more prejudiced, or that they perceived more racial prejudice

---

[9] Measured by respondents who answered 'very prejudiced' or 'a little prejudiced' in response to the question 'How would you describe yourself…as very prejudiced against people of other races, a little prejudiced, or not prejudiced at all?'

towards them. In the same survey a question about perceptions of discrimination by public organizations found that all minority ethnic groups (but especially those of Black Caribbean, Bangladeshi, and Mixed Race origin) believed that they would be treated worse by the Prison Service than individuals from other racial groups (Ferguson and Hussey 2010). However, the majority response for all ethnic groups was that there would be similar treatment of racial groups in prison (the range was from 38 per cent of Black Caribbean respondents to 55 per cent of Chinese respondents); 60 per cent of white respondents believed that they would experience the same treatment as other racial groups.

Jacobs' (1977) and Carroll's (1974) qualitative studies of the prison paid particular attention to black prisoners' racial identities which were increasingly politicized in the 1960s and 1970s. Such a focus has not been a feature of prison studies in the United Kingdom and this is a gap which the current book hopes to fill. The literature on racial and ethnic identities can be broadly subdivided into the social psychological and the sociological (for a review and critique of the former, see Phoenix 2010). Current sociological thinking has stressed the fluidity of identity. Hall's (1991/2000) seminal work on 'new ethnicities' focused on the multiple dimensions of identities, emphasizing their state of flux, immutability, complexity, and historical and spatial specificity. His analysis is invaluable in highlighting the contingent nature of identity, particularly its ambivalent and always-being-formed qualities. The diversity of identity belies any attempt to compose singular ethnic or racial categories. This clearly has relevance for understanding interactions between prisoners of diverse ethnic and cultural groups in the fraught environment of the prison. The deconstruction of identities encompassed in Hall's work and others has also been influenced by debates around intersectionality in which Brah and Phoenix (2009) recognize simultaneous oppressions of race, class, and gender and how they are lived in the everyday through multiple subject and subordinated positions (see also Crenshaw 1989; 1993).

The influence of the 'new ethnicities' paradigm has also, by implication, been to affirm the need to interrogate whiteness and to reflect on it as a racial formation and identity positioning (Phoenix 2010). Garner's work (2006; 2007) emphasizes the relational element of ethnic identities; whiteness can only be understood set against blackness and other racialized identities but the precise meanings of whiteness vary according to local racial regimes in which power relations are inscribed. In addition to whiteness as supremacy, Garner refers to a body of whiteness studies, including the pioneering work of Ruth Frankenberg (1994) which observes the invisibility of whiteness and its power (at least to white people themselves) despite its normativity and dominant presence. Garner is also alert to the plural trajectories of whiteness. While whiteness may offer privilege and status, the position at the top of the racial hierarchy is contingent and is mediated through the internal boundaries of class, gender, and sexuality. This idea of whiteness as contingent hierarchy acknowledges multiple positions whereby, for example, the material base of working-class white experience inscribes particular patterns of oppression and consciousness which are markedly different from middle-class white people. At the same time, Garner recognizes that while whiteness is a fluid and constructed identity, it still offers in many cases privileged access to power and material resources. The validity of these claims for the prison environment is fundamentally of interest and is picked up again more fully in the empirical chapters of this book, particularly in light of some research which has been suggestive of black dominance in prison social relations.

The ambivalent state of race relations in Britain has also preoccupied Paul Gilroy (2004; 2005). Gilroy's contention in his recent work is that Britain is suffering from a 'social, cultural and psychological blockage', termed 'postimperial melancholia' resulting from its traumatic loss of empire, but it also displays convivial multicultures in its metropolitan and urban centres (Gilroy 2006: 27). Gilroy uses a diverse range of examples from an unhealthy obsession with victory in the Second World War to the ongoing xenophobia towards refugees, asylum-seekers, and migrants to illustrate the paralysing anxiety, confusion, and bewilderment associated with this melancholic state as Britain finds itself home to non-white Britons and new migrants. At the same time, arguably, the latter fact produces vibrant, messy multicultures in which racial difference is minimized. Gilroy seeks to celebrate this display of conviviality, tolerance, and justice which is revealed in routine, everyday interactions where difference is regularly encountered. There is empirical support for Gilroy's analysis in qualitative studies of friendship, school, and neighbourhood relations which indicate racial difference as ordinary, subsidiary, and incidental (Rampton and Harris 2009), although this does not mean that racial boundaries are automatically effaced (Back 1996; Frosh, Phoenix, and Pattman 2002).[10] Even in the case of today's Muslim folk devils, Kyriakides et al.'s (2009) research in two multi-ethnic Glaswegian and Bristol neighbourhoods suggests a destabilizing of nationalist exclusionary impulses towards Muslims. Cultural hybridity is accepted; for example Scottish-accented Muslims can demonstrate and be 'allowed' to belong to the nation. However, national belonging remains circumscribed by any displays of foreignness or stereo-typically 'Asian behaviour' which prompts exclusion from national belonging. I argue further for the relevance of this body of work for the criminological terrain of prison social relations in Chapter 4.

Institutional Racism and Race Equality

Understanding contemporary prison social relations must be contextualized within the massive policy and legislative developments of the last decade. The Macpherson Report (1999) which examined the Metropolitan Police Service's investigation into the racist murder of black teenager Stephen Lawrence, labelled the police and other institutions of government 'institutionally racist'. Martin Narey (2001: Foreword), Director General of the Prison Service at the time, accepted that this was also true of prisons and that there were 'pockets of blatant and malicious racism within the Service'. A Race Relations Advisor and a Muslim Advisor were appointed to the Prison Service in 1999 (Joly 2007). At the same time, the Director General was beginning to talk publicly about prisons becoming decent, 'fair and humane' places and these sentiments served as a backdrop to wider aspirations for change in the prison system (Liebling 2004). However, the specific lightning rod for a major reform programme in the case of race equality in prisons, was the CRE's (2003a; 2003b) formal investigation into the Prison Service. This was sparked by the racist treatment of Claude Johnson, a black prison officer, who had won employment tribunals in 1995, 1996, and 2000, following his victimization at HMP Brixton. Additionally reports of brutality and racism among prisoners and staff had emerged in two other prisons, HMP/Young Offenders' Institution (YOI) Parc in Wales and Feltham YOI.

[10] Ali (2003) has been critical of this body of work for failing to acknowledge the gendered nature of these social interactions.

The CRE 2003a report on these three prisons identified 14 areas of failure based on their examination of practices and experiences at the three prisons. The team found that the general atmosphere in prison was supportive of racist abuse, graffiti, harassment, and discrimination, which negatively impacted on minority ethnic staff and failed to protect prisoners, with a poor response to complaints and issues of discipline, and the presence of informal recruitment and promotion practices. Problems were also uncovered in the provision of religiously appropriate services, particularly for Muslim prisoners, an inadequate supply of goods for minority ethnic groups in the prison shop, and a lack of assistance to meet the literacy needs of Irish travellers. Another failure related to the poorly managed use of discretion which was influenced by officers' use of negative racial stereotypes, including, for example, seeing groups of black prisoners congregating as a gang threat. This harsher treatment also included the unauthorized use of punishments and a culture of unaccountability. At the same time, black prisoners were more vulnerable to drug testing and minority ethnic prisoners risked being transferred if they raised complaints about prison officers. The complaints system itself was policed by officers, effectively discouraging submissions, and the quality of investigations was poor. There was also an indication of inconsistencies in the use of discipline, determinations of status in the incentives and earned privilege (IEP) scheme,[11] and access to work parties. The CRE concluded that most of the problematic practices in the three prisons were underpinned by the absence of management oversight, entrenched operational staff cultures, and inadequate race relations training.

Feltham YOI came under further scrutiny in 2000 when white prisoner, Robert Stewart, murdered his Asian cell-mate, Zahid Mubarek, with a table leg in a vicious racially motivated assault. The two had shared a cell, seemingly harmoniously, for six weeks before the fatal incident.[12] The public inquiry into Mubarek's racist

---

[11] This scheme aims to encourage responsible behaviour by prisoners, encouraging effort and achievement in work and other constructive activity, and to ensure the disciplined and therefore safer environment for prisoners and staff (see PSO 4000).

[12] Although rejected by the inquiry team as without foundation, there were rumours of prison officers engaging in 'gladiator' gambling which involved betting on the outcomes of putting unsuitable prisoners together in shared cells (Keith 2006).

murder, led by Lord Keith in 2006, found that Stewart had experienced a troubled, unloving home life and several prison sentences. There were indications that he had a severe personality disorder and his earlier behaviour in Hindley Prison had been disruptive and on occasion bizarre, often involving potential or actual harm to himself or other prisoners. Although not charged, Stewart had also been involved in a pre-planned fatal stabbing of a prisoner at Stoke Heath YOI, although later he appeared to be compliant and well behaved.

Significantly, letters written from prison by Stewart included a 'plethora of racist comments and on occasion threats'; including a criminal incident (Keith 2006: 279). Very little of this and other information indicating Stewart's racism and violent unpredictability was systematically collated in his various prison files which accompanied him to Feltham; hence his being placed in a cell with an Asian prisoner. Along with prison officers' failure to consider the tattoos on Stewart's head (a cross with RIP insignia reminiscent of Ku Klux Klan symbolism), and racist abuse used by prisoners and staff, the Keith Inquiry (2006) concluded that there was a 'deplorable' climate at Feltham where race equality was not part of core operational business. The inquiry team acknowledged that Stewart's intense dislike of Feltham prison was fuelled by his feelings of isolation and vulnerability as a white, northern prisoner among 'London gangs', many of whom were black. Stewart had claimed that the violence inflicted on Mubarek had been with the aim of securing a transfer from Feltham.

The negative findings of poor relationships between prison officers and prisoners reported by the CRE (2003a; 2003b) investigation have been confirmed in other research studies and inspections. Cheliotis and Liebling's (2006) analysis of the Measuring the Quality of Prison Life (MQPL) survey in 49 prisons in 2003–4 showed that minority ethnic membership (black, Asian, and Chinese/other) was the most significant predictor of perceptions of poor race relations. Even 9 per cent of white prisoners felt that black and Asian prisoners were treated unfairly compared to them. The proportion for minority ethnic prisoners was 42 per cent for black prisoners, 41 per cent for Asian prisoners, and 30 per cent for Chinese/other prisoners. These negative beliefs were closely linked to prisoners' views about prison officers' unfair exercise of their discretion in distributing privileges, controlling discipline, providing access to information, and responding to requests and applications. Their generally lower ratings on measures of dignity, trust, family contact, and order have significant implications for establishing penal legitimacy among minority ethnic prisoners (Sparks et al. 1996; Tyler 2010).

A thematic inspection carried out shortly after the CRE formal investigation by Her Majesty's Inspectorate of Prisons (HMIP) (2005) described prisoners and staff inhabiting 'parallel worlds'. Staff largely assumed positive race relations while some prisoner groups catalogued familiar concerns about their inferior treatment compared to their white counterparts (see also Edgar and Martin 2004). In contrast, white prison staff described their policing of racial tensions between prisoners as being an issue and expressed concern about them being falsely accused of racism by minority ethnic prisoners (see also Beckford et al. 2005).

HMPS agreed a huge reform programme of race equality in prisons taking account of the findings of the CRE (2003a; 2003b), the Keith Inquiry (2006), and HMIP (2005). This included making race equality an integral corporate and operational priority monitored through rigorous performance and policy assessment targets (PSO 2800), as well as changes to the racist incidents and complaint systems. These efforts have been reinforced by legislation (first in the Race Relations (Amendment) Act 2000 and then in the Equalities Act 2010) which require public authorities such as prisons to avoid unlawful racial discrimination and to promote equality of opportunity.

The NOMS (2008) *Race Review* five years later reported significant improvements in the management of race equality and a perception that blatant forms of racism and racial discrimination had been excised from the prison service. Improvements included better food choice and canteen items for diverse groups of prisoners and meeting Muslim prisoners' religious needs, but minority ethnic access to education and offender behaviour programmes was still limited (see also Cowburn and Lavis 2009). Moreover, race equality was still not necessarily core business for the prison service, and minority ethnic prisoners were more negative in their assessments of their treatment by prison officers, particularly with regard to IEP, work allocations, discipline, and segregation, and concerns remained with the complaints and racist incidents reporting and investigation mechanisms (see also HMIP Prisons 2009 focusing on women prisoners). The data on outcomes revealed that black prisoners were 30 per cent more likely to be on the basic IEP level with few privileges, 50 per cent more likely to be in the segregation unit, and 60 per cent more likely to have force used against them than white prisoners, perhaps because of negative stereotyping or cultural misunderstanding. These are areas of routine prisoner–staff interaction where discretion plays a key part in outcomes, whereas in more formal processes, such as adjudication, racially disproportionate outcomes were not found.

In its recent thematic inspection relating to Muslim prisoners' experience, HMIP (2010) uncovered similar negative assessments of the prison regime among Muslim prisoners, particularly those who were mixed race or black. In particular, they were less likely to feel safe in prison, reporting higher levels of assault by staff and experiencing imprisonment in a more coercive manner than non-Muslim prisoners. Survey findings pointed to more problematic staff–prisoner relationships largely in relation to a minority of staff who often assumed that Muslim prisoners were linked to terrorism and extremism and therefore categorized as a high security risk (see also Liebling, Arnold, and Straub 2012's study of Whitemoor prison). More positive views were expressed regarding religious needs being met in the HMIP inspection, although it was felt that pertinent issues like the cross-contamination of halal food were not well understood (see also Beckford et al. 2005).

Muslim prisoners in Beckford et al.'s (2005) qualitative study of a local prison, high security prison, and a YOI, felt that worship facilities for Muslim prisoners were inferior to those of Christian prisoners. There were some concerns about the compatibility of Islam observance with the constraints of both the prison regime and a prisoner body of mainly Christian and non-religious individuals. There were also perceptions of discrimination in work allocations to the most attractive jobs, and views that prison officer racism was latent or more subtly expressed in actions where Muslim prisoners were disadvantaged. Prison officers equally felt that some minority ethnic prisoners falsely claimed discriminatory treatment, 'playing the race card' (see also Crewe 2009). Some prison officers believed that self-categorization as 'Muslim' was simply used instrumentally by prisoners to access certain entitlements such as special food and time out of cells.

Absent from most of these studies and reports, valuable though they are, is a sense of the 'racial temperature' of the prison in *interactions between prisoners*, particularly as not all conflicts and tensions will come to the attention of prison officers. Whilst the racist murder of Zahid Mubarek was a tragic, yet seemingly isolated[13] incident, we have little empirical foundation on which to judge the everyday nature of prisoners' relationships across racial, ethnic, and national boundaries. The primary focus in race equality research and policy has been to produce more positive and less discriminatory vertical relations between prison officers and prisoners which are, of course, of profound importance, but less attention has been paid to horizontal relations in the prison milieu. This is despite there being a general public sector duty in the Equalities Act 2010 for prisons to foster good relations between individuals who have a protected characteristic (for example, race and religion) and those who do not. This last requirement has received the least attention in both prison equalities work and prison research. This was one of the spurs for the research study on which this book is based.

We have limited quantitative findings which give some measure of the nature of prisoner–prisoner relationships but none of the contextual flavour of the extent, if any, that prison life is racialized. NACRO's (2000) snapshot survey of nine prisons, for example, reported that 51 per cent of prisoners considered relationships between prisoners of different ethnic groups to be okay, with 27 per cent believing them to be good and 7 per cent very good. Only 13 per cent believed relationships to be poor or very poor, with Asian prisoners most negative in their evaluations. Such snapshots tell us little about whether such relationships are okay because of physical avoidance or whether this extends to friendship and solidarity in dealing with the pains of imprisonment. But this does compare very favourably with the 61 per cent of the British population surveyed by Ipsos MORI (2006) who believed relations between different ethnic groups to be good.

The HMIP (2005) thematic inspection of race relations, *Parallel Worlds*, found that racist bullying was most often experienced by Asian prisoners across all prison types (juvenile, young offenders, women, and adult men). This seems likely due to their being regarded as physically weak and passive in prisoner hierarchies (Sparks

---

[13] Notwithstanding, Gadd and Dixon's (2011) psycho-social interpretation of Stewart's actions, drawing on Gilroy's (2004) work, points towards the significance of Britain's melancholic sense of cultural loss as motivating race hatred. In this sense, Britain's national culture is implicated in violent racism rather than being just the actions of a disordered individual.

et al. 1996), although Crewe's (2005) research in Wellingborough prison suggests a repositioning when Asian prisoners gain status as dealers in heroin. Enriching our understanding of the racialized dynamics of horizontal relations in prison can shed light on prisoner hierarchies in the late modern prison. The presence of verbal and physical racist abuse and bullying among prisoners has been observed in some reports (CRE 2003a; Ellis, Tedstone, and Curry 2004; HMIP 2005), but seems to be largely peripheral to life inside in other studies of prison life (Sparks, Bottoms, and Hay 1996; Edgar, O' Donnell, and Martin 2003). There is a hint of physical threat in Harvey's (2007) study of young adult prisoners; white prisoners in Feltham prison who were not from London admitted finding black prisoners intimidating. Crewe's (2009) study of Wellingborough prison asserted a 'fragile calm' in prisoner race relations, with racial tolerance and hostility coexisting, although the latter was exaggerated in white prisoners' accounts. White prisoners were especially critical of claims of racism made, in their view, erroneously or mischievously, and were often resentful of the collective and solidary orientation of Asian prisoners. In the only recent study conducted in women's prisons, Kruttschnitt and Hussemann (2008) (like Carroll 1974) found that white prisoners' sense of their own racial identities came to the fore in prison, reflecting that they were for the first time in a minority position. Both white and black Caribbean prisoners experienced each other to be rude and, for black prisoners, this was, on occasion, perceived to be racist.

More work is needed to understand the dimensions of solidarity and dominance in prisoner hierarchies in the late modern, ethnically, religiously, nationally diverse prison (although see Crewe 2009). We have little idea about the role, meaning, and positioning of ethnicized (including white) masculine identities in prison life. Acknowledging Goldberg's representation of the 'monster Muslim', we also know relatively little of the meaning of Muslim identities for preservation of the self in prison, at a time when Muslim prisoners have been assumed to be ripe for politicization and extremism in policy and media quarters (but see Spalek and El-Hassan 2007; Hamm 2009). At the same time, the impact of the increase in the Muslim prisoner population (up 140 per cent since 1994, but still only at 12 per cent nationally) on social relations between prisoners who are more commonly unobservant or of Christian faith has not been extensively studied. A better sense of whether prisoner friendships and coalitions exist or are deeply

divided—as Wacquant (2001) suggests is true in the United States— is needed. Similarly, whether prisoner hierarchies are diffuse and fragmented or patterned by majority or minority race, ethnicity, or religion has not been subject to recent empirical research. The importation of street-based ethnicized gangs (now largely acknowledged to exist in the United Kingdom, see Goldson 2011) into prison has also fuelled media stories but there is very little empirical research with which to assess such claims (but see Liebling, Arnold, and Straub 2012). Nor is there any sense of whether there is tolerance of racial or religious prejudice in everyday life inside as compared with life in outside communities.

In reflecting on claims of minority ethnic separatism in Britain's northern towns following the 2001 disturbances between young Asian and white men and the police, Amin (2002) suggests that we need to consider the 'daily negotiation of difference' in public spaces like cafes, parks, and shopping centres. This needs to extend also to the 'prosaic negotiations' of everyday life in sites where contact is compulsory, such as workplaces, educational institutions, youth centres, and sports clubs. Of course, contact is effectively compulsory in the very public and mixed space of prisons, and these are places where individuals are culturally displaced and social relations are destabilized. We might assume positive prison social relations based on the significant minority ethnic composition of the prison population. Yet, as Amin (2002: 969) asserts, colour composition tells us little of the nature of interactions within that space: '[h]abitual contact in itself, is no guarantor of cultural exchange', possibly instead leading to established ethnic practices becoming embedded in social life. This was certainly evident in the US prison studies of the 1970s, leading Jacobs (1979: 23) to comment that '[i]t is hard to imagine a setting which would be less conducive to accommodative race relations than the prison'.

As Goodman (2008) suggested at the start of this chapter, little is known about the contemporary dynamics of ethnically diverse prisons—the interracial, intra-racial, and cross-national interactions between prisoners at work, in classes, during association, on the wings, and during exercise. How, if at all, are ethnic identities specifically articulated in prison social relations in England? Is there any sense of racial solidarity and, if there is, are these identities politicized? Or is the rather dystopic vision of Wacquant (2001) applicable to England and Wales with race acting as a 'master status' and source of extreme tension? Or do, to use Amin's

(2002: 959) phrase, 'the micropolitics of everyday social contact' in the prison owe more to Gilroy's (2006: 32) concept of multicultural conviviality thereby eschewing the United States as the 'the inevitable destination of our racial politics'? What role, if any, do racialized prison masculinities or religious identities play? Are these categorical and biographical identities mobilized to mitigate or resist the pains of imprisonment and institutional control? These questions have informed the study of prisoner identities and social relations at Rochester YOI and Maidstone prison and in Chapter 3 I outline the methodological approach used.

3

The Art of the Possible: Epistemological Turns and Counter-turns

'neither blacks nor whites...talk honestly about race in the other's presence' (Duneier 2004: 101)

At one point, as I am explaining how much and how long I intend to be around, and how we want to get a deeper more detailed insight into prisoners' lives, C says, 'the only way you can really do that is to do the time yourself, that is it, you can't really know how it is unless you've been there' (Fieldnote: 30 May 2007, Maidstone prison).

In Chapters 4 to 6 I outline the multiple ways in which 'race' was actuated, resisted, contested, and sustained by individual agency (Knowles 2003) in the social world of two men's prisons in southeast England—Rochester Young Offenders' Institution and Maidstone Category C prison. Examining the nature of horizontal relationships in prison and testing the racial temperature of the late modern English prison seemed more readily accessible using a qualitative approach. The study's aim was to get beneath the survey and ethnic monitoring data to examine how race relations are *felt and experienced by prisoners* inside. Trying to unpack the ordinary and the mundane of daily life inside the prison, to understand how difference is negotiated and the role of prisoners' racial, ethnic, religious, and masculine identities in coping with imprisonment and in prisoner hierarchies, seemed best studied using in-depth interviews and including an observational and interactional component to judge the nature of the interactions between prisoners *in situ*.

I have chosen, like others, to reflect on the epistemological foundations of the study and to include its methodological details here in the body of the book, rather than relegate them to an appendix. I believe that they reveal elements of the story of the prison just as much as the substantive analysis contained in the subsequent chapters. Importantly, they also set the boundaries of what is possible in qualitative work generally, and how this is further constrained in the unique environment of the late modern prison, where the researchers are observers of those 'doing time', as C suggests, but are ultimately far removed from its most fundamental element.

Reflexivity and its Discontents

In the first week of fieldwork at Maidstone prison Rod Earle and I met Warwick, a first-time prisoner from the Caribbean. It was immediately obvious that he was struggling to understand prison—how he got there, how he could get in contact with his family in the Caribbean, whether he could survive on his Rastafarian-influenced vegan diet, whether an appeal might help to get him out, and whether he might be vulnerable to deportation. His bewilderment and fear was palpable and a reminder of how the prison disorients in just the way Goffman (1962) described in *Asylums*. Even though we struggled sometimes to understand him as he used patois and had a broad Caribbean accent (and neither of our origins lie in the Caribbean), his pain and trauma was evident, and it was upsetting to see someone so obviously 'out of their depth' and in need of help. Over the following weeks it was noticeable that as we regularly bumped into Warwick around the prison, his attention was almost always directed at me rather than Rod. During one of these conversations I learned of Warwick's professional singing aspirations. Somehow before realizing it, I had agreed to bring in a blank CD so that he could record his voice. Even though I had warned him that I would need some time to buy a CD and also to fathom the procedures for bringing it into the prison,[1] I found myself being literally pursued by Warwick whenever I saw him. He interrupted my discussions with other prisoners, came into an interview room when I was conducting an interview with another prisoner, and later told me off for not seeking him out. At one point, the chaplain saw me

---

[1] I accept that this was a risky strategy that could easily have placed me in a compromising position. The fact that it did not was down more to luck than sense and I believe that Crewe's (2010) approach not to bring anything into the prison for prisoners is by far the safest.

in the chapel with Warwick, and he joked that he could see that I needed saving, and he did not mean by God!

These kinds of encounters will be doubtless familiar to anyone who has done research in prisons. What seemed important to understand, given the study's intentions to explore prisoners' identities, was not why Warwick sought our assistance as researchers but why he chose one member of the research team and not the other. It is certainly possible that Warwick saw in my personality or demeanour something more approachable and engaging than Rod. It could be that my gender signified to him a more willing listener, or that I might be able to provide more emotional support, or my London accent may have seemed more familiar to him. Yet, the fact that one of Rod's fieldnotes records that Warwick, on one occasion, was 'delighted' to see me, exclaiming 'Rastafari' on seeing my loxs (dreadlocked hair), suggests that my race played a significant role in this particular research relationship.[2] Other interactions between myself or Rod and other prisoners confirmed that the race and gendered dynamics of our mixed research team might have wider epistemological and methodological implications.

Increasingly, ethnographic and qualitative research has recognized that researching others cannot be disconnected from researching ourselves in that the field under study is inevitably affected, even constituted, by the researcher, their biography, positionality, values, and ideological and disciplinary perspectives (Davies 1999). These issues come to the foreground even more when the research questions are themselves centrally concerned with difference, as they were in this study of prisoners' identities and their impact on social relations inside. Reflexivity requires that we make visible the production of racialized, classed, and gendered power relations in the research process in order that we may mediate the different constructions of social reality which emerge (Gunaratnam 2003; Ali 2006). Krumer-Nevo and Sidi (2012) propose that we write in ways which minimize othering using narrative accounts, dialogue, and laying bare our emotions in order that we can expose our processes of interpretation to the reader. The alternative, according to Pearson (1993: viii), is that the 'researcher, however, carefully disguised in either fieldwork comportment or textual display, is always the elephant in the room'.

[2] Fieldnote 4 July 2007.

In contrast, for some scholars reflexivity can be a sham. Skeggs (2004: 128), for example, warns that it can all too easily facilitate an exploitation of other people's suffering to produce an academic bourgeois self which plays with power and authority. Claims of reflexivity can provide a platform for claiming an authenticity or realness of experience which is spurious. In a similar vein, Hobbs (1993: 62) deplores the confessional tales of the ethnographer 'who was nearly arrested, almost beaten up, and didn't quite go crazy'. Such accounts seem superficial when the 'daily grind of survival' continues for research subjects, and academic careers (like my own) are built on the back of brief 'flirtation[s] with the terrible immediacy of life amongst the lower orders'.[3] Other critics of the reflexive turn shun its emotionality which pays too much attention to exploring anecdotes and is overly subjective (Crewe 2009), or engages in rhetorical stances (Carlen 2010). Moreover, as Lofland and Lofland (1995: 11) note, 'even when exceptionally well executed, reports analysing autobiographical data are often viewed by readers as borderline self-indulgence: when only competently executed, they are likely to be labeled "narcissistic" or "exhibitionist" and simply dismissed as uninteresting'.

While I have sympathy with these criticisms, in light of our research experience in the prison field, I struggle with the belief that there is an unmediated, singular reality to be narrated, that researchers should simply 'tell it like it is' (Hollway and Jefferson 2000; see also Young 2011), excising themselves from the research process and professing their textual account to be a neutral representation of the social world. This seems to me to be akin to the experimenter who meticulously excludes his/her role and that of any other (supposedly controllable) extraneous variables in order to test the effect of the independent variable on the dependent variable. I agree with Wahab (2005: 30) that it is problematic to assume that 'the gaze of the text/author is universal, unsituated, neutral ahistorical, acultural, and an unquestionable production'. Indeed, it is the wholeness of the account and its conversational tone which qualitative researchers revere, actively rejecting objective positivist methods for their empiricism. Yet the dynamics of a conversation are inter-

---

[3] I did, however, become engaged in public service work, for example acting as a 'critical friend' on the Independent Advisory Group for the National Offender Management Service (NOMS) *Race Review* (2008).

active and one in which the researcher is actively present, and this active presence cannot be ignored.

I am equally unconvinced that the emotionality of prison research can be airbrushed out. Surely, it is only by exposing our emotional reactions to the prison experience, placing them in the foreground, that the readers of our work can judge our interpretations and 'the problem of our own susceptibility to "sensitized topics"' (Liebling 1999: 164; see also Harding 1987; Bosworth et al. 2005; Krumer-Nevo and Mirit 2012). I became aware of one such reaction soon after we began the fieldwork in Maidstone prison. Having spent eight months interacting with and interviewing 18- to 20-year-olds at Rochester, I was unprepared for my misgivings about doing the same with the older white men at Maidstone prison. At Rochester my initial concerns centred on my ineptitude with using keys around the prison (underlined by one dream I had of facilitating the escape of a prisoner who looked remarkably like Hannibal Lecter[4] and thus 'spoiling the field' for future researchers!). But at Maidstone prison I became aware of a fear of trying to engage white prisoners who represented for me the 'white bogeyman' of a 'white racist thug' resurrected from my childhood:

Some of these people [prisoners] look scary to me. Some of them look like the stereotype of a kind of white racist thug. And I found some of them quite frightening....There's a kind of style and a countenance of a kind of older white man...that I find really quite frightening cos it takes me back to when I used to...I'd be shouted at in the street, and I'd be like racially abused, and it would always be by, you know, white men, often who were kind of bulked up, that were tattooed...(Research co-interview, 8 May 2009)

As it turned out these fears were not completely misplaced, supporting Duneier's (2004) claims that black and white people may not feel free to talk honestly about race in the other's presence. For Rod, there was an initial indication of racialized[5] animosities

---

[4] A serial killer in the film *The Silence of the Lambs*, played by Anthony Hopkins.

[5] Whilst Goldberg (2009) is not a fan of the term 'racialization', I have found it useful, following Rattansi's (2005) lead, to use it to signify a more dynamic and multidimensional process than a binary view of racism, which recognizes the potential role of race, ethnicity, nation, gender, class, and sexuality in contributing to disadvantage and inequality. Usefully then, racialization takes account of intersectional plurality, the importance of simultaneous positioning across many categories

among some white prisoners in the self-cook areas of Maidstone prison, and importantly, he picked up comments which might not have been articulated in the same way in my presence:

A young white guy, very white, shaved head and a baseball cap is standing nearby and I ask what he's cooking. He says 'Just toast, not like these fucking guys, doing their fucking rice, fucking rice eads'—not proper food is it'—I'm not sure if he's making a kind of racist remark. The groups around the cooker are mixed, there is a curry being made, rice cooking and the cooks are non-white, and there is a white guy frying fat chips. (Fieldnote, 23 May 2007)

Likewise, in Rod's interview of Abbott, a prisoner at Rochester prison, it seems unlikely that he would have agreed to have been interviewed by me. Abbott spoke of not wishing to speak to minority ethnic prisoners and ignoring them and walking away if they spoke to him. He wanted to differentiate himself, as white and *English* from 'ethnic minorities, not even minorities now, majorities…the African minorities never say they're English, they say they're British, so I'd like to be separated from that'. And in Maidstone it became clear that several white prisoners had much to say about issues of racism, but for them, Rod again seemed to present a more receptive audience for their perspective. This point is illustrated in these interview extracts at Maidstone:

It is my experience, since I've been in here that the most noticeable form of racism as a word comes from ethnic minorities accusing the authorities of racism because they're not getting their own way. (Ralph, white British, no religion)

…the white and the black issue. Um, can be used in so many different ways, you know, um and I think it's unfair that the coloured people will use that against the white people as a racial sort of thing. (Piers, white British, no religion)

I return to this theme of using the so-called 'race card' in Chapter 6.

There were other indications that the nature of our research team, mixed in terms of gender, race, age, religion, and social class,

of difference which will depend on power relations (Crenshaw 1989). More than this, however, racialization can accommodate the ambivalence and contradiction of actions which seek to make superior or inferior groups on the basis of their race, ethnicity, faith, culture, or nationality. It requires empirical investigation of actors, institutions, processes, policies, and practices which act to apply labels, making race salient as well as taking account of the role of processes of stratification linked to class, gender, and sexuality.

meant that we were directly implicated in the study right from the beginning of the fieldwork, reinforcing my feeling that Warwick's sidelining of Rod, discussed earlier, was racialized. After hanging out, watching, and interacting with some young Rochester prisoners during B wing's association, Rod recorded the gist of a conversation that we had back in our office on C wing:

Coretta says all the black guys are telling her stories of the racism they face in the prison from the screws [prison officers]. It seems very striking, that they all have the same story, and want to tell her. She asks if I am getting the same and I have to say that I'm not. My interactions seem to be rather more mundane, low key, chit chat. I am worried about this as it seems a critical point of the project, and says something about the significance of identity—mine as a white researcher, and Coretta's as someone with whom such stories are meant to register. (Fieldnote, 26 July 2006)

While this raised concerns for Rod about his access to understanding minority ethnic prisoners' identities, my anxieties about moving around an adult men's prison with a majority white population were partly assuaged by the knowledge that the novelty of my presence in the prison excited attention and direct interaction with prisoners. As active participants in the research process then, our subject positions appeared to influence how and who we engaged with in the prison, and importantly, also who we avoided, at least in the early stages of the research (Hertz 1997). In my case, it was unclear whether this was connected to my race or gender or both but it was a pattern we noticed in both prisons:

The prisoners are all offered squash [after the Sunday church service] and there is a lot of milling around. Several prisoners gather around and ask who we are, what we are doing. It's nice that they are coming forward, we chat a bit, but I get the feeling Coretta is the centre of attraction/attention. There are a lot of glances toward her from small groups, some guys approach and get close, seemingly just to smile, a bit goofish, in her general direction and wander to exchange glances with mates, like they've checked her out. (Fieldnote, 6 August 2006, Rochester)

There are already people with food plates moving around in the [Kent] wing. The place has a bit of a crackle to it, a sense of alertness. Coretta's presence is immediately logged by people around the entrance area....Two black guys standing together indicate an interest to us, and we approach to explain who we are, Coretta talking to one, me to the other. Mine seems mildly annoyed that I am preventing him from engaging with Coretta, as his mate is, and he doesn't seem very interested, his eyes keep flicking to his left where Coretta and his mate are talking, his body also turning, though he doesn't entirely disengage. I don't feel I have his attention or interest, but I know who has. He even tries to grab a passing friend, also black, saying 'hey, hey, this guy wants to talk to you'. (Fieldnote, 6 July 2007, Maidstone)

Of course, the novelty factor in such situations can quickly wear off, but it did seem to provide somewhat of a privileged access to minority ethnic (and some white) prisoners in a way which was denied Rod, as a white man. Issues of racism against minority ethnic prisoners were more easily raised and aired by minority ethnic prisoners in my presence than in Rod's. Practically this meant that more of the informal contacts who were from minority ethnic groups, and who also became interviewees, were interviewed by me than by Rod. This also seemed to explain why our initial hopes to conduct an ethnically mixed group interview at Maidstone prison were not realized, as it became obvious that black prisoners were not prepared to join a mixed group and preferred to be interviewed in a black-only group which was facilitated by me. In the end, ten prisoners joined the discussion, which proved impossible to moderate and structure at the same time. It was often heated and rather difficult to control with requests to talk one at a time frequently ignored so that transcription was impossible. A smaller, mainly white group interview (of four white and one mixed race prisoner) was more easily arranged and we were both involved in conducting this.

The influence of our subject positions can extend beyond collecting data into the interpretive process (see Phillips and Earle 2010). During an observation of freeflow[6] outside Medway wing in Maidstone prison, Rod and I read the collective movement of prisoners quite differently:

Today it seems like one big group, maybe 100 prisoners, all together moving loosely. It's more tightly packed than the one I saw previously, and there is less calling. Coretta nudges me and says, 'See, how it is grouped according to race' or something like that and I feel myself snap to a different kind of attention; where I had been noticing a tighter knit whole group, she had seen ethnic grouping, and I wonder what is wrong with my way of looking that what leapt to her attention, leapt over my head. I look again,

---

[6] Where prisoners are unescorted by officers between the wings and place of work, education, gym, etc. It is a time of informal congregation in the rigid schedule of the prison day, allowing prisoners from different wings to chat, organize trade, or engage in illegitimate activities.

and in the crowd, which is loosening as people peel off to Medway while others proceed to Weald, it is obvious that black guys are bunched together and white and white-ish guys are also in groups, 3–4, or 4–5, with little overlaps here and there. (Fieldnote, 4 July 2007)

The research in Rochester and Maidstone prisons did not show that boundaries across race were impermeable, however,[7] and I concur with Phoenix (1998) who has argued that such effects are unpredictable and should not be assumed to occur in every research situation. The multiplicities of identities come into play in any kind of encounter. Given the choice to be interviewed by myself or Rod, for example, Anthony, a white prisoner at Maidstone prison, chose me, because he found 'it proper easy to talk to women'. The interview was long and informative, marked by commonalities of class, parental status, and age, where race did not impede access. Anthony had admitted that he would not have been able to 'open up' and express his feelings in an interview with a male researcher (see Phillips and Earle 2010). Similarly, Rod's interview with Melvin, a black Muslim prisoner at Maidstone, was rich in outlining his experiences of racism outside prison, his concerns about discrimination in prison, and his religious conversion to Islam.

There were predictable challenges of negotiating gender and sexuality. I was very unsettled by a prisoner regularly working outside on one of the wings at Maidstone prison. He was uninterested in talking about the key questions of the research study, preferring to flirt with me. At the end of one of these brief encounters, as I turned away he reached out and stroked my hand. This felt more of a violation than a sexual grope and I was thereafter very uncomfortable in his presence, but instrumentally decided I needed to keep him 'on side' rather than risk the research being disparaged on the wing. This was a reminder of the dangers of overfamiliarity in a setting where prisoners are starved of intimate heterosexual relations, and had the effect of making me more wary in subsequent interactions with prisoners. It is also a reminder that it is too simplistic to assume that the hierarchical power relations of the research endeavour flow in only one direction, from researcher to research participant. Rod struggled with a prisoner who insisted on being interviewed but only after he had aggressively confirmed that Rod

---

[7] Twine (2000) described 'racial subalterns' in Brazil seemingly being more comfortable discussing race and racism with a white researcher than with her, an African American.

was not gay. Feeling uneasy about being in close contact with a prisoner who was glassy-eyed, clearly under the influence of drugs, it was an uncomfortable and stilted interview, where Rod felt 'hostility, antagonism toward me, like he was looking for an excuse to wind me up or worse' (Fieldnote, 19 October 2007). The absence of any common ground between them seemed to preclude full engagement in the interview for both parties.

Access to men's interactions with each other is also likely to be deeply circumscribed, possibly even inaccessible to women researchers. Pearson (1993) suggests that whilst you do not have to be a competent burglar to provide a competent ethnographic account of an active burglar, researchers' identities may preclude the immersion required of ethnography. One example he uses is of a woman researcher trying to be a 'fly on the wall' to men's conversations in the pub (see also Bandyopadhyay (2006) on her limited access to men in an Indian prison). I have much sympathy with Pearson, and in the prison I was never fully comfortable hanging out on the landings without invitation or seeking out particular individuals. Nor did I feel at ease in joining in at pool during association, not least because this is not a recreational activity at which I excel.[8]

Similarly, in discussions about masculinity, Sallee and Harris (2011) found that male students sexually objectified women when being interviewed by a male researcher but advanced their rejection of these gendered norms in interviews with a female researcher. Other studies have similarly suggested that men emphasize their dominant heterosexuality, power, and superior knowledge in interviews with women researchers (Pini 2005). It is undoubtedly the case that men can find it difficult to express views about their own masculinity and can be sensitive to questions in this area. They may view the interview as a means for demonstrating their masculinity or as a threat to their masculinity (Schwalbe and Wolkomir 2001). One vivid example of this was in the first interview at Maidstone prison with Anthony. Asked what he thought women looked for in a relationship with men, he became slightly aggressive and defensive. He seemed to project his anxiety onto me by asking me to answer the question, and interjecting with an incongruous 'yeah, babe', going on to say:

[8] A request to work out with prisoners in the gym was declined, presumably because of my gender.

I dunno you tell me, you're a woman. Eh, that's alright, that's alright for me to say innit? You're a woman.... Yeah, but I mean, what you've just asked me there, that's for you to find out innit really? It's not for me to produce anything for you; it's for you to find out. You want to know what your man wants…What actually makes your man happy? How does it make him happy? How do you build up to having that happiness with your man, do you know what I mean? That's all you've got to work on all the time you know. You shouldn't have to work on it, you should be happy anyway, you know. (Anthony, white British, Christian, Maidstone)

It was an uncomfortable moment in the interview but it did not seem to have a lasting effect on its depth and fluidity. Anthony's response did, however, make sense when considered alongside what he saw as a painful betrayal in his last intimate relationship.

It is also not unusual for researchers to be challenged by qualitative research with sex offenders. Women may experience sexualized conversations, flirting, or inappropriate gestures, while male researchers may be invited to collude with offenders' presentations about their offence (Blagden and Pemberton 2010). Rod, for example, chose to change the subject when a prisoner on Thanet wing, who had been convicted of rape, described his lack of trust of women so as to avoid colluding with the man's denial and absorption in his own victimization. Highlighted also was the difficulty of asking questions but being unsettled, unprepared, or simply uncomfortable with the responses, a feeling particularly pertinent to the interviews with vulnerable prisoners on Thanet wing. Arthur, for example, convicted for sexual offences against children, described a homosexual relationship with a former prison officer, then his cottaging (casual homosexual sex in public places), as well as his married life with children. It is also not hard to be swayed by the sensationalist stereotyping of sex offenders— Rod recorded a seemingly involuntary thought whilst observing prisoners from Maidstone's Vulnerable Prisoners Unit, 'scanning a template across them to see which one fits the stereotype "sex-beast" "misfit" "inadequate" "weirdo-perve" conscious of the prejudice which informs such thinking' (Fieldnote, 21 November 2007). At other points there is a clear difficulty of maintaining a neutral stance:

In my mind is the appallingly low conviction rate for sexual assault and rape, the difficulty in securing a conviction, also the persistent denial of men who rape, that they have done so, a wilful twisting of sexual violence to normal sexual activity. (Fieldnote, 18 July 2007)

Notwithstanding, doing research in prison is a humbling experience. Pain seems to be etched onto prisoners' bodies; they tell sad and anguished stories about their lives outside to which the pain and devastation of incarceration is added. As neither researcher nor prisoner is naive enough to assume that these multifaceted experiences are affected or alleviated in any way by a single, academic study, there remains inherent to social research a fundamentally exploitative essence which Hobbs' (1993) acerbic comments hinted at. Nowhere was this more evident than in an interview I conducted with a foreign national prisoner in Rochester prison. Declaring that he would commit suicide if faced with deportation, it was particularly hard to justify opening up his raw emotional state to interview questioning while he was living with such desperate uncertainty.[9] Of course, regardless of whether or not he was interviewed by me, his immigration status was still insecure, but it was situations like these which ensured that the feelings of voyeurism never really went away.

At an affective level, our access to what research participants are saying or doing is also subjectively filtered through our own emotional lens. During an interview with Manu, a black Central African prisoner, who was serving his first sentence at Rochester, I found myself unable to ask further probing questions about his family and their influence in his life as he talked about his mother's death five years previously. Still in the midst of grieving for my own mother who had died just before the fieldwork started at Rochester, I found my eyes welling up with tears as Manu talked. He told me about how he had realized that 'life is actually harder than I thought it could have been' as he prayed in his cell, feeling depressed that he had let his mother down by being in prison. The enormity of his pain while being contained behind bars was overwhelming for me. A similar experience occurred when I interviewed Mark, who believed that because of his mother's severe health problems he was unlikely ever to see her again. In neither case did I share my own experience; in the interview moment I felt that this would be an insensitive indulgence. But in this way, it emphasized my power to hold back, to maintain control in our encounter, to refrain from allowing our common experiences of pain and grief to be aired. As Hertz (1997) reminds us, the questions we ask of research participants, but also

---

[9] I ensured that one of the wing officers was made aware of his state of mind following the interview.

those which remain unasked, and how we listen to what is said and ultimately how we understand, are all connected to our identities as researchers.

Capturing the Prison Experience: Ethnographic and Qualitative Approaches

Engaging reflexively with research participants is challenging in a place where ontological insecurity is part and parcel of life inside. Ethnography bears the promise of getting to the nub of this lived experience, offering the opportunity to immerse ourselves in the social world of prisoners, listening to conversations, observing social action, and participating in the scene, in an attempt to uncover the sense and meaning social actors attach to the complexities of their everyday lives. I was hopeful that Rod Earle and I would be able to get a deep and textured feel for the prisoner societies in Rochester and Maidstone prisons by observing them at close quarters, and then combining these insights with material gathered from semi-structured narrative/biographical interviews. This was attempted by being in the prison three to four days a week, usually from 8am to 4.30pm or 12.00pm to 8.15pm with some days when we were both present in the prison. In total, we spent eight months at each prison (Rochester Young Offenders' Institution (YOI): July 2006 to February 2007; and Maidstone prison: June 2007 to February 2008). These prisons were selected as both included a large number of prisoners from the urban areas of London where minority ethnic men are overrepresented as offenders but their 'catchment' area extended to Kent, Sussex, and Essex where white ethnicities predominated in criminal justice populations.[10]

The research prisons

Rochester YOI stands in rolling countryside just outside the Kent village of Borstal. It was built in 1874, taking its name from this village which later came to be used as a generic term for the penal discipline, industrial training, and treatment of boys aged 16–21

---

[10] These prisons were within reasonable travelling distances from our home locations which was important given the need to spend long periods of time at the prison and to cover early mornings (usually 8am to 8.30am) and early evenings (6pm to 8pm) when prisoners are unlocked and out of their cells.

years, established in Part 1 of the Prevention of Crime Act 1908. Visited by Alford (1909) in 1902, it was then the largest prison after Dartmoor prison, consisting of 240 acres. It retains the brick boundary wall from this early period, and along its western edge is Sir Evelyn Road, named after the founder of Borstal and prison reformer Sir Evelyn Ruggles-Rise (Forsythe 1990).

As Garland (1990) notes, prison architecture maintains a certain style to be palatable to the eyes of the public and for me the sand-coloured high walls and barbed wire lent Rochester the feel of a barracks or military compound. On my first visit, I stood outside the gate, observing the notices on the walls—the blue plaque detailing the Prison Service's race relations policy which immediately impressed me, and on the Visitors Centre, details about the criminal risks of bringing drugs into the prison. It took me a while before I realized that you have to ring a doorbell to alert the gate staff of your arrival and the public entrance to the prison is through an imposing wooden door—just like in *Porridge*, the prison sitcom I watched the repeats of throughout the 1980s.[11] Having travelled from my home in south-east London, I was aware of the changing topography as I moved from urban to suburban and then Rochester's semi-rural surroundings. I wondered how minority ethnic prisoners had felt on being transported here from the inner London boroughs just like *Porridge*'s main (white) character, Norman Fletcher, who ends up in a prison in a remote, rural area very distant from his London home. Rochester stands adjacent to the predominantly white rural idyll of the 'garden of England', as Kent is known, a far cry from the urban areas many prisoners have grown up in. However, the Prison Service website suggests that the prison is actually a popular choice for London prisoners because of the ease with which families and friends can visit by car or train.[12]

At the time of the study Rochester consisted of five residential wings (A–E) which held just under 400 young men aged 18–21 years. There was an education block with a small library, a health care centre, a gym, a contract services workshop for assembling fruit punnets and sorting clothes, an unused painting and decorating

[11] Coincidentally, Maidstone prison was used by the BBC in some of its filming of *Porridge* (see Jewkes' (2006) discussion about the depiction of prison life in this popular sitcom (see also Johnston, H. 2012)).
[12] This was presumably also the case in the 1990s when the infamous Reggie Kray, East End gangster, was held at Maidstone prison.

workshop (which was later converted into a multi-faith area with sinks for ablutions), a hairdressing salon, a wood working workshop, a computer suite for IT training, and a waste management workshop. Dotted around were small expanses of grass which were well tended by prisoners with beds of brightly coloured plants in stark contrast to the functional sterility of the main buildings. There were also football pitches and exercise yards framed with high perimeter fencing, a patch of brownish-green grass, and a grey concrete path around them. The administrative offices, visits room, chapel, and the room for Muslim prayers, completed the buildings.

Wings B, D, and E were the original Borstal wings—long, narrow, rectangular buildings over two floors. The upper floor had landings running the length of the building, with metal railings and a bridge in the middle at each end from which a metal staircase descended to the ground floor. The corridor inside ran the length of the block with cells on each side. The following gives an idea of the configuration of a typical cell (one on E wing):

the cell door[s] with its narrow vertical window slit, probably a foot long and two inches wide, covered by a metal flap. Next to it, the name card, sometimes with a photo of the prisoner. The cells are small, cramped ... Spartan, rough, institutional.... Most have a battered tubular metal bunk bed, with pale green sheets and green blankets down one side, nearly the full length of the cell. On the other side, in the middle is the stainless steel sink unit, then a small desk and chair. At one end or another the two shelf wardrobe units are stacked on top of the other. There are some pictures on the wall, (an officer says 'as you can see the usual form of decoration, tits and arse, predominates'). There are also some drawings, of cannabis leaves, spliffs, hiphop graffiti-style lettering. The air feels stale and stuffy and I ask about ventilation. The officer pulls aside a blanket pinned roughly across the window [there are no curtains] to reveal the vent. It can be turned to open or close, but I can't see how it would make much impression. With two guys inside it must be very stuffy. The toilet is off to one side ... (Field-note, 4 September 2006)

The ground floor typically consisted of a wing office for prison officers, another office or interview room, kitchen facilities, and an open area used for association with pool and table tennis tables. During evening and weekend association prisoners had free movement around the wing for one to two hours depending on their Incentive Earned Privileges (IEP) status; they could make phone calls, take showers, and play cards, dominoes, pool, or table tennis.

A wing was the resettlement unit with a more relaxed regime reserved for selected prisoners awaiting imminent release or transfer to adult prison. C wing was the Induction Unit where prisoners came for their first week before being allocated a more permanent cell on one of the other blocks. It was a more modern building than the other original Borstal wings, built over two storeys. It was U-shaped with two spurs in a long corridor containing the cells either side, some shared and some single cell, with showers upstairs. The windows were narrow slits with concrete beams over glazed interiors. There was a servery off to the left where prisoners collected their meals to take back to their cells. The walls were painted light blue to waist height and then magnolia above. There were numerous posters and notices including ones on suicide prevention, race relations, bullying, and so on. One hand-drawn joke poster advertised the installation of a new swimming pool for residents and another offered an Easter egg hunt.[13] Alongside the wing office there were 11 wooden document trays labelled 'Apps'; these were for prisoners to place their application forms for visits, courses, benefits, and the like. CCTV cameras nestled discreetly in most corners, shooting film in colour to the monitors in the main wing office. Each wing had access to an exercise yard—a tarmac enclosure surrounded by high wire-mesh fencing.

We were based in an office in between the staff room and wing office on C wing. Its location was convenient for observing the morning routines of prisoners getting ready for work and education, seeking assistance from officers, and putting in applications. At these times it was noisy and we caught snippets of prison life: the loud jangle of keys; the clanging of metal doors as prisoners were unlocked and locked up; frequent tannoy announcements. Prisoners and prison officers could be heard conversing, laughing, and sometimes shouting. Our office was a place to go when prisoners were locked in their cells (often for around 15–17 hours a day), where we could enter contemporaneous and reflective fieldnotes on the laptops we brought into the prison. It also provided a sanctuary and respite from the demanding nature of observing and engaging prisoners in conversation about their lives inside. At these times, the wings were quiet, and the sounds of the outside world—cars, children, people walking by, were noticeable by their absence.

---

[13] This example of 'gallows humour' was actually on D wing.

Maidstone prison was designed by the architect Daniel Asher Alexander and was built on a 14-acre site, completed in 1819 at a total cost of £200,000 (HMP Maidstone 2009). Unlike Rochester, it was constructed from the distinctive Kentish rag stone. Its imposing walls are one of the first sights you see as you drive into the town of Maidstone. It was the site of public executions outside the prison, and during the period 1868–1881 12 executions were conducted within the walls of the prison. At the time of the study, the prison consisted of a large range of buildings of different sizes and architecture, reflecting the considerable attempts to maintain it as a functional prison over the years. Some of the early restorations had been carried out using convict labour, and some, such as the Round Tower at the centre of the compound, are now English Heritage sites. It had the feel of a medieval castle village with its high, heavy walls made of great stone blocks, its alleyways between closely packed buildings, and the large round tower in the middle with its huge oak doors. This housed the prison's administrative offices with a nearby visits room at the front of the prison. Its Victorian drains were being renewed at the time of the research which made moving around the site difficult as footpaths were restricted. There was heavy plant equipment on the site and it was swarming with building contractors. Noticeably too, there was a ring of 'dead space' between the interior perimeter fencing and the exterior walls of the prison which were part of the town. This fencing was an attempt to disrupt the flow of drugs into the prison, some of which could be thrown over from the other side of the wall.

There were four residential wings (Weald, Kent, Medway, and Thanet), housing just under 600 category C prisoners; the latter wing exclusively accommodating vulnerable prisoners, many of whom were sex offenders. Weald wing had a dilapidated, neglected, and claustrophobic feel to it. Towards the end of the fieldwork it was closed when legionella bacteria were found in the water supply. Kent wing was much bigger, and higher than the other wings, in the old style architecture of the original prison. The spurs radiated from a central block, each with three landings of cells, but because the interior was open up to the roof it had a cavernous feel. Medway wing was built in the 1960s and its architecture was square, angular, and functional. A wing office was situated near the front, with a gloomy corridor leading off towards a laundry, another office for staff, and bare rooms housing pool and snooker tables, plus a couple of interview rooms. There was a small garden area with a square of grass containing a flowerbed planted with lettuce and herbs. A central staircase led up to the first and second floors and two spurs on either side where the cells and showers were. Thanet wing had been refurbished, with an extension housing the servery, recreational, and self-cook areas, and with a small garden. It had a different atmosphere with an open, airy foyer, a fish tank, and bookshelves, perhaps reflecting the average older age of prisoners held there. The cells were on two elevated landings.

We had an office in the health centre which was some way from the residential wings. There was an education block—a series of classrooms and art room, and a small library containing various materials including the black newspaper *The Voice*, an Arab language paper, and a travellers' newsletter. On the site there was also a bricklaying workshop, used intermittently, a well-equipped computer software operating systems workshop, a print workshop, and a fabric recycling workshop. The chapel had the feel of a Baptist church without the ostentatious ornamentalism of Catholic buildings. It was large, but spartan, with a high vaulted ceiling and stone steps leading to the altar. It was also used for Muslim prayers with a curtained divider. Somewhat incongruously, outside there was a large statue of Buddha.

Observation and interaction

In retrospect, at Rochester our observational work was made more difficult by occurring over such a broad area. While concentrating time on a single wing, or a single site within the prison (such as on the education wing, see Bosworth 1999) may provide only a limited picture of prison life, it may facilitate the development and maintenance of ongoing relationships with a smaller number of prisoners. We chose instead to spend short observation periods across a number of key sites within the prison: workshops, classes, all residential wings, particularly during association (6–8pm on weekdays) and the morning unlock period (8am to 8.30am at Rochester and 8.10am–9am at Maidstone), gym, exercise yards, Christian Sunday services and Muslim prayers, the visits room, and during freeflow. The heavily structured pattern of daily life provided relatively few opportunities for informal interaction, so the periods of formally permitted 'association' were precious to both prisoner and researcher alike. In Maidstone more observational time was concentrated on two wings, Weald and Medway, with less time spent on Thanet and Kent wings, the latter of which was known locally as the 'Beirut wing', to signify the chaotic nature that sprang from a larger number of prisoners, many of whom were perceived to be aggressive, and to some degree, 'out of control', because of entrenched drug use.

As Crewe (2009) has noted, there is an insecurity to observational work in prisons. In the beginning, it is hard to initiate, difficult to know where in the prison environment to locate yourself, what kind of pose to strike, or what to say which will be seen as inviting of interaction without being intrusive and voyeuristic. Ultimately it is the prisoners' place of residence and for some even a home (Klare 1960). As such, prisoners can emerge from the showers semi-dressed, they may be trying to relax after work or making phone calls to family and friends without interruption, and research breaches these moments of attempted privacy. Only some of these insecurities about observational research pass as more time is spent in the field.

However much researchers narrow their observational field, doubts often remain that they are missing the real action (see also Crewe 2009). Even the experience of the male researcher, Rod, whose gender did not automatically impede access to the more private realm of male interaction, indicated that there were severe limits on observing more than cursory interactions between prisoners unless you are deeply immersed in prison. On reflection, I agree with C's comment at the start of this chapter. I have come to believe that such immersion is not possible in a prison unless the researcher is serving a prison sentence themselves or conducting the research covertly (but see Sparks et al. 1996; Bosworth et al. 2005). It is very difficult to understand the denial of liberty and the invasion of privacy when you can come and go as you please and are not locked continuously in a small cell for more than 12 hours a day. Undoubtedly, more can be gleaned from being in a cell overnight when prisoners converse via the water pipes, hearing what is said while people are showering or hanging out in small groups in cells during association, and observing the non-verbal cues as people pass each other on the stairs or landings; many of these scenes are hidden from the view of researchers. Participation is not an option.

Observational research in prison is not, however, without value. The early interactions with prisoners were particularly

instructive because these informal chats revealed the presentation of a 'harmony discourse' by prisoners when asked casually
about race and social relations inside. As I discuss in Chapter 4,
to some extent this was confirmed through observation of the
public spaces of the prison, but these reflections and perceptions
were then undermined by the content of the in-depth interviews.
Harris and Rampton (2009) have urged caution in using only
interviews to gauge the significance of race and ethnicity amidst
other social relations, arguing that they privilege literal statements separated from social action. The interview material in
this study combined with the observational material helped to
flesh out the ambiguities and ambivalence around race and ethnicity in the late modern multicultural prison. The observational
and interactional period also provided an opportunity to learn
about the rhythm and routines of everyday life in prison, and to
learn the language of the prison (terms such as 'freeflow', for
example), which established a certain credibility when the interviews were under way. Simply being there also made it easier to
approach prisoners selected as part of the random sample, to
seek their consent to an interview.

Because of the foregoing discussion I prefer now to regard the
study as *qualitative* rather than *ethnographic* because I feel that the
formal semi-structured depth interviews provided more with which
to answer the key research questions than did the observational
and informal interaction components of the study. Or to be more
generous, perhaps it is simply more accurate to recognize that all
fieldwork requires improvisation and compromise, and will include
failings of one kind or another. As Buchanan et al. (1988: 53) have
aptly observed, organizational research is best seen as 'the art of the
possible'.

Interviewing prisoners

As the study's focus was to fill the research gap by exploring prisoners' horizontal relationships and examining the influence of identity on social relations *between prisoners*, I chose not to interview
prison officers. I was anxious that a security lens might distort prison officers' views of race relations among prisoners which would
be difficult to penetrate. Previous research had also found that victimization by other prisoners was rarely formally reported to prison officers and did not usually come to their attention (Edgar et al.

2003).[14] Furthermore, I anticipated that gaining access both formally from the governor and informally on the wings would be politically sensitive if it was regarded as yet another study of prison officers' practices with regard to race equality. Finally, I also worried about being associated with the 'govs'[15] and was less than convinced that Carroll's (1974: 11) approach in Eastern Correctional Institution, of avoiding role conflict by 'temporally segregating' his relationships with white prisoners, then black prisoners, then prison staff, could work in the smaller confines of an English prison. An incident which occurred during the observational work at Rochester YOI indicated that I had probably made the right decision:

I went over to Contract Services and the govs there asked if I'd like a cup of tea. I got them to point out a white prisoner to me who was on our random sample list. When I approached him and explained the study he seemed amenable and agreed to an interview which we scheduled for the following week. I then spent 15–20 mins chatting with the officers,…Then a white prisoner sent up by my scheduled interviewee came up to tell me that he didn't want to do the interview anymore. When I went down to check this with him, allay any fears, etc. he just confirmed that he didn't want to do it. By this time he had been talking with an Asian prisoner who asked how he'd been selected. I told him and also said that it wasn't a survey, that there weren't right and wrong answers, but that I was just interested in his opinion. He confirmed that he didn't want to do it. I immediately felt that it was because I had been seen sitting with the govs and perhaps was overly associated with them. A definite mistake on my part…(Fieldnote, 18 January 2007)

There are a whole series of methodological concerns which relate to interviewing incarcerated offenders but these largely relate to the appropriateness of asking them about their offending behaviour (Bernasco 2010). Whilst the interviews we conducted in prison did pick up on prisoners' criminal activities when asking about their pre-prison lives, this was not an explicit objective of the study.

[14] The CRE (2003a) and the Keith Inquiry (2006) similarly found that prisoners displayed racist attitudes, but few incidents were reported to prison officers. At Rochester, 24 racist incidents were reported involving only prisoners at the time of our fieldwork, of a total of 61. Of the 81 racist incidents recorded during the period of our fieldwork at Maidstone prison, only six involved complaints about prisoner–prisoner abuse.
[15] Short for 'governor', of management level in the Prison Service, but actually used more widely like 'screw' to cover all prison officers.

The interview sample was selected to reflect the socio-demo-graphic profile of the prison at the time of the study. In Rochester prison this consisted of informal contacts with whom we had estab-lished a rapport during the initial period of the study, which lasted almost three months. To avoid the possibility of our sample only including prisoners with particular stories to tell, ulterior motives, or who were especially vocal and sought us out, we included a 'ran-dom sample' of prisoners in each site.[16] The split between informal contacts and 'random sample' was 58 per cent/42 per cent in Rochester prison and 62 per cent/38 per cent in Maidstone prison. In Rochester, a small number of prisoners identified by the admin-istration as vulnerable prisoners were included in the sample because their difficulty in coping with prison life might shed light on aspects of prisoners' social relations.

The 'random sample' was constructed once the interviews with informal contacts had been concluded or scheduled. It had purpo-sive elements to it and was stratified only on an ad hoc basis. It was devised by working out the proportion of interviewees that we had from the informal contacts who fell into the social categories based on ethnicity (using self-ascriptions), religious faith, and nationality. These were compared with the prison population in each prison using information provided by race equality officers. We then worked out the required numbers across each of these categories to make a total of 60 interviews in Rochester YOI and 50 interviews in Maidstone prison (see Table 1). These numbers were calculated to ensure reasonable sub-sample sizes in order that we could attempt to analyse the experiences of, for example, foreign national prisoners. We then drew an nth name from the Local Inmate Data-base System (LIDS) prison roll beginning with ethnicity, followed by religion and then nationality in order to construct a total sample that was broadly representative of the whole prison population. Two specific problems were associated with this approach. The first was that there were occasional errors in LIDS where prisoner eth-nicity, nationality, or religion had been misrecorded and this there-fore required further adjustment in order to meet the interview targets. The second was that the ethnic monitoring data was unable to locate those of Gypsy, traveller, or Roma origin, so that these

[16] Professor Alison Liebling and Dr Ben Crewe from Cambridge University's Prison Research Centre acted as invaluable consultants in the early stages of the project. It was Ben's useful suggestion to include a 'random sample'.

Table 1: Socio-demographic profile of the samples and prison population[1]

Ethnic Origin/Ethnicity[1]	Rochester N	Maidstone N	Total Sample N	Total Sample %	Both Prisons %	National Population 2006/7
White	30	29	59	54	62	73
British	25	21	46			
Irish	1	2	3			
Other	4	6	10			
Black	18	15	33	30	27	15
Caribbean	6	8	14			
African	12	7	19			
Asian	6	3	11	10	5	7
Indian	1	-	1			
Pakistani	3	3	6			
Bangladeshi	2	-	2			
Mixed Race	5	2	7	6	5	3
Other ethnic origin	1	1	1	1	2	1

Religion/Faith

Christian	34	24	58	53	52	52[2]
Muslim	13	11	24	22	16	11
Other	1	2	3	3	6	4
No religion	12	13	25	23	26	33

Nationality

British	47	39	86	78	82	85
Foreign	13	11	24	22	18	15

Notes:
1. Based on self-categorization but aggregated to the HMPS/Census equivalents.
2. Based on data for June 2006 (Berman, 2012: 20).

were possibly under-sampled in the study. Moreover, given the small number of Asian prisoners in prison (5 per cent nationally) and their internal heterogeneity, the interview samples produced a predominantly black–white sample. Of all those approached for the random sample, six prisoners[17] at Rochester declined to be interviewed, and a further three were released before the interview could be scheduled. At Maidstone, there were three refusals and four released or transferred.[18]

Previous research with incarcerated offenders has found that many are motivated to participate in research studies because of the cathartic and therapeutic effects of being interviewed or, more prosaically, momentarily to escape the intense boredom of life in prison (Copes and Hochstetler 2010). To these motivations, Sparks et al. (1996) have added sounding off without repercussion, alleviating loneliness, and providing contact with the outside world. In a co-authored paper with serving prisoners, Bosworth et al. (2005) reported that some prisoners want to educate those outside prison about its failings and to have their views and perspectives validated. If relieving the boredom of prison encourages research participation, there are, of course, occasions when you face competition. After observing one of the Sunday church services in Maidstone prison, we came up short in trying to arrange interviews in the afternoon; watching Formula 1 motor-racing and the men's final at Wimbledon was evidently more appealing than doing a research interview.

The rationale for conducting fewer interviews at Maidstone was that the initial interviews were of greater duration than those conducted at Rochester. There, prisoners who were aged 18 to 20 years tended to tire at around the same time. We surmised that in most (although not all) cases this was not because there were uninterested in the nature of the conversation and questions asked, but that they were not used to speaking intently on a one-to-one basis. Rochester interviewees yawned around one hour into the interview and appeared less able to concentrate on the questions being asked. As this was not the case at Maidstone prison, we decided there to supplement the individual interviews with two group interviews.

---

[17] Of these, three were white British, one was black and one was white, both of foreign nationality, and one was British Asian.

[18] All of these were of white British origin.

The interviews took place in various locations around the prison, but mainly in spare offices on the wing.[19] Although prisoners could not be paid for their interviews, which would have been my preference, we provided a Mars bar and bottle of water, as an implicit thanks for their participation and this seemed to be greatly appreciated.[20] The small digital voice recorder sparked considerable interest among the prisoners but did not seem to make them overly nervous, perhaps because of its discreetness.

Broad, open-ended questions were asked about the neighbourhood in which the prisoners had grown up and lived, their friendship groups outside, family relationships, influences and values, ethnic identities, and experiences of prejudice and discrimination. This then moved into discussion about prisoners' experiences inside: their friendship groups; support and emotional experiences; ethnic identities; masculine identities and sense of self; inter-ethnic mixing; prisoner hierarchies and bullying; arguments and fights; and views on the presence or absence of racism in prison. These questions were prefaced by some brief introductory questions on age, length of sentence, pre-prison employment, languages spoken, partnership status, and whether the prisoner was a parent. The schedule was structured to enable a content analysis using NVIVO 7, a qualitative data analysis software package, which inevitably tends to fracture interviews as extracts of responses are coded as nodes. The semi-structured conversational tone allowed for a narrative analysis to examine the stories prisoners told as they attempted to 'impose order on the flow of experience to make sense of events and actions in their lives' (Reissman 1993: 2). These narratives were particularly apparent in stories told about beginning offending, with regard to intimate and family relationships, particularly with fathers, and in the retold stories of particularly difficult episodes of their life inside. In the following chapters of this book, particular attention is paid to events and the meanings

---

[19] The interview began with interviewees receiving a research information sheet which covered the study's purpose and details of the consent process with an indication that we would have to report harm where planned, either to self or another person. This was interpreted liberally. One prisoner turned up to do an interview with a hangover after consuming too much hooch the night before. In no cases were prisoners reported to prison officers for rule-breaking.

[20] This was at the suggestion of a governor who recognized the value of chocolate bars to prisoners. But see King and Liebling (2008: 446) for problems with such an approach.

attached to them by prisoners, but also to see beyond these singular understandings, to consider the way prisoners create stories and how these can be interpreted. This proved particularly valuable and insightful in hearing how white prisoners talked about race equality policies in prison, for example, which is touched on in Chapter 4 and addressed more fully in Chapter 6.

After conducting 11 interviews in Rochester it was clear that prisoners struggled with answering questions about their 'identity', which was often interpreted to mean personality (see also Evans and Wallace 2008). As the primary interest was in understanding prisoners' ethnic, masculine, and religious identities, we revised the questions to ask about these more directly. Initially we tried to avoid leading prisoners to talk about these specific identities, hoping that they would naturally emerge where prisoners believed these to be relevant to how they perceived their sense of self, but this did not, in fact, happen. Therefore, somewhat reluctantly, we asked about these elements of their identities more directly in the revised interview schedule.[21]

It is, of course, likely that at least some of what was said in interview was a construction of how the prisoner wanted to be seen. Their narratives present an impression of a person who is coherent, also portraying an identity with which the interviewee is comfortable. There was little available in the prison environment[22] which could verify the accounts provided in interviews. Notes were made following each interview to reflect on its tone, content, and narrative, which included, on occasion, doubts about the veracity of some aspects of the interviewee's account, or the extent to which a particular sense of 'performance' had been witnessed. The rule of thumb that we followed in incorporating accounts about which we were sceptical was to include memos attached to the interviews to record these doubts in the data file. In relation to their inclusion in the findings these were rejected for their content (although not nec-

---

[21] The interview schedule was revised one further time when the interviewing began at Maidstone prison. Questions on prisoners' masculine identities were reformulated in part to reflect the older ages of prisoners there, but also in an attempt to elicit more detailed responses than had been possible at Rochester.

[22] Relevant documents were collated which had relevance for examining racial dynamics in prison, including recent inspection reports, race equality annual reports and other documents, racist incident data, the governor's weekly bulletins, the *Rochester Life Behind Bars* magazine, and *Inside Time*, the national prisoner newspaper.

essarily their narrative), unless they could be supported by the observational work or unless the themes were supported in a substantive number of other interviews.

A final issue relates to the presentation of the empirical material in the subsequent chapters. Pseudonyms have been used, selected for their association with particular ethnicities, faiths, and nationalities. Footnoted throughout is the detail of particular prisoners' ethnicity, faith, and nationality. An immediate contradiction lies in, on the one hand, critiquing and partially rejecting the idea of race as a social and political construction and recognizing the fluidity of ethnicity, and on the other hand, naming, labelling, and foregrounding identities. As Kalra (2006: 459) notes, this is the 'problem of having to name a subject before it can be explained...this does not let us escape from an initial identification in ethnic/racial terms' but risks reifying and fixing cultural difference while trying to do the opposite (see also St Louis 2009). There seems no easy solution to this problem, but I have tried, where possible, to avoid the ways in which interviewees' quotations can sometimes appear disembodied. I hope to be able to convey something of the texture of prisoners' lives beyond and within the prison by providing details of prisoners' lives beyond these categorical identities.

Concluding Comments

In this chapter I have presented an account of the research process which lays bare the methods used, some more successfully than others, to consider the obstacles to carrying out ethnographic research in carceral environments, and to attempt a reflexive approach. As such, it is clear that the research undertaken did not fully conform to ethnographic principles. The study did not achieve deep immersion in the full range of prisoner experience which might have enabled a more meaningful understanding of racial dynamics in prisoner relations, but this is the counterfactual that can never be known. The chapter also engages with the human, interactive aspects of social research which pattern any form of social interaction in everyday life. In conversation, we forget to ask things, we misunderstand or misinterpret what is said, we give an answer to a question that was not asked, we ask a question in a way that we did not mean to, we contradict ourselves, we deliberately or mistakenly conceal certain bits of information, or we make assumptions about what will be said, and often conversations are not fully concluded. The practices of using an interview schedule attempt to ameliorate some of these problems, but our biographical identities flow through and may also influence perceptions and understandings. Partial truths and revealing insights are perhaps the best we can ever hope for in social research, and the idea of narrating a single reality will always be a chimera.

4

Ethnic Identities, Faith, and the Dynamics of Multicultural Con-Viviality

> It is possible both to speak of prisoners as a class or group and, at the same time, to recognize this class to be internally fragmented. (Jacobs 1979: 21)

The story of prisoners and their lived experience in prison must be understood within the context of their pre-prison life (Irwin and Cressey 1962). In line with the importation model, social relations in the multicultural prison will be shaped to some degree by near and distant experiences of multiculturalism outside prison, an issue addressed in the first part of this chapter. Moving further inside, the chapter examines the multiple ways in which white and minority ethnic and faith identities are (re)constituted within the confines of the prison. The performance of ethnicity in public and private space provides an insight into the presentation of self in a uniquely totalizing environment. Yet, ethnicity, like other identity forms, is relational. Our own self-identification stands in contradistinction to what it is not (Fanon 1967/2008); as Hall (1991/2000: 147) put it, 'the self [is] as it is inscribed in the gaze of the Other'. Once identity practices are recognized, they are reacted to by other prisoners, and of course, prison officers. The role of the latter is considered more fully in Chapter 6 of this book. Here, using five 'clips' (compositions of fieldnotes and interview extracts) of what Amin (2002) calls 'prosaic encounters', I map the variegated contours of 'living diversity' in the late modern prison. In so doing, I consider how social relations in prison are shaped by prisoners 'doing ethnicity' while 'doing time', at the same time recognizing the intersectional nature of identity where faith and nationality are also inscribed.

Much of the discussion will centre on the complex relationships between mainly white and black prisoners. This reflects the composition of Rochester and Maidstone prisons of which only 5 per cent are Asian, only slightly less than the proportion in prisons across England and Wales, and even this figure is somewhat inflated by the foreign national population (MOJ 2011a).

Inside and Outside the Multicultural Comfort Zone

In Goffman's (1961) framework of socialization into the total institution, he referred to newly arrived prisoners' fear of physical contamination by other prisoners. Having to live shoulder to shoulder and cheek by jowl with other prisoners deemed inferior in status was central to the degradation process that prisoners experience. Rochester and Maidstone prisons also bring into enforced proximity, individuals who differ, in terms of their previous residential location, but also their identities shaped by race, ethnicity, faith, and nationality. Most, but not all, prisoners originate in the South East, particularly from urban London and suburban towns and semi-rural areas in Kent.

The mid-2007 population estimates put the minority ethnic composition of inner London where many Rochester and Maidstone prisoners originated at 33 per cent and 29 per cent in outer London (ONS 2009). For these prisoners, exposure to cultural difference was common and many tended to be comfortable with ethnic difference because it was something they had grown up with and been socialized into. Racial boundaries were diffused through the common experiences of growing up together, hanging out on the same estates, attending the same schools, and, on occasion, living in the same households. It was often at the forefront of the way such prisoners described their own neighbourhoods, with most valuing neighbourhood diversity. In this sense, as Gilroy (2004: xi) has suggested, the cohabitation and interaction of people from diverse cultural groups has 'made multiculture an ordinary feature of social life in Britain's urban areas'.[1] This ordinariness is referred to by Gilroy as subversive as it seems to represent the collapse of a

---

[1] There is now a burgeoning literature which describes the modalities of 'everyday multiculturalism', recognizing solidarities, border crossings, tensions, exclusions, and inequalities (see, eg special issue of *Journal of Intercultural Studies* 31(5)).

rigid and exclusionary racial categorization. As Daniel,[2] a Maidstone prisoner, put it, 'I don't really think it's got to do with your skin colour anymore, it's just who's got things in common'. Rafael and Pete's accounts also epitomize this perspective:

[I've got a] couple of Turkish friends, got a couple of Jamaican friends, a lot of African friends…three or four [white friends]…everyone mixes together. Like we all group up…we just grew up together…(Rafael, black African British, Christian, Rochester)

I had a load of black mates…it was just normal…we all went to school together. In fact my oldest friend um since we was six, he's black…his mum and dad still see my mum…I mean we, as I say, we all played football together and um obviously there was like name calling like there would be, like there is, you know, but it was never, what can I say, class was the be all and end all like it is today…where I lived where my mum is to this day still we live in a block of ten maisonettes and one summer we counted all the children there and in these 10 houses there was 96 kids, so there was Africans there and white people, black people, Indian people, Chinese people, you know. (Pete, white British, Christian, Maidstone)

Similarly, although Egon[3] had only come to England aged 14, and had never before seen black people, he spoke warmly of positive friendships, adding that 'five years I've been in this country, never had fight with them, problems with them or racism with them'.

This is not to deny the sometimes fractious nature of minority ethnic relationships, however. Hostilities between, for example, black Africans and black Caribbeans were not uncommon. Gary,[4] a Maidstone prisoner, had been called 'racist' because of his passionate hatred of Jamaican yardies.[5] A seemingly long-standing distrust and significant degree of separation between black and Asian communities in London also surfaced in some prisoners' accounts of their neighbourhood experiences.[6] Clinton,[7] a prisoner at Rochester, was from east London where he had a couple of Asian friends from 'day dot', but he was adamant he did not need to make

[2] Of mixed race British, Christian origin.
[3] Of white Muslim origin, from a Baltic state.
[4] Of black Southern African, Muslim origin.
[5] Members of Jamaican gangs.
[6] Harris (2006) has traced this to historical conflict during the British Empire which placed Indian labourers in direct competition with African and Caribbean labourers.
[7] Of black African British, Christian origin.

any new ones. However, as Alexander (2000a) reminds us, encounters are complex configurations in which racialized identities form only part of the picture, alongside territory, age, local history, family, peer group, and personality.

In sharp contrast, we can see, using the 2001 census, that of the 376 local authority districts in England and Wales, 81 per cent contain a lower than average proportion of minority ethnic groups.[8] Put another way, most white people live in districts where they comprise 97 per cent or more of the local population and minority ethnic groups make up 3 per cent or less (Simpson 2007). In Kent, minority ethnic groups as a whole made up just 3 per cent of the residential population in 2001, although this had risen to 8 per cent in 2009 (Kent County Council 2011), undoubtedly affected by Dover as a main point of sea entry for economic migrants and asylum seekers. Thus, some of the prisoners in Rochester and Maidstone prisons lived in what Johnston et al. (2002: 608) have called 'host society citadels' where multiculturalism is not lived beyond the ubiquitous curry house or Chinese takeaway, and is in fact mostly happening somewhere else (but see Nayak 2003). Yet as Clarke and Garner (2010) observed in their study of predominantly white areas in Plymouth and Bristol, racialization is far from absent in these contexts. Their study threw up distinct othering processes among white working-class and middle-class respondents. These centred on contested claims over welfare entitlement, competition for employment, and a disgruntlement with what they saw as the privileged position of minority ethnic groups in British society, issues which also have resonance in the prison, as explored in Chapter 6.

It was evident that many white prisoners from the towns and suburbs of Kent, East Sussex, and Essex had encountered few minority ethnic people until they entered prison. For them, the social geography of race (Frankenberg 1993) consisted of a map of whiteness with the odd lone black or Asian pupil in their class at school or neighbourhood. Preston[9] mentioned that his Essex town had only 'the odd foreign family'. There was a recognition that they had lived in areas which were inhospitable or dangerous for minority

---

[8] Mid-2007 population figures estimate the minority ethnic population of England and Wales at 17%. This includes those of white Irish and white other ethnic origins. If these are excluded the figure is 12% (ONS 2011b).

[9] Of white British origin, no religion, at Rochester.

ethnic groups. Micky,[10] a Rochester prisoner from a Kentish town, talked of his peers using terms such as 'nigger, fucking wog', while avidly disavowing racism himself. Jason admitted despising Kosovans who harassed 'our girls'. John expressed a virulent, racialized hatred and fear of what Gilroy (2006: 31) calls 'reverse colonisation' which explained his move from London to Kent:

I'd say give it another 50–60 years there'll be hardly any white people left there [south-west London]. They've taken over London already. We live on the outskirts in Kent and that now, we can't even go to our own fucking ends [neighbourhoods] like, we have to live in Kent. But soon they're going to take over Kent as well. The Pakis are already taking over Kent, aint they? So there'll be nowhere for us to live in peace mate, nowhere. (John, white British, no religion, Maidstone)

Such residential spaces were often hostile to those of minority ethnic origins, and generally avoided. Sami[11] recognized the enmity shown towards foreigners, finding it to be a 'scary time' to be in Kent as a minority ethnic individual. However, racialized hatred was not solely the preserve of the majority ethnic group; it existed among minority ethnic individuals and was on occasion aimed at white and Asian young people. In his east London neighbourhood, Yohan,[12] a Rochester prisoner, recalled his friends targeting lone white people to rob. While professing not to like this racialized targeting, Yohan was willing to accept it because 'that's the way people make money'. Gary, from Maidstone, had similarly found that his white friends were vulnerable to threats of violence from a friendship group which was entirely black:

Like it was just madness like because…They will try it on with my friends like, some of my friends, do you know what I'm saying who are not black like. They will try to put it on them and I'm like no, do you know what I'm saying, it's not happening. (Gary, black southern African, Muslim, Maidstone)

These experiences of living with multiculture or monoculture provide the contextual backdrop to how racialized social relations between diverse groups become accentuated and intensified in prison.

---

[10] Of white British origin, no religion.
[11] An Arab Muslim of West Asian origin.
[12] Of black African British origin, no religion.

Doing Ethnicity, Doing Faith Inside

Ethnicity, self, and disavowal

Self-identities are shaped by the labelling and categories imposed by the state (Rattansi 2007). In the Prison Service, data on the ethnic origins of prisoners is tied to the 16 codes used in the census (Prison Service Instruction 14/2003). Abbreviated codes were quoted at ease by some minority ethnic prisoners; Martel[13] referred to himself as a W9 (White Other) using the Metropolitan police ethnic codes. However, immediately apparent in interviews with other prisoners was their reluctance to submit to state processing of their ethnicity. This resistance to classification, a defining feature of the disciplinary prison according to Foucault (1975), might reflect a refusal to erase a personal identity which is so integral to the dehumanizing conditions of incarceration (Goffman 1961). This defiance in the face of state attempts at ethnic objectification could be seen in the context of the regular forms of categorization which frame prisoners' lives inside—from OASys[14] risk scores to Incentives and Earned Privileges (IEP status)—and in which power relations are deeply inscribed as prisoners experience often arbitrary designations (Crewe 2009; Crewe 2011a).

For most white prisoners, at least, there was a fundamental disconnect from the subject of race and ethnicity. Their ethnicity was generally invisible, obscured from them as part of the majority ethnic group in British society. Questions of ethnic identity and the use of standard ethnic monitoring codes were often baffling to those for whom ethnicity is regarded as something only possessed by those of minority ethnicity. Matthew, at Maidstone prison, for example, told us, after prompting, that he was 'white, just normal' and as Alfie put it, 'I don't feel white ... I'm still the same person as a Black and Asian, Chinese people ... they're still the same person as me ... we all growed up from the apes'. Barry found ethnic monitoring a 'disgusting' invasion of his privacy and he deliberately subverted categorization by recording himself as 'a black Afro-Caribbean Chinese cross ... just to piss them off'. For other prisoners, like Dimitri, a white minority ethnic prisoner at Rochester, there was a vigorous reaction against being defined using a predetermined template:

---

[13] Of white Western European, Christian origin.

[14] Offender Assessment System used by the prison and probation services to determine reconviction likelihood, offender needs, and sentence planning.

What do you mean? I'm not an ethnic group, I'm just Dimitri. I don't class myself as any ethnic group. If someone want to ask me where do I come from, I come from [Mediterranean country] and I don't class myself as any ethnic group. I'm just Dimitri and I don't feel this little communities with ethnic groups and whatnot, I don't care, I'm not interested. I don't get involved in that. (Dimitri, white other British, no religion)

This chimed with Nayak's (2003: 173) view of whiteness as 'the ethnicity that is not one' and is consistent with much of the empirical and theoretical work on the perceived normative character of whiteness where white ethnicities are imperceptible, denied, or regarded as devoid of ethnic content. White British ethnicities had an evacuated, vacant quality as if emptied of their former imperial glory, reflecting an 'intense desire to refill the painfully empty shell of national identity', as Gilroy (2006: 38) has put it. In Ray et al.'s (2004) study of racist offenders they similarly described a powerlessness associated with whiteness which brought shame, resentment, and anger towards Asian residents and businesses. White ethnicities stood in stark contrast to 'culture-rich' black and Asian ethnicities where communal and family loyalties were prioritized, something perceived as lacking in white communities (Gilroy 2004; Gadd and Dixon 2011). As will be revealed later in the chapter, this was often a source of bitterness.

But there was also a multitude of minority ethnic prisoners for whom ethnicity had a latent, undeveloped quality, lacking any personal, social, or political meaning. Martel and Brassard (2008), in examining the construction of female, aboriginal identities in a Canadian prison, suggest that the imprisonment experience itself may prompt a readjustment of self-identification and some ambivalence around ethnic identities (see also Schmid and Jones 1991). They found that some aboriginal women prisoners disavowed their ethnic identities to avoid stigmatization in the prison. There was, however, no evidence of this at Rochester or Maidstone prisons. Regarded as something suspiciously prescriptive, ethnicity was actively portrayed as simply a formal descriptor rather than being at the forefront of lived experience. Here a Maidstone prisoner, Andre, resisted attaching any significance to his official and social ethnic ascription:

I'm black British innit…Like I was living in England innit. Black British. It's who I am innit, I don't really…it's me innit, I'm just me innit. I don't really look at it. Um, I'm not…I'm not into all of that, that's all bullshit, you know what I mean, black this, black that, white this, white that.

The sentiments expressed by many white and some minority ethnic prisoners reflected a desire to see themselves and others simply as human beings, not defined by their race or ethnicity. Sahmir,[15] a Rochester prisoner, explained that 'ethnicity is not really a big thing…nobody takes it as a main mark. It's more on the lines of who you are personally. Not your race as an individual, exactly'. Such sentiments do not hold up much prospect for communal identification around race as depicted in Carroll's (1974) and Jacobs' (1977) studies of US prison life and in Wacquant's (2001) assertions of race as 'master status' in prison social relations.

Where elements of ethnicity were owned rather than denounced by prisoners—most often in the case of minority ethnic and Muslim prisoners who described cultural practices and symbols which united them with others similarly ascribed promoting a collective self—these identity stories equated ethnic identification with culture. This was a dynamic Barthian (1969) sense of self bounded by an historical sense of shared culture and heritage (often described as 'roots'), but not absolutist and limited by essentialist characteristics. Dexter[16] used a similar characterization of pride in his 'roots', also connected to his family. In this sense, ethnic and racial identities are impossible to know as coherent, singular, fixed essences, but they operate to situate individuals in a collective past which configures the present and are, as St Louis (2009: 566) asserts, 'phenomenally real' and ontologically felt. However, the fluid boundaries of ethnicity allowed permeation from, or penetration into, the cultures of other ethnic groups, and there was among British national prisoners a strong sense of being British. Tarun regarded himself as a 'British born Indian', as a patriot, someone who expressed pride in being British. Similarly, this was how Asad, a Rochester prisoner, put it:

It's important because I am British, you know, I'm in this country I'm in Britain so I would like to be a citizen of Britain, you know what I mean. And Bangladeshi I would like because it's my, you know, culture. And I like speaking a different language in my family, you know what I mean. (Asad, Bangladeshi British, Muslim)

A sense of pride in a white English or white British identity was not totally absent. John was happy to be called a 'white English bastard',

---

[15] Of Asian British, Muslim origin.
[16] Of black African British, Christian origin.

for example, and Jason described stories his grandfather had told him about Britain's role in the Second World War which made him proud. For others, this pride was relationally understood. Stuart, for example, said that he was proud to be white and proud to be English, evoking the beauty of white girls as a key element in this, but also recognizing white privilege in the job market as something unavailable to minority ethnic people.

Cultural symbols and practices

Prisoners demonstrated the significance of their cultural origins in other important ways, differentiating themselves and upholding cultural behaviours practised outside. Black Caribbean and African prisoners sported a range of plaited or twisted hairstyles (corn row, chiney bumps, two strand twists), while the trend for natural styles on road was also followed inside with longer afros, 'loxed' (dreadlocks) hair, and shaved styles which were clear signifiers of racial difference. As Mercer (1994: 100–1) has noted, hair is the 'medium of significant statements about self and society...constantly processed by cultural practices which thus invest it with meanings and value', having both an aesthetic and political resonance in the devaluing and revalorizing of diasporic blackness (see also Spellers and Moffitt 2010). Hair offered black prisoners some expression of individuality and collective presentation, depending on the skill of available wing barbers, in a way that was seemingly less significant for white prisoners:

One guy has a completely 70s look, and seems completely unaware of any stylistic issues. He has a big shaggy brown beard and a big mop of thick wavy brown hair. The fact that he is actually quite small and slim makes it all the more anomalous... For black guys, mainly, it seems there are more styles and a greater uptake in them. Plenty have short or shaved bald heads but then there are plaits, loose afros, afros bunched into two little bobbles... there are dreadlocks and there are braids. (Fieldnote, 17 October 2007)

Talking 'slangs' on the wing, 'rude boy' or 'street' talk was also a source of connection and a means of performing identity for many black prisoners of British nationality. During association, black prisoners would often be seen playing dominoes with an exuberance which was often deemed threatening by prison officers. The loud, competitive banter and the strategic slamming down of the domino pieces appeared to signify a potential threat to social order. This type of official reaction reflects cultural ignorance, providing a reminder of vertical power relations in the prison, as officers present a direct challenge to, and control of, displays of ethnicity.

Distinctive styling of hair and clothes was less common among white and Asian prisoners, but like Bartollas et al.'s (1976) study of an Ohio juvenile institution, emulations of black prisoners' urban expressions, tone, and dress style were not uncommon. Rochester prisoners, of all ethnicities, often went 'backsy' with their emerald-green prison-issue trousers or grey jogging bottoms worn well below their hips showing their (ideally designer) under-shorts. This is, of course, one of those cultural trends which has flowed between road and prison, and beyond into urban (Sharma, Hutnyk, and Sharma 1996; Frosh, Phoenix, and Pattman 2002; Nayak 2003) and mainstream youth culture (Wacquant 2001; Shabazz 2009). The black music (grime, slow jams, garage, hip-hop, dancehall, and lovers' rock) which could be heard on the wings and was popular with prisoners of all ethnicities could also be viewed in the same light.

Food represents another vehicle for 'identity work' in everyday life. Ugelvik (2011) has argued that prison food symbolizes the loss of home and family and operates to remind prisoners of their stig-matized status but can also offer a site of resistance. He describes the ways Norwegian prisoners circumvent the established rules of the prison to enhance prison food or to cook their own in their cells. In these acts prisoners can demonstrate autonomy and maintain an emotional connection with family and community, facilitating a positive sense of self inside. This is all the more essential, Ugelvik suggests, for the minority ethnic prisoners of Oslo prison for whom traditional Norwegian fare is poorly regarded. Creative chefs use traditional Norwegian staples like the large rations of milk they receive to produce Russian cheese, clearly a challenging task in a small cell. For Ugelvik (2011: 61) these culinary activities are a 'manifestation of an ethnic community', although he provides little evidence to support the claim that this represents 'resistance against the positioning of the immigrant prisoners in Norwegian society at large'.

The self-cooking facilities at Maidstone prison were a significant feature of social relations on its four wings. Relatively rare in the prison estate, they provided communal cooking facilities for pris-oners to supplement or substitute prison-provided meals. The self-cook area had an industrial kitchen feel to it, with magnolia painted walls and stainless steel cooking equipment, food preparation surfaces, trolleys, and fridges. Usually, there were large cookers with six to ten gas rings, a couple of ovens, and a separate grill. The self-cook areas condensed and revealed the ethnic diversity of the prison as no other place did (see Earle and Phillips 2012). Observations noted how at morning, midday, and evening periods of association the cook areas were thronged with people and a hive of activity. The value of this facility to many prisoners was on a par with that of the gym.

The self-cook area was a place of cultural exchange and sharing, of food, tools, resources, and ideas which contributed a sense of sociality to the prison. Food of all kinds was cooked by prisoners of different ethnicities; they were not constrained by anything other than their culinary skills. Considerable ingenuity was demonstrated where prisoners did opt to cook cultural favourites, particularly following outside rituals of cooking on a Sunday. White English prisoners, especially at the weekend, were observed frying eggs, grilling bacon and burgers, making beans or cheese on toast, eating curry, and cooking apple crumble. Cypriot and Turkish men took time over the making of yoghurt, and preparing Kattimeri, a paste of flour, oil, almond, and cinnamon which was poured into a piping tube and then gently fried. These were skilled cooks, one of whom, 'the cake-maker', would bake cakes to order for special occasions like a fellow prisoner's birthday. Caribbean men could be found cooking up jerk chicken, rice and peas, dumpling, punch, and macaroni, while African men prepared groundnut stew and rice. In these performances of identity, prisoners could maintain something of their lives outside, drawing on their own cultural resources and the rather limited material resources available in prison.

Religious participation

The imagery of jailhouse religion is a cynical one. It connotes a manipulation of prison authorities and parole authorities to achieve special consideration—fewer restrictions inside the facility, and eventually, early release entirely. The image is so common that we were surprised to hear so little confirmation of it in our interviews. (Clear et al. 2000: 63)

Christianity was deeply implicated in the expansion and reform of the modern prison in the 18th and 19th centuries. As Ignatieff (1989) has observed, there was an attendant evangelical spirit in the work of prison reformers like John Howard, who were concerned to purge the sins of the lower orders through a programme of solitude, rigorous discipline through hard work, and religious instruction. The intention was to isolate the criminal from corruption, but also to uphold existing class relations (McGowen 1995). While this dispensing of correctional punishment through divine justice accorded with the social climate of the times, in the late modern period the influence of Christianity has waned considerably. The Prison Act 1952 established a chaplain in every prison and the right to worship but, as the quote by Clear et al. indicates, religious participation is often now viewed suspiciously.

Most prisoners in England and Wales are recorded as being of the Christian faith (49 per cent in 2008) or they have no religious affiliation or beliefs (34 per cent in 2008),[17] while around 12 per cent are Muslim, up from 5 per cent in 1994 (HMIP 2010). The largest ethnic constituent of the Muslim population is Asian (42 per cent) but a further 34 per cent are black, 13 per cent white, and 7 per cent mixed race. This contrasts with the general population, where South Asians made up 74 per cent of Muslims in 2001 (Dobbs, Green, and Zealey 2006).[18] These figures underline the internal diversity within the Muslim prisoner population which cautions against reducing them to a simple common denominator of religious affiliation. In the current study the Muslim prison population included those of British Pakistani, Bangladeshi, black Caribbean, black African, mixed race, and white origin, as well as foreign national prisoners from countries in Southern, Northern, and East Africa, the Middle East, South Asia, and the Balkans. The population figures, of course, tell us nothing of the degree of observance in prison.

Whilst outside prison, as Macey and Carling (2011: 123) note, 'a general tendency towards secularisation is accompanied by a sharp reassertion of conservative identity by a minority within the minor-

---

[17] Figures for the population as a whole were 23% in 2010/11 (ONS 2011a). In Rochester and Maidstone prisons, a significant proportion of prisoners also expressed a notional allegiance to Christianity, often reflecting fleeting childhood participation, say at Sunday school, or a kind of default Christianity which stood at the opposite end of the spectrum of active religious practice.

[18] It is commonly noted that ethnicity is multi-layered for this group, with faith integral and intrinsic to a sense of self, at the core of being (see also Jacobson 1997). The small number of Asian Muslim prisoners in the sample prevented a specific exploration of this (but see Beckford et al. 2005).

ity', religiosity can be a source of solace and coping during incarceration. It is recognized that prisoners may experience a heightened state of stress in the critical moment of entry to the prison, and religious faith assisted some prisoners in this difficult time. Salif,[19] a first-time prisoner at Rochester, recalled how a focus on practising his faith had eased the transition to prison life and removed much of the acute fear he had of prison based on sensationalist media accounts. He had entered prison refusing to talk to anyone and trusting no one. Two days after he was imprisoned he attended Friday prayers in the prison's multi-faith area and had been welcomed and made to feel more comfortable by the Imam. The Imam and other prisoners served as an important resource for socialization into the prison environment and for ongoing social support and sociality. Ianos,[20] also at Rochester, vividly described how on entering prison 'it feels like you're going to die in that moment', a sentiment reminiscent of Goffman's (1961) ideas of the mortification of the self. Ianos' Christian faith, through a trust in God, had helped him to reduce the fear that he had felt in the beginning. Prayer was a means to promote positive feelings which he described as 'feeling soft', lighter after the intense anxiety which accompanied him initially. A religious amity was a further benefit in coping with prison. Anan, a prisoner on Thanet wing at Maidstone, described a level of genuine generosity among those who practised the Christian faith. Religion provided a refuge from the enormity of his position, as a sex offender, a stigmatized other in society and in prison:

…there is some healing, a lot of healing um people get from their faith, especially here in prison. Because being in prison alone especially in this day and age, getting out with a criminal record, you know what that mean.…But then in the chapel as you go and your faith strengthens you even start to begin to realise that all those fears sometimes may not necessarily all be true…(Anan, black East African, Christian, Maidstone)

The calming effects of faith, the sense of catharsis, even of spiritual healing was central in accounts of some prisoners who drew on a previously existing—even if partially practised—faith and those who had turned to religion for the first time. Xavier,[21] a Maidstone

---

[19] Of Pakistani British, Muslim origin.
[20] A white Eastern European, Christian prisoner.
[21] A white Muslim prisoner from a Baltic state.

prisoner, had experienced something of a religious reawakening, which he felt had brought inner happiness and self-understanding.

Prison forces a confrontation with oneself, it is a time to contemplate the *why* of one's imprisonment, often producing painful feelings of guilt which may be relieved by religious participation (Clear et al. 2000). In some cases, there may be a kind of religious fatalism where prisoners believe they have been 'saved' from the dangers of 'roadside', that God has intervened in their lives to bring the relative safety of prison. Sami[22] experienced a revitalization of his faith and his prison sentence was reinterpreted as a 'message from God', a divine intervention. For him it provided a purposeful and meaningful route to self-control and religious salvation, operating as a powerful counter to embitterment and self-hatred (see also Maruna, Wilson, and Curran 2006). Such beliefs put a positive slant on incarceration, as prisoners were saved from moving further along the destructive paths they were pursuing outside, and, simultaneously, suggesting some higher purpose beyond the penological concerns of retribution or rehabilitation. It can also provide a route to self-forgiveness, eliciting hopeful thoughts for an uncertain future (see also Maruna et al. 2006; Kerley and Copes 2009).

The demands of religious practice lent themselves well to the physical and emotional space which opened up for prisoners during their incarceration. The seemingly limitless time available in the prison, where little constructive is occurring and prisoners are stultified, alone in their cells, in moods of self-reflection and rumination, contrasted sharply with the fast-pace chaos of lives on road without stability or 'free time' (Earle 2011b). Prisoners like Asad,[23] at Rochester, talked of being unable to meet the requirements of Islamic worship on road, but having time to pray five times a day from his cell. Other prisoners referred to enjoying the self-discipline and structure imposed by strict Islamic observance:

Because I do follow my religion, so as a Muslim, it's a lot of things you have to do and its strict as well....If you pray and you do your religion things, your time goes by and that's one thing that's good about it. (Aniq, Bangladeshi British, Rochester)

Obviously I'm more focused innit. I try to pray five times a day when I can. Read the Qur'an more, I read the Qur'an now and again. I practice

---

[22] An Arab Muslim of West Asian origin.
[23] A Bangladeshi British, Muslim prisoner.

my faith more now than I did on road, innit, because well, mostly all, I've got is, got more time innit, so you know, it's something constructive innit. (Sammy, black Caribbean British, Rochester)

Not all prisoners felt able to avail themselves of this positive spiritual path; for Lawrence,[24] at Maidstone, his sinful behaviour put God out of reach. He resisted what he regarded as a religious self-deception, acknowledging his repeated returns to prison and his continued reliance on 'puff' (cannabis) which challenged a belief in the possibility of religious salvation. Others, like Melvin,[25] also at Maidstone, were less self-rebuking, more willing to acknowledge that anything in prison which helps the 'drive down an easier road to get home' was acceptable given that 'you cling onto anything you can do to help you get through your time in prison'.

Religiosity might also be of value in presenting a repentant self to the Parole Board, although this was raised rarely by prisoners. More common was the attempt via attendance at worship to gain out-of-cell time which was precious among all prisoners. Attending church was a way of passing time; 'just to keep the day rolling', was how Anton[26] explained it. 'Kickback' time, 'something to do', an opportunity to socialize with other prisoners, especially those from other wings also propelled prisoners towards church services on a Sunday. Dexter,[27] a Rochester prisoner, talked about his church attendance as 'one of the highlights of the week', an opportunity to break the routine and boredom of the long weekends spent exclusively on the wings.

Some prison officers at Rochester were sympathetic to this instrumental need (as one officer said, 'That's all they're here for really, a five-wing association'), while others were deeply suspicious that religious services provided a cover to further illicit business opportunities, and hence their watchful approach as they remained alert to any negotiations or disturbances during the service. Such suspicions were bolstered by the Sunday church services, which resembled the atmosphere of a school assembly with prisoners fooling around, giggling, making an occasional 'farting sound', engaging in either the lame singing of hymns, or the reverse, exaggeratedly hamming it up and singing excessively loudly. The sermons, some-

[24] A black Caribbean British, Christian prisoner.
[25] A black African British, Muslim prisoner.
[26] A black Caribbean British, Christian prisoner at Rochester.
[27] A black African British, Christian prisoner.

times preceded by amateurish acting out of a parable by outside Christian volunteers, presented opportunities for ridicule, humour, deliberately mistimed amens, inappropriate or out-of-sync clapping, and snatched time for chatting. It is little wonder that prison officers were sceptical of prisoners' religiosity but it was not entirely absent, and some prisoners seemed genuinely to appreciate the content of the service, bowing their heads solemnly in prayer, enjoying the singing, and some respecting the sentiments of the sermons (particularly when the message resonated, as with the 'let he who is without sin cast the first stone' adage).

In contrast, at Maidstone prison fieldnotes recorded the tone of the Sunday service as more 'sombre, more well-attended to and more seriously participated in', very possibly because of the maturity of the older population there:

The service is predictably dull, consisting of hymns, and formal prayers. The singing is strong though, and there is none of the sense of play that characterised Rochester's services. The mood is serious. (Fieldnote, 8 July 2007)

The conduct of Friday prayers for Muslim prisoners was also markedly different. Observed by Rod Earle, these religious meetings had upward of 50 prisoners in attendance at Rochester and Maidstone prisons, reflecting diverse ethnic and national origins, although largely non-white. There were fewer prison officers on active watch and their countenance was relaxed rather than wary (Earle 2011b). It is not clear whether this signified a respectful or disinterested distance and separation from the 'alien' Muslim other:

There is shushing as one guy stands and 'calls' or chants what I assume is the calling to prayer....It is generally quiet and 'observant'—a small group close to me at the back continue to talk quietly...the attention of over 50 guys in the one room, seems focused, is held by the ritual or routine or whatever it is. I wonder what it is that is holding their attention, what has suspended the normal rules of conduct, the conduct that is usually so boisterous, with loud chat and the exchange of insults or jokes, etc. Is it the relevance of the readings, the relevance of the message, or is it the integrity of the messenger?...The distance the officers sit away from the prayers is interesting....They are all sitting at the far end of the very long visiting block, the four officers that are mandatory for this size of gathering. I wonder if it is out of respect or a wish to keep their distance, to avoid something 'foreign'. It seems they feel there are no security reasons for them to be in close but I wonder if they would keep the same distance if it were an orderly gathering of white Christians. (Fieldnote, 6 October 2006)

Reversions/conversions[28] to Islam

Religious conversion in prison is not an uncommon experience (Maruna et al. 2006) and yet such practices have come to be viewed cynically. 'Jailhouse religion' carries with it assumptions of duplicitous insincerity, with bogus performances crafted to secure advantage in doing time. As Maruna et al. (2006: 162) wryly note, 'finding God behind bars seems somehow too convenient to be believable', and this was certainly the case at Rochester and Maidstone prisons. Dominic,[29] at Maidstone prison, was the only prisoner to be interviewed who claimed to have used religion as a ruse to gain some form of privilege. He claimed a Mormon allegiance which meant he could substitute tea or coffee with hot chocolate.

However, it is at least as plausible to see religious conversions inside as linked to an emotional and spiritual need to seek personal change and self-development, following the identity crisis wrought by incarceration. Religious conversion can allow the presentation of a pro-social identity. Importantly, as Maruna et al. (2006) suggest, conversion narratives are significant as subjective phenomenon for what they tell us about individuals' sense of self. It is therefore unhelpful to view them as objective events, and they are perhaps best interpreted as either a revitalization of an existing faith identity or as a search for a new transformative affiliation which prompts new ways of self-understanding.

Samson, a black African British prisoner at Maidstone, for example, had been searching for an alternative belief system to help understand his current predicament converting to Islam while he was awaiting sentencing. This, often desperate, attempt to find a new framework with which to interpret life experiences has been documented in other studies of prison conversion (Maruna et al. 2006). Schooled as a Christian, having been in the church choir, he had rejected his faith in his teenage years. His prison sentence had come at a time when he was reaching the zenith of his legitimate professional career and he talked bitterly and with anger about his disillusionment with Christianity, feeling 'betrayed by God, betrayed by the church'. Samson personally identified with being racially persecuted and felt that 'Muslims had become the new

---

[28] As it is believed that all are born Muslims those that actively choose the faith are technically regarded as having *reverted* rather than *converted*.

[29] Of black Caribbean British, Christian origin.

black', experiencing abusive police harassment and state surveillance. Likewise, in Liebling, Arnold, and Straub's (2012: 52) study of Whitemoor, the attraction of a Muslim identity was linked to a politically disadvantaged position where unfair state practices supported social inequalities. Over time Samson had relinquished his Islamic faith when he had reached the conclusion that the anger and disappointment he felt inside was not to do with his faith. Simultaneously, he acknowledged that his partner's refusal to convert from Christianity would scupper their plans to marry. At the time of interview, Samson had turned towards another religion, attracted by its philosophical orientation, and being asked to 'look within yourself for the answers'. He regularly attended a service and group discussion at the prison and described its calming effects on him, how it made 'utter sense' to find and understand the origins of his suffering in prison. There was no indication in Samson's long interview and informal discussions on the wing which suggested that he had been motivated to convert to secure physical protection.

Typically, there was little sympathy for the view that religious converts were inspired by a spiritual searching as Samson had. Instead, conversion was regarded as a 'quick fix' to the insecurities of prison life (see also Spalek and El-Hassan 2007; Hamm 2009; Liebling, Arnold, and Straub 2012). Particular scorn was reserved for those prisoners, many of whom were British black Caribbean or black African, who were 'churched' as children, having grown up in traditional or evangelical Christian communities, who choose to convert to Islam in prison. For Bradley,[30] a Rochester prisoner, raised as a Muslim, converts were, in his view, motivated to 'look cool', wearing their faith almost as a fashion accessory. He described it as 'the new phase that's going round London, it's a fast fame religion'. The ulterior motive of this new-found faith was argued to be physical security through the universal protection of the cohesive Muslim bloc, often referred to as 'a gang' (see Chapter 5). This is how Rufus, who had converted on road seven years previously from Christianity to Islam, saw it:

…most of these black guys in here have only turned Muslim in prison so they're protected, do you understand what I'm saying….if you're Muslim and something happens to you and a Muslim brother's there, no matter who it is, an officer, inmate, all the Muslim brothers are going to jump in

---

[30]   Of mixed race British, Muslim origin.

for you because you're a brother...(Rufus, black Caribbean British, Muslim, Maidstone)

There was little patience with intermittent observers of Islam who were judged against the template of the 'proper Muslim', infecting perceptions of Islam to a degree with illegitimacy. As Gavin[31] at Rochester resolutely noted, 'they [Muslim converts] won't do all the stuff they need to do like praying five times a day...so they can't be real really'. Held in less disdain were those prisoners, like Douglas, a white British prisoner, who had converted some years previously. In his case, his conversion had occurred while living in Afghanistan. Some practices had waned, but Douglas insisted that he stuck to the basic principles of the religion, avoiding pork, sitting whilst urinating, and ensuring cleanliness.

Interestingly, there were no corresponding criticisms for previously non-practising or more 'relaxed' Christians to be 'proper Christians' and fastidiously observe all tenets of the Christian faith. Views about the partial practising of the Islamic faith tended not to acknowledge that it was common for prisoners to depend on a faith during hard times; this was how Lennard put it with regard to his Christian faith:

sometimes when things aint going right for me I tend to like read a Bible...And when things start getting a bit better, I tend to forget that. Do you understand? I just start thinking more positive a bit and when they gets negative, I start just trying to find a way out of it, like, I mean in here like, like your religion is a way out of it for me anyway, I know it is for some people. But then I get outside and things will be alright and like I won't go church a lot...(Lennard, mixed race British, Rochester)

While spiritual reasons should not be automatically dismissed as a reason for religious conversion, it would be misleading to imply that physical protection was not sometimes a motivating factor, although this was not advanced as a reason by any interviewees.[32]

Paul, a black African British prisoner, presented during interview as a troubled and somewhat vulnerable young prisoner, and his account of Islamic conversion and observance was more equivocal

---

[31] Of white British origin, no religion.

[32] There was no evidence of coerced conversion at Rochester and Maidstone nor did we observe any proselytizing by Muslim prisoners. In contrast, Liebling, Arnold, and Straub's (2012) recent study of Whitemoor high security prison found examples of bullying and violence where prisoners resisted conversion attempts.

than Samson's. Paul had been raised in inner London in a lone parent household alongside several siblings, but without his father,
who lived in West Africa and with whom he had little contact. As a
child, Paul had attended an African church which he remembered
fondly as being lively and fun, although time-consuming with day-
long services and night vigils unlike 'white people's church'. Attend-
ees had dressed smartly and were fully engaged in the singing with
enthusiastic clapping, and Paul himself had served as an altar boy.
He went on to describe dangerous street relationships that had
developed on road as he got older and he referred to experiences of
being bullied, as well as some threatening interactions with previous associates in various prisons.

At the start of his current sentence, Paul recalled a pervasive
Muslim influence in prison by which he had initially been uninflu-
enced. Later, with time on his hands, he had taken to studiously
learning about Islam in a way which he contrasted with his following of Christianity as a child. His recall of some of these lessons was
rudimentary and confused, but Paul mentioned also being influenced by the political teachings of Malcolm X. A developing racial
consciousness seemed to him to be incompatible with elements of
Christianity, which did not promote freedom, justice, and equality
with the same prominence as Islam. Paul discussed, for example,
the incongruent handcuffing of his slave ancestors in church who
were praying to the same God as their slave masters. Fleeting comments suggested that he also did not agree with the ordination of
gay priests in the Anglican Church. Significantly, although discussed rather disjointedly in interview, the equality of man before
God appealed to Paul because of his experiences of being bullied
and exploited on the streets. What attracted Paul to Islam was
'putting together my life experiences and what Islam teaches
you...[to] give me more understanding about myself'. Despite this
growing political consciousness and spiritual reflection, Paul was
not a committed Muslim in prison and he assumed that this partial
observance would continue when he was released when he would
be once again distracted by other pursuits:

When I go home I'll still say I'm Muslim, even though I don't...I'm not
praying properly because I get periods where like I pray like but then I'm
the type of man I just get carried away as well innit, so I'll stop praying,
like I will smoke weed, and if I'm doing that, it's either one or the other
innit, I know what I believe in but I just...like certain times Friday if
I don't feel...if I don't wash that day I won't go, like I respect the religion

in certain ways, but if I'm going to be any religion it will be a Muslim, I will be a Muslim, that's what I believe...I'm going to try and go to the mosque [when released] but I know how it is, sometimes I might forget, forget about it, but I might even all forget about it for two years and just work and do what I'm doing, or...I don't want to take things too serious. Because if I start praying five times a day and do all that every day like my brains just different, I'll get too serious about that as well and I know how I am. Like I'll start acting stupid, so I won't, don't want to take it that serious.

Paul could be seen, then, as a 'casual convert', dipping into aspects of the religion which were comforting and supportive in prison, whilst only partially practising the faith and recognizing his own limitations to preventing full participation. Although Paul refrained from depicting his conversion as about his own personal safety, given his expressed vulnerability it seemed possible that his conversion was largely, although not exclusively, strategic. Liebling, Arnold, and Straub's (2012) study of 12 Muslim converts in Whitemoor prison similarly paints a picture of multifarious reasons for Muslim conversion with more than one factor influencing individual decisions. Those cited by prisoners included: needing to make sense of life in the context of long sentences; psychological coping and the provision of a structure for prison life; becoming part of a brotherhood or family which could provide care, support, and protection; and in a small number of cases, active rebellion and opposition to prison staff and the administration.

Finally it should be remembered that religious identities like any other are not immutable; they are fluid and changing, and as Clear et al. (2000) note, this may occur across prison sentences, or even during a single incarceration. To use religion as a prop is understandable. The extent to which religion may be used as a technique of safety will be at least partially dependent on the degree of threat present in the prison environment (Liebling, Arnold, and Straub 2012). Moreover, whilst not emerging as a key issue in the study of Rochester and Maidstone, Her Majesty's Inspectorate of Prisons' (HMIP's) (2010) recent thematic inspection on the experiences of Muslim prisoners did also find markedly higher levels of fear and feelings of being unsafe among Muslim prisoners compared with their non-Muslim counterparts in Category C prisons. These perceptions were informed by concerns about prison officer intimidation and victimization and threatening behaviour by other prisoners.

Foreign national identities

Foreign national prisoners accounted for 18 per cent of the population at Rochester and Maidstone prisons, where they comprised an internally diverse category of citizens mainly from various European, African, and Asian countries. The variety of experiences prior to sentence, and prospects afterwards, even among the small numbers encountered during fieldwork, defied aggregation. They were however, all too frequently, marked by trauma and distress. From our observations and interviews it was clear that foreign national prisoners tended to see themselves as a distinctive grouping among prisoners in Rochester, and were recognized as such by other prisoners. A few prisoners explicitly stated that they did not mix with foreign nationals, sometimes citing language barriers as an insurmountable obstacle, but their indeterminate status in the penal system also seemed a factor:

I don't really talk to them [foreign nationals] because they keep themselves to themselves, don't really talk to no one, they're just waiting for their deportation aint they? (Luke, white British, no religion)

As with earlier research (Cheney 1993; Richards et al. 1995; HMIP 2006; 2007a), we found evidence of informal networks of support among foreign national prisoners. The common difficulties of communicating in a foreign language, and of having little or no incentive for developing anything other than rudimentary functionality in English, was recognized as a bonding agent among some of the foreign national prisoners. Sometimes this involved efforts to help 'induct' new prisoners to prison life, or to assist with translation and interpretation, and liaison with immigration solicitors and government officials. Sami, a Maidstone prisoner, explained it in more oppositional terms with the additional promise of collective security:

The first thing would come to your mind if you are a foreign national is to go and talk to someone who is a foreign national like you. Not from your religion or region, no just foreign national whether he's African, Asian, Turkish, whatever ... Because you want to avoid the local people, prisoners because you know it's like an instinct, everybody know it, they are the troublemakers in any country in the world, the locals are.... Foreigners are the ones who are weaker and just want to get along with their life.... If he talks shit, he talk crap, it don't matter, I'm here with him I'm talking to him I'm pretending I'm listening ... I'm protecting him, he's protecting me. The troublemakers pass by, they ignore me because I'm with a group. (Sami, Arab Muslim, Western Asia)

The politics of migration reverberate inside the prison and have had significant ramifications for the experience of foreign national prisoners. Far more than British national prisoners, foreign national prisoners' concerns were not with everyday life in prison, but with their circumstances at the completion of their prison sentences. At the time of the current study many foreign national prisoners were caught up in the aftermath of the political crisis when it had been revealed that some 1000 prisoners had been released without consideration of deportation as indicated in the Criminal Justice Acts of 1991 and 2003 (Bhui 2007). The constant threat and anxiety of deportation shaped these prisoners' experiences. For most prisoners the eventual prospect of release is a defining feature of their existence, a shared resolution, and a common ending that each will eventually achieve. Imminent release is usually greeted with eager anticipation. The end point of a sentence for a foreign national may bring only more apprehension, and this uncertainty of the ending preoccupied almost all of the foreign national prisoners we spoke to.

For Egon, a white, Muslim, Rochester prisoner whose origins lay in the Balkans, this political refocusing on deporting foreign national criminals left him feeling agonizingly anxious about his immigration status. Like others, he had been 'driven mad' in his frustrated attempts to obtain information from prison officers. Similarly, Stefan[33] was less than ten days from the end of his sentence but he was still unsure of his status. Ianos[34] felt aggrieved that his loss of liberty was not regarded as sufficient punishment. He had decided not to appeal deportation if it was sought, but he would return illegally to the United Kingdom, if necessary. Likewise, Umar, a Pakistani Muslim prisoner also at Rochester, described the worry and strain that these uncertainties created and their impact on prison life:

…yesterday my interview with immigration yeah, and I tell him what happened to me Friday, my sentence is finished yeah. But what happened to be would they tell me what's going on yeah. He said 'I don't know, I don't know'. I tell him I've done the 7½ months yeah, still you say I don't know, don't know, no way, tell me, my future is going too blind, yeah, tell me innit. But he can't and I come back and stress because three days is left of

---

[33] Of white Christian origin from a Baltic state at Rochester.
[34] Of white Eastern European, Christian origin at Rochester.

my sentence is finished yeah but I don't know if I am released or not. I'm stressed. In the soash [association] time yeah, the officer sees me that I'm stressed. He says, 'Come Umar, play pool with me'.

The likelihood of further detention for an unspecified period with an unspecified outcome—a state of limbo—was undoubtedly extremely distressing. Jackson, a Caribbean prisoner at Rochester, had experienced exactly that. He had completed his prison sentence but was being held with a deportation order pending as he sought political asylum. Resignedly, he referred to the irregular visits to the prison of immigration officers which made organizing legal representation difficult, their absence when expected, and the impossibility of finding out anything about the progress of his case. Wearily, he saw himself as 'just here doing a prison sentence that's finished…its hard but I've just got deal with it'. This double punishment of imprisonment then deportation or its threat is what Fekete and Webber (2010) refer to as 'enemy penology' and Bosworth sees as representing the virility of the state in demonstrating sovereign power over non-citizens (Bosworth 2011). I now turn to consider interactions between prisoners of different ethnic, religious, and national origins.

Prosaic Encounters: The Daily Negotiation of Ethnic Difference

At a surface level at least, many prisoners at Rochester and Maidstone prisons accepted difference in everyday prison life. They acknowledged the reality of diversity, and racial and ethnic difference was rendered unremarkable and unexceptional, something they were at ease with. Frankie,[35] a Rochester prisoner from London, commented, 'with like fifty of us that's been on this wing for ages, we all know each other, it doesn't matter if you're black, white, Indian…you'd all be together'. Similarly, for Dominic[36] at Maidstone, the array of different ethnicities in prison made the significance of colour somewhat obsolete. He described prison as a 'boiling pot' where relations 'gets melted up' so that he would 'walk over to the yardies, I will talk the deepest patois and then I will walk from there and I will go and talk the biggest cockney to the white boys. And then I will go and talk Turkish to the Turkish boys'.

[35] Of white British, Christian origin.
[36] Of black Caribbean British, Christian origin.

Fieldnotes recorded many other positive inter-ethnic inter-actions, including an enthusiastic repartee between two black British national prisoners, of Nigerian and Jamaican origin, in a contract services workshop at Rochester prison. In a huge, noisy, high-ceilinged room, with prison officers seated in an office in a gallery above, prisoners chatted while preparing plastic fruit punnets for later filling. Many worked quickly to maximize their piece-rate wages, while others chose to work at a slower pace which allowed them to talk alongside co-workers. Whilst sticking bubble wrap onto the empty punnets, I listened as Sacha[37] and his friend spent their time 'racially' abusing each other and claiming the superiority of African or Caribbean cultures. The humorous mood survived even when one called the other a 'jungle monkey'.[38] Similarly, in an education class at Rochester, where banter and humour often seemed of more importance than engaging with the topic being taught, I heard a white prisoner ask warmly of a black friend, 'how are you doing little batty [pejorative Caribbean term for a gay man]?'[39] The slur was accepted in the 'light-hearted'[40] way in which it was intended.

Prisoners from the suburban and semi-rural areas of Essex and Kent, who had limited previous exposure to minority ethnic and faith groups, also generally expressed positive sentiments about difference. Sometimes prisoners' accounts pointed to the educative potential of diversity; learning about halal meat or the social significance of tribal lineage in Congolese and Nigerian communities in Britain and Europe were examples given by Rochester prisoners who valued learning about other ethnic religious and cultural practices. Habitual contact could also produce empathy towards linguistically disadvantaged and politically oppressed foreign national prisoners.

At Rochester prison, explicit racism was so highly stigmatized that a self-declared racist, a swastika tattoo-bearing member of the National Front, had frequently to be segregated for his own protection. Incidents were also revealed in which groups of black prisoners responded aggressively to expressions of racism by other prisoners, with news of their response rapidly spreading around the

---

[37] Of black African British, Christian origin.
[38] Fieldnote, 3 January 2007.
[39] Fieldnote, 25 July 2007.
[40] This is not intended to deny the homophobic nature of the comment.

wing and across the prison.[41] As Ant[42] noted, 'If a white person said to a black person, wog or nigger, it's fighting in the showers, that is'. Such retaliatory actions were viewed as entirely legitimate and morally appropriate by prisoners. Such abuse might even allow prisoners to flout the inmate code of not 'grassing'. Neal[43] explained that 'if you tell a guard that someone's racing you or being racist to you that's not snitching, right. That is standing up for your own religion and your own culture or what you are'.

At Maidstone prison, racism was suppressed; there was no legitimate channel for it in the public spaces of the prison, although, as I discuss below, it had emerged in the private areas of the prison. Melvin[44] remembered a heated argument between a white and black prisoner. When the white prisoner, in anger, shouted 'Oh you black...', Melvin was amused at his slip-up because 'you can't say that in prison because you know you'll get your head kicked in'. Likewise, Vanni[45] claimed that religious insults would be 'catastrophic' for social relations there, adding 'you never mark someone else for religion'. Similarly, John,[46] also at Maidstone, observed that insulting Islam would 'touch a raw nerve' and lead to violent retribution. If a prisoner dared to say 'fuck Allah', 'it doesn't matter what you say after that, they're going to fucking stamp on your head'.

However, asked more directly about inter-ethnic friendship groups, Rochester and Maidstone prisoners described ethnic separation in the prison based on shared cultural understandings and commonality rather than rigid lines of racial or ethnic division. Prisoners described 'feeling better with', 'safe', having 'more in common with' those who came from the same racial or ethnic group as themselves. Arcel[47] perceived himself to 'get along with everyone' but he admitted to having more in common with black people ('it's just the way it is'), or white people who had 'the black sort of culture', who enjoyed similar music.

[41] Michael, another white British, Christian prisoner, described how 'JJ', having used the 'nigger' epithet after evening lock-up, had been stamped on and had his head flushed down the toilet by a group of black prisoners the following morning.
[42] Of white British, Christian origin.
[43] Of mixed race British, Christian origin.
[44] Of black African British, Muslim origin.
[45] Of white Southern European origin, no religion.
[46] Of white British origin, no religion.
[47] Of black Central African, Christian origin.

Observations of inter-ethnic interaction in the stark, uninviting exercise yards at Rochester were largely consistent with prisoners' accounts. A patch of grass, framed by a concrete path, and tall wire perimeter fencing did not feel conducive to sociality, but did allow prisoners time outside, off the wings, and out of earshot of prison officers. As this fieldnote recorded, interactions between prisoners were not limited only to those from the same racial or ethnic group, but there was a loose, low-key, ethnic component:

The guys quickly settle into two large groups at either end of the yard, with some pair groups, scattered in between and one of four/five. Of the two large groups, one is basically white, though there is one tall South Asian guy among them. The other is black....There is some to and fro. One guy goes over to the smaller black group, stays for a while and then comes back. Another guy from the black group goes over to the white group, and comes back after a few moments. The hour passes without any significant shifting around...(Fieldnote, 8 September 2006)

These are not indications of exclusive relations but there was a consistency with which these broad groupings formed in different parts of the prison. Seating preferences at the weekly church services in the chapel seemed to reflect a similar patterning of same-race cliques as in this example:

I am interested in the places that prisoners choose to sit in—which pews they are drawn to and why. The choice appears to be ethnically bound with small groups of mainly younger black prisoners, alongside some older white men, but all grouped together. There are only two exceptions—two younger white men—one at the front and one at the back.

	W		W				
B	B	B	W	W	W	W	
W	W	W	B	B		B	
	W						
		W	W	B	B	B	B
		W		B	B	B	

(Fieldnote, 8 July 2007)

Likewise, when hanging out in the self-cook areas at Maidstone, some prisoners eat as they stand, chatting to other prisoners in small groups or pairs, 'mostly same ethnicity, but some sense of mix as well' (Fieldnote, 28 June 2007). As we stood in the outdoor spaces of the prison to watch the freeflow movements, these also suggested a degree of separateness along ethnic lines—'Guys coming out of D-wing, in mainly black or white groups, or pairs, lighting up fags, stopping to talk' (Fieldnote, 11 September 2006).

However, amid the buzz of the more playful atmosphere of young Rochester prisoners at the pool or table tennis tables in evening 'soash' (an abbreviation for association) or during their relaxed saunter across the prison complex during freeflow, where fist-to-fist greetings or handslaps, youthful chattering, and play-fighting occurred, the divisions appeared less static with more fluidity between groups. White, black, and Asian individuals tended to cluster together but these groupings did not appear to be conflictual and the boundaries were permeable with some mixing within groups. Nathan[48] even went so far as to call the prison 'a civil society', where cultural understanding was actually facilitated by the bringing together of diverse groups who learned to live together; this is the multicultural prison of the 21st century. This was the way Sami, from the Vulnerable Prisoners Unit (VPU) (Thanet wing) at Maidstone prison, explained it:

I mean you can't see African, Jamaicans, Asian, everything in one place outside. You can't see it. Here you see it all the time with people just under one roof. You see them everyday, you eat with them everyday, you play with them everyday, you fight with them everyday so you know everything about these cultures, the way they think, the way they behave, what they eat....you learn a lot of...I mean these are good things to learn in prison actually it's not only bad things. (Sami, Arab Muslim, Western Asia)

It is certainly feasible that the difficult and potent mix of social isolation, continual surveillance, and enforced proximal living in the prison promoted a desire among many prisoners to simply make life more bearable for each other and themselves. It is also consistent, however, with the social psychological insight of Allport's (1954) 'contact hypothesis' where exchanges with different racial and ethnic groups is assumed to reduce prejudice and increase tolerance. Prisoners identified the removal of choice in movement and location, and co-presence was as central to the ensuing social relations. 'You have to [mix] in here though don't you because there's no choice about it is there?' observed Michael,[49] a

[48] Of white British origin, no religion.
[49] Of white British, Christian origin.

Rochester prisoner, 'because on road you can avoid that mixing with people but in here, like, *you're all here*' (emphasis added).

The prevailing discourse of racial accord was also detected by Back (1996) in his study of urban youth cultures. There, white and black people had forged a solidarity inflected by class and locality, which he called 'neighbourhood nationalism', which seemed partially to dispense with racial division.[50] It is also suggestive of a spirit of unity and tolerance reminiscent of the shared solidarity of prisoners described by Sykes (1958) and Sykes and Messinger (1960). It could therefore be viewed as an adaptive response to one of the pains of imprisonment, namely the forced and close interpersonal contact with individuals that the prison engenders, which may be mediated through friendly relations and harmony.

In the remainder of this chapter, I use five 'clips' of observed or reported social action using extracts from fieldnotes and interviews with prisoners in prison life at Rochester and Maidstone prisons to elucidate what Elam and Elam (2010: 191) refer to as a 'full accounting of race', indicating the multifaceted ways in which diversity is lived in the multicultural prison. These clips reveal the complexities of racialization in late modernity exhibiting both continuities and discontinuities with old patterns of racism. The first 'clip' must be viewed within the context of the earlier discussion on cultural transgression and hybridity as it presents an unusual social stage in the prison world.

Cultural Fusion: A Performance Poetry Workshop at Rochester YOI (Fieldnote, 13 January 2007)

A young white, female writer-in-residence worked with a group of 18 prisoners, seven white and the rest black over several weeks to produce a performance poetry workshop at Rochester prison.

The prisoners performed their prepared lyrics to musical backing tracks, presented to a small audience of peers. The contest begins with a black prisoner reading a poem, rap style into the mike; his lyrics are 'conscious', lamenting the self-destructive tendency of black urban youth, with appeals to 'my niggas' to live a better life. The rhymes are clever and the delivery confident and neatly rhythmical. Another guy seems to be a popular goof-ball type of character as everyone laughs at his lyrics, about prison and wing life, and he plays to them with some funny and clever rhymes about

---

[50] This was more successful in the case of white and black young people, but less so in the case of those of Vietnamese origin.

screws [prison officers] and wing order. Next, a white prisoner comes to the mike and apologizes for not being 'used to this' but gives a powerful and popular fast chat rap about hard living on the edge and the need to live right and move away from crime.

Some of the deliveries are awkward and inept, though the crowd was, somewhat 'officially', supportive. Another white prisoner comes to the mike and pours out a vitriolic rap aimed at the judge who sent him down—it is full of misogynist references to his wife and other 'bitches' and other violent sexual imagery; he gets a massive reaction. The poem of a foreign national prisoner with an African accent deals with war and the hypocrisy of governments who preach peace on the streets and wage war in other countries. His delivery falters as he attempts to achieve the required speed and expressive virtuosity, but the audience is good-humoured and he receives both gentle ridicule and harsh encouragement. The set closes with Jonathan[51] from B-wing who has been interviewed as part of the study's 'random sample'. He starts with a swift talking and rhyming rap—a story, funny and anecdotal, with lots of puns. His ultra-fast chat stylings drew from his itinerant immersion in a criminal lifeworld that extended from the ports of Kent to the suburbs of London and beyond. When finished, he is pulled back to the mike and he launches into an almost unintelligible garage rap. The delivery is so quick fire it assumes a staccato rhythm of its own, with only the occasional word recognizable. Jonathan won the contest by popular acclaim.

In many senses, this represents the cultural hybridity, about which sociologists of race have long opined as a characteristic feature of the changed times of late modernity (Brah 1996). The cross-fertilization and fusion of sometimes disparate cultural styles and practices represents new emerging plural and hybrid identities which displace notions of fixed, closed, and homogenous racial identities tied to biological origins. Harris (2006) has demonstrated, using sociolinguistic data, that young British schoolchildren of South Asian origin express cultural identities which are fundamentally British, spatially anchored in 'Londonness', but with the diasporic inflections of South Asian community languages, but also incorporating some Jamaican Creole and African American vernacular English. Prisoners' talk too was peppered with London and black Caribbean expressions—'innit', 'you get me', 'do you understand'—and some white prisoners attempted (often unsuccessfully) to suck their teeth in disdain. The cachet of black cultural forms meant that, if used correctly, white prisoners' credibility could be

---

[51] Of white British, Christian origin.

boosted inside. The performance poetry workshop similarly represents hybridity. That this can be achieved within the confined environs of the prison is, in many ways, extraordinary.

Taking Amin's (2002) lead, we can see prisons as potential spaces of mixedness, connection, even transgression and boundary-crossing. There is, however, a cautionary note in the hybridity literature which is relevant for understanding social relations among prisoners. As Nayak (2003) has emphasized, hybridity has its limits; it can still shift remarkably quickly to re-imposing racial boundaries of belonging and exclusion. In his study of white masculinities in north-east England, while young white people incorporated symbols of black youth culture, they simultaneously engaged in racist talk which demonstrated a white chauvinism. Researching young masculinities in London, Frosh et al. (2002) also note that even those who espouse the irrelevance of race may simultaneously reproduce negative, racialized ideologies of superiority and inferiority (see also Hughey 2011). Indeed, there is more than lived cultural fusion to Jonathan's prison experience; I return to examine this later in the chapter.

'Doing Multiculturalism'[52] in the Self-Cook Area I: Extract from Ruhi's Interview at Maidstone prison

Ruhi, a prisoner from North West London, of British Bangladeshi, Muslim origin, talked of growing up in an ethnically mixed area which had 'loads of cultures…like Middle East, Jamaican, Asian'. This was reflected in his groups of friends at school and in the neighbourhood, and having grown 'up that way, just never known any different', Ruhi was unfazed by the diversity of Maidstone prison. He had a quietly authoritative prison presence about him. He was quietly spoken and highly regarded, it seems, by all on the wing, and not just because he is serving a long sentence for violence.

[W]e do the food boat thing [clubbing together of money to buy ingredients and cook food in a small group]. I mean like Christmas is coming up. I mean I've got like a friend of mine cooks…cooks with me, two other lads. One of them's from the same background as me and the other one isn't. But it's not so much, it's just that we know them and they wanted to cook and it wasn't a problem doing that. But with Christmas coming up and I've got like a couple of pals on the wing, we all sit together, we've said well we'll get together for Christmas and we'll just buy a load of stuff and we can have a proper Christmas.…when you have a self-cook area in a prison, a lot of people tend to share food as well. Like the Turkish people make yoghurt and if I haven't got any, they're more than happy to give me

---

[52] Taken from Gilroy (2005: 439).

some of their yogurt and things like that. So it does help to socialize people and make people more comfortable with each other...Everybody does different things on there. I mean like a person upstairs, all he does is bake cakes. He's a white person, I would say he's in his late 50s and like he likes curries and stuff. So like he'll bake a cake and say well are you lot making a curry today, you can have some of the cake, give us a bit of curry and some rice. And he likes things like that. He'll make shepherd's pies and he likes roasts and things like that, but he can't cook a curry a lot of the times, so he'll ask one of us to do it. And it's not a big thing. If I'm cooking down there and he's got all his stuff there and he's got a bowl. All I've got to do it...he chops it all up, all I've got to do is just put it in there and make sure I cook it properly for him same as mine.

If you came onto the wing on a Saturday you probably will see a lot of black and Asian lads down there. But personally I reckon about 95% of the wing uses it....I suppose the reasons you probably see a lot of black and Asian lads, is because like a lot of the servery food, we wouldn't eat it at home or wouldn't eat if we were outside. We don't normally eat boiled potatoes or mash potatoes and things like that. So we cook food that we were brought up on. I mean like...we cook Chinese, we cook Italian food, curries, we have...like on a Sunday we have like roast chicken and things like that. You get a few arguments in the cooking area....I mean a lot of the times prisoners do tend to be aware of other people. Like when I go down and cook, if somebody's cooking bacon say, he'll say look, you know, I'm cooking some bacon, it's only going to take me ten minutes, just move your...Like I'll move my pot out of the way, let him cook, then do it that way. And if I go down there and, you know, if you've got a vegetarian and I'm cooking chicken, if he says something to me or it's some old person, you do tend to move it.

In this account we see a young Muslim prisoner and an older white prisoner exchanging food types which each enjoy, working collaboratively under restricted conditions. There is cultural differentiation and overlap in Ruhi's account of his daily cooking arrangements at Maidstone prison, including how use of this precious resource is successfully negotiated. Ruhi demonstrates aspects of his ethnic identity in his cooking but he is not bound by this identity in an exclusive sense. In a similar way, these prisoners described the sharing and eating of food across racial boundaries, which are not constrained by difference, and which reflect the hybridity of food tastes in the early 21st century:

Yeah, I eat with a Jamaican, he'll come and eat with me. I cook for the Turks, they come and eat with me. I cook with them, so whatever I cook today, they taste it...Everybody really mixes with each other well. (Gamal, white North African, Muslim)

Like on Saturdays I've got this Turkish guy. Um I'll give him some mince-meat and he'll cook the koftas yeah. That's like a Turkish dish. And then this black guy, I'll give him like some chicken, he'll do chicken, rice and peas. And then I will do like um I do a variety of things. Like yesterday I did a Korma curry. Um I do, Monday I do Kentucky chicken with wedges and salad, you know. (Daniel, mixed race British, Christian)

My girlfriend is white and both of my baby mums [his children's mothers] are white and when they used to cook it would be like lasagne, pasta. And one of my girlfriends is Irish, it would be boiled bacon and cabbage everything like this, and you know, stews and shepherd's pies and chips and fish, you know what I mean....I make banana cakes, banana fritters and things like this, but certain people like on this wing used to make carrot juice and that and certain of the white guys liked it and you know they started making carrot juice and things like that. But they wouldn't have known about it, you know what I mean. (Rufus, black Caribbean British, Muslim)

This is presumably what Gilroy (2005) means when he discusses the creative spontaneity of convivial multiculture which must be seen for its political potential as well as its cultural power, although, of course, Gilroy did not have the prison in mind in this depiction. The exposure to the other is managed and negotiated, demonstrating perhaps that the 'supposedly unbridgeable gulf between civilizations can be easily spanned' (Gilroy 2005: 439), an example of the 'unspectacular ways in which people live with and across the cultural complexities of sameness and difference' (Back 2007: 148). Racial difference is rendered insignificant in making live bearable and survivable in the prison (Gilroy 2004). Yet, the reported accounts of racial harmony, the cultural fusion demonstrated in the poetry workshop, and the observed relaxed inter-ethnic interactions at Rochester and Maidstone prisons belied more complex racialization and conflict among prisoners. As Amin (2002: 969) reminds us, '[h]abitual contact in itself, is no guarantor of cultural exchange. It can entrench group animosities and identities, through repetitions of gender, class, race and ethnic practices', and the following clips illustrate the aptness of this quote for the underlying tensions in prisoner society.

'Doing Multiculturalism' in the Self-Cook Area II: Extract from Barry's Interview at Maidstone Prison

Barry was a white British man (with no religion) in his mid-forties. He had been self-employed in various businesses during his time living in London and abroad in several continents. He had attended a grammar school and gone on to gain a university degree. He had little experience of ethnic diversity in his childhood, claiming that a black man would only likely be seen on a visiting cricket team in the area where he had grown up. His recollections were of a traditional 'charming' racism where he had, for example learned a Royal Academy of Music-accredited piano tune called 'The Coon Song', and where everyday racism was accepted, even encouraged.

The one thing that does cement...the groups together in this prison in particular is the self-cook....And you'll find that the three or four Asian lads on the wing stick together because they cook together, they eat together. The West Indians all have their...and again I'm not being racist, but this is genuinely what they're like, they have their fried chicken, rice and peas, and they eat it all the time. I'm not stereotyping them...Except it does cement the racial barriers. There's three or four Italians on the wing and they all eat and sit together and talk together. They probably would anyway, but even more so because now you see them all sat...that's the Italian table. That's the Polish table...it goes back to the old question which I'm sure is part of your syllabus [interview schedule?] here, which is whether the racial and um cultural barriers and difference should be celebrated or broken down....I don't think you could ever break them down. Um and if you celebrate them too strongly then it becomes racism....

On uh on Kent wing there was a period where the Muslims complained so much about people cooking bacon that it was banned from the self-cook. And they tried to make that stick on Weald and on here, and I wouldn't have it, neither would any of the others. Fuck off, if you don't like it mate, I'm sorry, we can always fall back to the old baseline that this is a Christian country and if you want to be here, come and fit in. If I go and live in Dubai, I fit in with the Arabs, I observe Ramadhan. I don't walk down the street with a beef burger. And I do...you observe the traditions of the country that you're in, you don't try and impose your own traditions on them....Yes, it didn't last long on Kent Wing, didn't last long at all. But they play the race card, they play the race card. Say he's being racist, he's cooking bacon where I want to. Fuck off....Everybody does have their own pots and pans and if you want to keep them halal that's up to you. But they argue about there might be some bacon grease in the washing up basin and all that....They try it on all the time, they try and play the race/religion/Muslim card all the time. It is a Muslim thing....It has, it's made them so unpopular. I mean I've heard people on the wing saying openly that they do not want Muslims on this wing. And that's not healthy...When Weald Wing shut down, I got moved over onto Kent Wing and uh I couldn't get down to self-cook, which is the West Indians are the only ones allowed to cook okay. Nobody else is allowed to...but it's the fact that the West Indians are the ones who take over. Again, I'm sounding racist. I'm not at all, it's just an observation.

Elam and Elam (2010) suggest that we need to examine when and where race emerges and to consider the effects to which it is put in social action. In this account, the 'social stage' is the self-cook area, a highly valued, but discretionary facility which many prisoners prized for the opportunities it afforded them for socializing and providing a variety of food in ways ordinarily and routinely denied by imprisonment. The vitality of the kitchen allowed the performance of ethnicity, and as demonstrated in Ruhi's account, a cross-fertilization, but it also served as a site of strained interactions and deeply felt animosities, seemingly uniting and dividing prisoners. Barry hints at the cooking and eating of food together by white and black minority ethnic groups as reinforcing segregation. Yet he makes no comment regarding the congregation of white British prisoners whose separation is implicitly rendered unproblematic. This 'script' is a familiar one, a counter-narrative to the harmony discourse which is prevalent, particularly at Maidstone prison. It is continuously revealed in the implied challenge to the validity of Muslim prisoners' desire to avoid haram (forbidden or contaminated food), undoubtedly a tricky task with the restricted resources of the wings' self-cook areas. For Barry, these are unreasonable requests, because Muslims 'should observe the traditions of the country that you're in' not 'impose your traditions' on the majority. This, according to Gilroy (2006: 39), is a form of the 'fit in or eff off' assimilationism which fuses victimhood with superior culture. It is also, of course, a sentiment shared by a majority of the general population (Heath et al. 2010: 197). Yet, a Kymlickan (1995) perspective would regard such claims-making as an indication of the desire of Muslims to be recognized and represented in the 'prison polity', rather than as indicative of minority ethnic privilege and segregation.[53]

Barry is keen to assert that he is not personally motivated by racism. Given the negative stigma of being labelled racist in contemporary society (Ray, Wastell, and Smith 2004), white prisoners understandably fear being misunderstood and labelled as racist.[54] But Barry is also making a series of observations in which

[53] In *The Art of Listening*, Back (2007: 145–7) describes the arrest of Harraj 'Rab' Mann whose listening to The Clash's *London Calling* was deemed suspicious and seditious by police following an altercation with airport security staff. Instead of symbolizing integration into Britain's multiculture it was deemed 'terrorism incognito'.

[54] Such fears are heightened by the demonstratively violent and immediate way in which racism may be policed in prison.

an apparently zero-sum game is being played; where respectful treatment and recognition of minority ethnic groups' cultural needs equals unequal treatment and disadvantage for the white majority, an issue I consider fully in Chapter 6. This is accomplished through signalling the worrying and unhealthy conflict that such claims-making has provoked. Lastly, the 'audience' for this play of race was, unsurprisingly, the white male researcher, not this author. This links back to the issue of reflexivity in Chapter 3 and underlines the impossibility of ignoring researchers' subject positions.

Whilst there is a grave danger in romanticizing the defensive comments of the white majority, where racism is seen as reasonable, the only narrative with which we try to understand lived multiculturalism (see Back 2009 on the problems with the book *The New East End*), I equally do not wish to downplay the feelings of exclusion that Barry expresses and the emotional labour involved in living diversity in prison. However, it is impossible not to observe how race animates the discussion of this material resource, precisely because it is regarded as a site in which black privilege displaces the traditionally assumed and implicit white privilege of the majority. The first Prison Service circular on race (Circular Instruction 28/1981) rightly cautioned against allowing any public spaces and facilities of the prison to be dominated by any one ethnic group. Our initial observations did suggest that the self-cook facilities were being dominated by black prisoners, upholding Barry's complaint, and this was particularly a feature of life on Kent wing [the so-called 'Beirut' wing]:

A small queue of white guys has gathered at the [servery] hatch. An almost corresponding number of younger black guys are starting to gather at the boundary of the cook area, pans at the ready...[Later] The food queue moves as the hatches are opened. The grouping is still fairly obvious, white guys in twos and threes, then black guys in twos and threes. (Fieldnote, 22 October 2007)

Even some black prisoners spoke of avoiding the cook area because of the stress and hassle involved in competing for the limited facilities, suggesting that this might be less racialized than Barry has assumed. However, over time spent in the prison, it became clearer that the social dynamics of Maidstone's self-cook areas were less rigidly divided than suggested in Barry's account, on both Kent and the other wings:

In the kitchen there are a few people getting busy in the cook area [on Medway wing]. One is Upal…A small bearded Asian guy with glasses…who is working with an older white guy called Dane, who everyone seems to know and like. Dane is expertly boning a chicken while Upal chops and prepares spices—'it's a curry' he tells me.…At first it is small groups, pairs, of white guys. One doing a saucepan of baked beans. Not a chatty guy, tall thin, tattooed skinhead, he says the food from servery is 'total rubbish', but then he and his mate seem to be only intent on replacing it with beans on toast. Meanwhile more elaborate preparations are taking place all round them. A large wok of beef mince is being stirred by a large Mediterranean/Greek-looking guy.…There are no screws [prison officers] in sight.…I'm amazed it doesn't cause any aggravation here but perhaps it is a modus vivandi they've developed, live and let cook.…Around the servery hatch a loose queue is forming.…I'd say it was more older white guys, but a mix of minority ethnicities sprinkled among them…(Fieldnote, 25 June 2007)

Moreover, as Anan suggested in interview, 'the English' prisoners were more often found in the prison cooking Sunday breakfast:

I think the English like um Sunday breakfast very much. All this bread in oil sausages and um roast potatoes, those kinds of things. So if you came over the weekend early in the morning you will find that place…those who are cooking breakfast and they will be mainly white guys to my surprise, yes. And I just don't know why few of them do real cooking over there on other days. (Anan, black East African, Christian)

The self-cook areas may be more attractive to minority ethnic prisoners because, as Lloyd[55] said, 'I wouldn't eat the food on road innit, so if I'd got the choice to cook my own food I might as well do it'.

Notwithstanding, the resentment that Barry felt was also expressed by other prisoners. Tommy told us about a conversation he had had with a white prisoner:

Yeah, like I say 'Are you not cooking today?' to a white guy and he'd be like, 'No, listen, if I go down there I'll end up stabbing them, I fucking hate them', you know what I mean. And they wouldn't, but that's why they're not down there. (Tommy, white Irish, Christian)

Yet there was also a recognition of the confined cooking conditions and the need for mutual sensitivity and respect in this valued public space. Several prisoners were also able to talk positively about

---

[55] Of black Caribbean British, Christian origin.

negotiating the use of the gas rings without argument, even when there was a potential for conflict over the cooking of non-halal and halal food. Xavier put it like this:

If someone's cooking bacon with a fryer you're not going to use the same fryer are you, so, as long as you are not eating it, not using the same pan or whatever, it's alright if he's next to me because it's not a big thing. We're all in prison, we have to respect them as much as they respect us, so it works…(Xavier, white other (Baltic state), Muslim)

This negotiation of difference was not always straightforward even among minority ethnic prisoners. Although religious, like racist, taunting was off-limits, the challenges of proximal living did, on occasion, jeopardize individual relationships particularly the demands of Islamic observance.[56] Gamal, a North African Muslim prisoner himself, struggled to accommodate his Maidstone cell-mate's strict Islamic conventions which included the setting of an alarm clock to wake for prayer at 4am. A move to a single cell prevented any serious conflict but not all prisoners were so accommodating. Ant, a white British, Christian prisoner at Rochester described a dispute with his Muslim cell-mate who asked for the television to be turned off when he prayed five times a day. Ant's perverse retort was 'I don't care, you're not having it [TV] off if I'm watching it at a certain time of day and I'm, "go pray in the toilet if you want to"'. A palpable friction punctuated individual interactions and prison social relations more generally.

The point about what is now increasingly referred to as 'everyday multiculturalism', is that wary and awkward interactions, like those in the self-cook area or in shared cells, coexist with the vibrancy of convivial multiculture, cultural fusion, and hybridity.

Negotiating Interactions With Minority Ethnic Prisoners: White Exclusion—An Extract From Jonathan's Interview at Rochester YOI

Jonathan was a young white British man in his early 20s who had lived in several seaside towns in Kent. He had served several custodial sentences and had a chaotic life in between times inside. He described himself as 'easy to get along with'. His relationship with his mixed race girlfriend had broken down when he had been imprisoned for a relatively long sentence. He prided himself on being able to categorise new arrivals to the prison by the state of their trainers. The first part of this extract describes Jonathan's time as a juvenile prisoner.

---

[56] Kerley et al.'s (2005) research suggests that religiosity may reduce arguing, and, to a lesser extent, fighting in prison.

[F]irst when I come in like I felt, as a little boy like, I nearly got bullied, you know what I mean, [black prisoners were] calling to my window and going 'White Boy', 'White Boy'. 'What mate?'—you know, I'm talking Kent and all that. 'What mate, how's it going?' And they're like, 'shut up, suck your mum like',[57] or like 'shut your door', you know, 'shut your window. . . . I used to lie, you know, when I was little I used to say I'm from London. If you just say Kent they're like 'you country bwoy, country bumpkin, osty boy', like this, and you'd go 'lrighht, yeah mate' and I get my head kicked in like just because I'm from Kent like, you know what I mean. So I used to say yeah I'm from London like. 'Yeah, what part?' Northwest. And you pick up like, where's the hardest area? 'Brixton, mate.' Whereabouts? Er, near the train station. It's a lie, you know. But now I just say I'm from Kent mate, why I'm a big lad now you know what I mean, so I'm like, so what are you going to say mate? . . .

[B]lack people seem to think that every white person is a mug . . . Because I get quite embarrassed by quite a few of the white lads being like that, coming down here just to get mugged off. Just because . . . it's not a racial part of it, it's just a matter of black lads look more intimidating like and they'd got dreadlocks, gold teeth, a little bit of an attitude and the way they talk. And you get a white lad and he says, 'hello mate, are you alright?', and you get a black lad saying 'Wha Gwaan! Pussy!', whatever, what's it. Right, what's more intimidating? So as soon as you realise the lingo yeah and you understand it. I talk like that in front of them, I switch, you know, I don't even mean to do it. . . .

[Asked about his friendship groups] . . . I'd be with the white guys, straight up. I'm not racist or nothing like that it's just black guys will obviously respect black guys more and white guys always respect white guys more. It's nothing to do with racist or anything like that. But I believe black people are more racist than white people, and that's what I've watched. And religion-wise yeah, Muslims yeah, they are highly racist. You're a Cafar, that means a non-believer, yeah. So if you're a Cafar I will not talk to you. So that's highly racism in my book yeah . . . I had an argument like the other day yeah, but it was behind closed doors like, a couple of cells up. And the kid said I looked like Elvis, we were having a laugh and a joke through the pipes and that, 'you look like fucking Elvis'. I said, 'you're funny mate' [unclear—00:23:13], you know having a laugh with him. I said, 'you look like Side Show Bob' mate, [character for TV series *The Simpsons*] you know, coming back to him, then 'fuck you I don't joke with white boys', you know what I mean. I said, 'why are you bringing the racial issue like?' And I can talk like that you know, because I like arguments,

---

[57] This is an example of 'cussing', an aggressive and gendered verbal contest in which masculinity can be demonstrated in defence of female relatives. It is discussed further in Ch 5.

I enjoy it you know, I've got a good opinion on it yeah. And I said, 'fuck it mate you're like Aladdin mate,' you know, not racial, and he said, 'why you being racist?'…and then my next door [cell neighbour] was stirring him up, he says 'oh you've got a magic carpet and you've got a monkey as a best friend' and all this. I said 'no mate, I didn't say that mate'. He said, 'you're racist, you're racist like, fucking you Cafar', and all this like. I was like, 'No mate'.

The anxiety and discomfort expressed in this account is testimony to the difficult terrain of race and ethnicity in late modernity. Far from inhabiting an uncontested position of power and privilege within the social hierarchy of the prison,[58] such comments reveal an uncertainty among white prisoners about how to navigate everyday contacts with black prisoners. Familiar and reassuring privileges of racial hierarchy are manifestly not what they were; they are less stable and heavily, openly, and constantly contested by black prisoners who take for granted their right to an equal, even dominant position in prisoner society.[59] Jonathan's account is particularly surprising given his success at the performance poetry workshop where he felt competent and comfortable enough to perform in front of an ethnically mixed group, including a large number of black prisoners.

What Jonathan's account also reveals is that for some white prisoners there is a understandable resentment about being tested or having their whiteness disparaged or evaluated negatively. Martin, despite growing up in an area of London with significant concentrations of black people, struggled with a black prisoner who challenged his choice of girlfriend:

…he said, 'Oh do you like black girls?' I said no. So he started calling me racist, blah-blah-blah, saying to people I'm racist and I thought that was unfair because it's up to me. Like it's not that I dislike black girls but do you know what I mean, it's not my type or whatever. So he's saying I'm racist and stupidness like that whereas I don't think that's racist…telling people I'm racist and shit, loads of trouble…I don't think he likes me for some reason, but I haven't done nothing to him. (Martin, white British, Christian, Rochester)

---

[58]   See also Haylett's (2001) work on the positioning of the white working class, which he has argued challenges dominant social systems of privilege as they pertain to class and race, as economic privilege and success are not 'naturally' assured.

[59]   See Ch 6 for a discussion of how some minority ethnic prisoners fatalistically assume a subordinate position in the racial hierarchy of the prison where prison officers have ultimate power.

Equally mystifying were the apparent contradictions of racist motivation depending on the race of the victim and perpetrator, as expressed here by Stuart, also at Rochester:

…it's just the way they talk, like, 'That little White ting, and that little White prick,' you know and 'White this and White that'…But if we're sitting there going, 'Yeah that little Paki cunt,' or 'Big black prick', then all of a sudden, we're, we're labelled as a racist. (Stuart, white British, no religion, Rochester)

It seems that Jonathan and other white prisoners are angrily struggling with the notion of being victims of racialized exclusion, where the cachet of blackness has facilitated a cultural dominance in the social world of these prisons. As Nayak (2005: 145) suggests, there is now an elasticity to blackness which is not solely negative, but is context-specific. As such, 'blackness is split, marked by an ambivalence that does not necessarily equate with "powerlessness"…the process of racialisation may render visible minorities more powerful in certain arenas and less powerful in others' and horizontal relationships in prison may be one of these.

A safe option requires that white prisoners at Rochester mimic the language, mannerisms, and dress of black prisoners, and this is certainly what Jonathan does, even lying about where he was raised so he can present a hard, urban persona, rather than a less macho suburban one. This capitulation to black ascendancy in prison was because, according to Saul,[60] 'if you don't speak like he does, you're like, he's like, well, you're not a part of me, you're not a part of, of our group' which could lead to victimization. In this sense the racial hierarchy in which whiteness is universally superior has been disrupted in the social world of the late modern, multicultural prison. The superior positioning of black masculine identities in prison was similarly discussed by Bartollas et al. (1976) in their study of a juvenile institution in Ohio, and research on youth cultures in the United Kingdom has shown that popular masculinity appears to be most closely associated with black boys.[61] There is, however, also resistance to the emulation of blackness as cultural hegemony in

---

[60] Of white British, Christian origin, also at Rochester.
[61] 'Hardness', showing a disdain of academic work and a rejection of school authority, sexual prowess, physicality, and cool dress sense are of paramount importance (Back 1996; Frosh et al. 2002; Archer and Yamashita 2003).

the prison;[62] it is ridiculed by some white prisoners who are bewildered by, even scathing of, this borrowing of cultural practice, perhaps because it signifies the emptiness of white culture and heritage. Daryl, for example, scoffed at white Rochester prisoners emulating 'how *they* [black prisoners] walk around' in an attempt to be part of these social groups inside. Gareth[63] confirmed that 'if you see a white guy hanging out with black guys, speaking like a black guy the other white guys will take the piss out of him a little bit behind his back'. But white prisoners also retained the option of returning to traditional narratives of white superiority as some derided the particular linguistic forms or 'street' words—such as 'Wha Gwan', 'Hey Blood', 'Fam', and 'Wasteman'[64]—commonly associated with black prisoners' talk. Seemingly less threatened by this were black prisoners such as Gary,[65] a prisoner from Maidstone, who recognized the differences between 'the white boys from London like think that they're so much like us that it's crazy…they've hung around with so many black people that's just the way it is like, it's just natural for them innit like', and those from outside London.

Racism Behind Doors?: Extract from John's Interview at Maidstone prison

The interview notes recorded by Rod Earle indicated this was a difficult interview where it had been hard to establish a rapport. Rod had described John as prickly, quick to take offence, and he exercised his prerogative not to discuss aspects of his personal and intimate relationships. His interview revealed a violent past and frequent references to using violence during disagreements. When asked about the ethnic mix in the neighbourhood where John lived, he said, 'Its [well-known area with large concentrations of minority ethnic groups], take a guess…Blacks and Pakis…I don't really like them. I'm not racist at all. I just like to stick to myself and that's it. My type of people really'. Rod noted that John would get animated when expressing his strongly felt racist and xenophobic attitudes ('fucking

---

[62] I am not arguing that this cultural dominance exists in any meaningful economic or political sense in outside society.

[63] Of white British, Christian origin.

[64] 'Wha' Gwan' is an expression in Jamaican patois meaning 'What's going on?' and 'Blood' and 'Fam' are used in reference to close friends or members of a peer group; 'Wasteman' is similar to the term 'loser'.

[65] Of black Southern African, Muslim origin.

foreigners'), but he was also aware of their meaning and looked to Rod to see if he was judging him negatively. John presented familiar concerns about foreigners receiving welfare support (estimated at £100,000). At a YOI, John had been cussed[66] ('suck your mum') by an Asian prisoner and he responded by insulting the Asian prisoner's faith (telling him to 'fuck Allah and eat the Qu'ran). He had later been attacked with a knife in retaliation by a group of Asian prisoners.

I don't think anyone actually cares in this day and age. I could walk out on that landing now and shout out, you dirty black cunt and no one would say a thing. They could walk out and say, you dirty white cunt as well and no one would say nothing…No one cares anymore. Come on, black people call each other nigger.…The thing is, if I went out there and I said black cunt and any one of them had come up to me I'd stick a knife in their face, so it wouldn't be worth their time.…the Muslims all stick together, and the blacks all stick together, but the white people don't.…you've just got for some reason the white people in here they just like to kiss everyone's arse and they're all running round with the Muslims and the black people.…If there was 10–15 black fellers out there lining up to fight me the only white person in here that would stand beside me is my cell-mate. All the other boys would be like oh it's nothing to do with me boy, don't want a bit of that boy. [unclear—00:28:17], and you look at them and thinking, who are you bruv, you're supposed to fucking stand side by side with us, you know what I mean, but it don't work like that, not at all. I don't expect it to. I've been in jail for nearly 6–7 years boy, I know exactly how it works…

Emergent in some white prisoners' accounts, like John's, was a perceived deep racial divide in prison, which was more prominent in the interviews at Maidstone prison than at Rochester YOI. Although such talk was not commonplace, several spoke of maintaining only a reserved level of interaction with black and other minority ethnic prisoners. Similarly to Carroll's (1974) and Jacobs' (1979) findings, minority ethnic solidarity was seen as assured in a way that white solidarity was not. These narratives are marked by ambivalence—they are infused with envy, disdain, and resentment—and were readily employed in reference to collective identification among minority ethnic prisoners. It appeared to be the rigid solidarity supposedly engendered by black prisoners and/or Muslim prisoners which was most acutely resented, refracted by its absence among white prisoners. Equally troubling to John was the equivalent of 'race traitors' who sought black interracial

---

[66] I discuss 'cussing' more fully in Ch 5.

company in prison and who could not be relied on to stand on the 'white side' if violence erupted.

James,[67] a prisoner at Rochester, noted that 'some [whites] don't just talk to blacks you can tell...[and] some blacks don't talk to whites but...nothing gets said like really out blatantly loud'. Some minority ethnic prisoners like Ramiz[68] also talked about how prisoners' racism would be hidden to a degree—'the way they act on the wing, they don't show they're racist or anything, but sometimes it just comes out of their mouth'. For the most part, prisoners acted prudently and did not let their prejudiced views be known. Prisoners, like Anthony, revealed an ambivalence in their accounts of social relations with minority ethnic prisoners. On the one hand, Anthony described easy friendships with black prisoners, sharing CDs (a favourite of his being reggae artist, Gregory Isaacs) and being disgusted by the racism directed at his friend by prison officers.[69] On the other hand, his talk carried hints of black cultural pathology, and he, perhaps incongruously, enjoyed the company of prisoners who held vehemently racist views.

For some other white British, Maidstone prisoners, like Matthew, the patterns of social relationships in prison were the fault of 'black racists' who 'stick to their own'. This seemed to lead to a resigned withdrawal and resentment taken behind closed doors. There was evidence in some of our interviews of the way in which expressions of racism had become thoroughly privatized as traditional affirmations of racial superiority could only be safely shared in exclusive white company,[70] which the crowded, enclosed, and structured prison environment tended to frustrate.[71] In this sense whiteness is not undefended; instead, there is 'white flight', social

[67] Of white British, Christian origin.

[68] Of Bangladeshi British, Muslim origin.

[69] Anthony offered to support his friend if he wished to submit a racist complaint.

[70] It is significant that the Keith Inquiry (2006) into the murder of Zahid Mubarek noted that his murderer, Robert Stewart, had notably only expressed his racism among white prisoners at Feltham YOI; it had remained hidden from black prisoners and prison officers (see also Commission for Racial Equality (CRE) 2003a). At Rochester, 24 racist incidents were reported involving only prisoners at the time of our fieldwork, of a total of 61. Of the 81 racist incidents recorded during the period of our fieldwork at Maidstone prison, only six involved complaints about prisoner–prisoner abuse.

[71] For Goldberg (2009) this privatization of race is central to the neoliberal project where racism is denied or explained away as non-racist.

withdrawal, and avoidance (see also Hughey 2011). The axis of the defence of whiteness often turns on notions of reverse racism; I look at the implications of this in Chapter 6.

Discussion

Consistent with Irwin and Cressey's (1962) 'importation model' of prisoner identities and social relations, there are multiple ways in which external identities impact on lives inside prison. Providing an emotional connection to home through the cooking of particular foods or the type of music played in cells, indicating a way to differentiate oneself and perform as an individual but also as part of a collective, and helping to cope with the psychological effects of imprisonment by seeking an inner peace and self-understanding through religious participation, are all examples. Yet, prisoners' identities are not exclusively bound by predefined cultural practices; they are not essential, immutable features of racial, ethnic, religious, and national identities. Instead, they are fluid, subject to flux, even flexible within the confines of the prison. Moreover, for many prisoners, these represent empty positions, ones which have become redundant, meaningless, and superfluous in late modernity, and this seemed particularly true of race, ethnicity, and (Christian) religious faith.

The observation of prisoner interactions together with their interview narratives portrayed the social world of the prison as a state of loose ethnic solidarities, cultural fusion, convivial multiculture, and racialized tensions. Hallmarks of this fragmentary and complex prisoner society could be seen in any number of the stories prisoners told about their lives outside and inside prison. Ruhi's matter-of-fact account of cultural exchange in the self-cook area seems to provide an apt illustration of Gilroy's (2006: 40) conceptualization of multicultural conviviality which is:

a social pattern in which different [urban] groups dwell in close proximity, but where their racial, linguistic and religious particularities do not—as the logic of ethnic absolutism suggests they must—add up to discontinuities of experience or insuperable problems of communication.

This comes more easily to the urban prisoners who have been socialized into a diverse multiculture at school, college, and on the housing estates in which many lived, or brought about through global migratory movements. It is more challenging for those who come from 'host society citadels' who may be straining to adapt to the changed times of late modernity. Some such prisoners exhibited tendencies collectively described by Gilroy (2004) as representing a state of melancholy linked to Britain's loss of empire. The implicit nostalgia back to a time when Britain was mighty, the dominant power on the world stage, seems to generate destructive prosaic encounters between the white majority prisoners and minority ethnic prisoners. This post-imperial melancholia is the uneasy counterpart of multicultural conviviality with which it coexists in the prison. This is especially the case in Maidstone prison where first and second generation minority ethnic 'settlers' live alongside the 'indigenous' older white prisoners who were only a generation or two away from the height of imperial nostalgia.

Thus, while multicultural conviviality is present, so is conflicted 'hidden' racialization which can also transcend the binary of a white racist–black victim typology. Racialized antagonisms were liable to surface in specific instances as tensions rose or relations became more stressed. However, the black–white polarities of old have been splintered beyond recognition by the more complex identity dynamics of Britain in the early 21st century, which include vacillating racialization and articulations of racisms which intersect with ethnicity, faith, class, and nationality. A black (and Muslim) cultural pre-eminence in the social world of the prison can be likened to the black hegemony of prison subcultures in the United States, referred to 30 years ago by Carroll (1974) and Jacobs (1979). Whilst Jacobs attributed this to the majority presence of black prisoners in many US correctional institutions, and their shared history of collective organization through race, the current study appears to signify the instability of social hierarchies where white privilege is no longer assured but black prisoners' assertive presence is more certain, albeit contested.

It is important to recognize that this cultural dominance does not equate to meaningful economic or political power in outside society. As Hill Collins (2006) has asserted, the widespread commodification of black cultural practices and symbols has not dismantled the black stereotype of hypermasculinity or the structural dislocation of black men in the economy (see also Connell and Messerschmidt 2005).[72] At the same time, the racial dynamics of the late

---

[72] For example there were extraordinarily high levels of young black male unemployment in the last quarter of 2011 (Office of National Statistics (ONS) 2012) with previous evidence that racial discrimination plays a significant part in this (Heath and Cheung 2006; Wood et al. 2009).

modern British prison are such that race is essentialized and reified, but also contradictorily, racial difference is rendered unremarkable. Conviviality, the relaxed minimization of racial difference where multiculture can be creative, vibrant, and above all, negotiable, is underscored by wary, unstable, and inconsistent social relations.

That social relations in prison appear to be brittle does not mean that multicultural prisons are on the precipice of communal disorder. The findings presented here are not intended to be alarmist with regard to social order. There is certainly much to be positive about, as the tensions described here are often constructively worked through by prisoners, and order is maintained. However, I do wish also to sound a cautionary note. In 1986, Ahmed Iqbal Ullah was murdered at Burnage High School in Manchester. The public inquiry into his death (Macdonald 1989) suggested that it was essential for schools to address the underlying racism which clearly existed in social relations in the school, and the same argument can be made in relation to prisons; both are sites where the dynamics of social interactions may fall under the radar of officials. We only need look to the circumstances surrounding Zahid Mubarek's murder to be reminded of the fragility and dangers of prison life marred by racism. In Chapter 5 I explore further social relations in Rochester and Maidstone prisons, paying particular attention to the variegated dimensions of racialized masculinities and their enactment in prison in attempts to sustain a masculine self inside.

5
From Boys to Men: Racialized Masculinities Inside

Masculinities, just like racial, ethnic, religious, and national identities, are not fixed. They are plural, fluid, and dynamic modes of being constrained by micro-level interactions, social-structural constraints, and cultural influences, in particular gender orders (Connell 1987; 1995; Connell and Messerschmidt 2005; West and Zimmerman 1987; Wetherell and Edley 1999; cf. Seidler 2006). Connell's[1] (1987) concept of hegemonic masculinity has remained a powerful conceptual device for understanding the cultural expression of masculine dominance over women. All men can be seen in relation to a valued, idealized, yet normative masculinity, stratified by class, race, and sexuality producing dominant and subordinated masculine positions. Connell (2005: 111) uses the term 'protest masculinities' to describe the gendered practices of the impoverished and powerless which describes most prisoners at Rochester and Maidstone prisons (see also Jewkes 2005). Their actions can often involve elements of what has been referred to elsewhere as 'hypermasculinity': an exaggerated form of key masculine conventions, particularly aggression, violent domination, and independence. These have particular resonance in the gendered space of the prison. The pains of imprisonment—the loss of identity with the removal of material possessions, the loss of autonomy, occupational status, heterosexual relationships, alongside societal rejection—can be particularly infantilizing and undermining of a sense of masculine adequacy. Elements of the inmate code proposed by Sykes and Messinger (1960) as a means for

[1] On her personal website, Connell refers to herself as a transsexual woman whose formal transition occurred late in life. The body of work, including that published as a man RW Connell, is also referred to in the feminine noun, and I follow this convention (see <http://www.raewynconnell.net/p/about-raewyn_20.html>, accessed 28 March 2012).

guiding social relations in prison in response to these pains fit neatly with the contours of hypermasculinity. Demonstrating independence through 'doing your own time', emotional strength through 'playing it cool', and presenting a tough persona, are all essential qualities of 'being a man' in prison.

The Performance of Violent Masculinity

Adaptation to the pains of imprisonment also requires the erection of informal hierarchies of power often achieved through violence between prisoners. According to Toch (1998), hypermasculine scripts are used by young prisoners who feel compelled to respond to any masculine challenges in order to reduce their risk of future victimization, just as in violent street cultures (Bourgois 1995; Anderson 1999/2006; see also Seaton 2007). Crewe (2009: 409) refers to this as a 'culture of calibrated confrontation' where prisoners have to act aggressively to pre-empt conflict or derision. Consistently found in prison studies (Jewkes 2002; Edgar, O'Donnell, and Martin 2003), it is no surprise that Rochester and Maidstone prisoners revealed similar concerns. This underlines how presentations of masculinity are subject to intense scrutiny inside, thus producing extreme insecurity:[2]

But this guy come to me trying to bully me for my burn, for my tobacco yeah…And um basically I whacked the poor kid round his head a few times and then I got done for GBH, yeah…And like the only way I felt to deal with it was to do that, and I thought um I can't tell the officers because of the pressure of um making me look like um like a snitch, small, that's how I feel innit…I certainly was scared and I was scared of what people would think of me as well. So I had that pressure as well. (Daniel, mixed race British, Christian, Maidstone)

…you're two inches taller when you go outside your door. And then when your door's shut at night you just, you just deflate.…when you're behind you're behind your door, this is your sanctuary…they're not locking you in, you're locking them out…(Douglas, white British, Muslim, Maidstone)

A pastime of schoolboys too (Frosh et al. 2002), unmasking 'fronters' or fakes, whose dubious claims of material wealth or criminal status were fabricated or grossly exaggerated, framed the anxious

[2] Ultra-masculine prison environments may undermine prisoner adjustment adding to feelings of isolation (Lutze and Murphy 1999).

'jockeying for position' at Rochester and Maidstone prisons (Edley and Wetherell 1997). This constant threat of exposure feeds masculine insecurities in prison, as such exposure led to violent retribution at worst and a ruined reputation and permanent lowly status at best.

The volatility of social relations where a shift from conviviality and friendliness to aggression and violence in minutes was because, as Barry[3] suggested, 'everybody's on a knife edge…everybody's potentially unbalanced'. Many prisoners had negotiated ways of avoiding violence—staying away from the flashpoints (pool, snooker, and table tennis tables, self-cook areas)—or not responding to provocative challenges when they occurred. Skilfully, prisoners attempted to manage the tricky balancing act of blending in, being reserved, but not too timid, friendly, but not too open, and chatty, but not mouthy in social interactions. However, while the comments of Daniel, Douglas, and Barry reinforced the findings of previous research, also repeatedly heard in prisoners' accounts was a denial of 'fronting' or mask-wearing, and a heartfelt belief that you *could* be yourself in prison, as Dexter noted:

I don't change for nobody. I'm same way I'm here the way I am outside.… I just stay the same. I aint got no reason to change. I don't need a new identity…I don't need to hide behind my personality, I'm me. It's very easy for me to be me. (Dexter, black African British, Christian, Rochester)

Yet, many of those who denied fronting a tough public image often relied on a hard reputation on road to protect themselves from challenges inside (see also Jewkes 2003; Crewe 2009). For others, this agential assertion of an autonomous self, the unwillingness to pretend or change, to claim an identity which is demanded by the prison experience, represents an inner fortitude, perhaps a resistant stance, which is in itself characteristic of hegemonic masculinity. For prisoners such as Nathan, 'fronting' carried the danger of losing one's sense of identity:

I try in prison to be the same person as much as possibly I can that I am outside. So when I get out of prison I haven't changed that much, I'm still me, you know what I mean. And like I mean Nathan one, come to prison, Nathan two, get out, Nathan one, come, Nathan two, and you just start getting multiple personalities…so I've tried to just remain who I am. (Nathan, white British, Christian, Maidstone)

[3] Of white British origin, no religion.

Writing 15 years ago, Sim (1994) argued that violence was uncontrolled, yet normative, particularly in young offenders' institutions (YOIs) like Rochester. While there was little evidence to indicate unbridled violent exploitation in Rochester, there was more masculine posturing and 'jockeying for position' than at Maidstone prison (see Wetherell and Edley 1999). Public displays of violence were deemed more common in YOIs than in 'big man's jails' where a certain maturity was expected. For this reason, some prisoners such as Dimitri,[4] serving longer sentences, looked forward to their move upwards in the system, away from the 'hype' (wildness, boisterousness) and 'child mentality' of Rochester.

A notable feature of gendered aggression at Rochester was 'cussing', which is calculatingly designed to hurt and humiliate the recipient because the cuss refers to female relatives in misogynistic, sexually explicit, and vulgar ways. Most often, mothers are the subject of cusses—as Arcel[5] observed: 'the magic words are "suck your mum"'. Sometimes it can simply involve a competitive, witty repartee of quick-fire insults which is taken lightly by both protagonist and antagonist, strikingly similar to 'the dozens', a feature of cool pose black masculinity in the United States (Majors and Billson 1992). Ian, a Rochester prisoner, explained the potential trajectory of cussing:

Well that's just escalated arguments....So basically if you are cussing and staying at that level but that alone, that level alone is hurting that other person so much that they've had the cheek to say something that's above the limit where you go. And in the end it either gets quashed, like say there's friends on both sides that just say no, stop that, and you got no arguments anyway. Or it will just end up in trading blows because of the simple fact that you crossed the line. (Ian, black African British, Christian, Rochester)

However, even when there seems to be a mutual engagement in cussing banter, it symbolizes a masculine contest in which men can assert their authority and excel in the humour stakes whilst also expressing supreme heterosexuality (Swain 2002). But the ritual can very easily spiral into physical aggression:

One boy cussed my mum and I cussed his mum back...he must have thought he could just spit on my door and I wouldn't do nothing about

---

[4] Of white other, Christian origin.
[5] Of black Central African, Christian origin.

it…I got hot water and put shampoo in it and when he went to do it again and I squirted it all in his eyes, and we had the fight the next morning…Yeah, I got five days loss of soash [association]. And he got down the block [segregation unit] for three days. (Martin, white British, Christian, Rochester)

In this way, protagonists can publicly display their masculinity through the chivalrous role of acting as the 'moral guardians of the sexual reputations of mothers, girlfriends and sisters' (Kehily and Nayak 1997; Wetherell and Edley 1999). In the male peer group of young prisoners, a reminder of absent, affectionate, and supportive female family members can touch a raw nerve at a time when prisoners are aware of the shame they have caused their families. As Michael[6] noted, 'you only ever get one mum'. In Martin's case, the relationship with his mother was less straightforward and he held her partially responsible for his offending. She had only visited him once in prison, on a previous sentence, as her regular and excessive alcohol use meant that she rarely had the resources to travel from their home in south London. Regardless, the convention is to respond to cussing with a return cuss and violence where necessary.

Where fights did take place, and they were more prevalent in Rochester than in Maidstone prison, and even less so in Thanet wing housing vulnerable prisoners, the ritualism of fighting inside often resembled the displays of almost-violence described by Fox (1977). Aggressive gestures, threatening language, and hostile posturing showed bravado and avoided ridicule serving, according to Fox, a rhetorical and symbolic function which minimizes the harm done by combatants (see also Marsh 1982). One such example had racialized overtones:

[T]here was like a boy down by the stairwell the other night on soash [association] and he was like started like giving…a few evils [aggressive stares]…And like me and him stood there side by side basically waiting and like before you know it you've got like 15 boys all crowding round…Like a lot of their [black] boys will come over and they'll be all just giving it mouth and then a certain black boy, one of the boys got lairy, it was one of his mates stepped in and he started standing there like clinching. So I said, don't clinch your fist mate, I said don't try and stand there and give me signs, if you're going to do something do it, do you know what I mean. Don't think I'm going to back down. And then that was it…you show you aint going to take no shit, you're willing to have him and then they think twice…(Jason, white/Gypsy, Christian, Rochester)

[6] Of white British, Christian origin, at Rochester.

Clearly it would be wrong to argue that violence only operates at a symbolic level. Both Rochester and Maidstone prisons were, on occasion, the site of horrific violence; stories were recounted of pool balls stuffed into socks and used as a cosh, or kettle-boiled water used to scald, and razor blades used to cut. Wing cultures also influenced the crafting of violent performances. At Maidstone the legendary Kent wing, the 'war zone' or the 'Beirut wing', where it was 'dog eat dog', exemplified how drug use had been allowed to proliferate at the time of the study (HMIP 2007b), bringing violence where addicts had unpaid debts or were involved in cell thefts. We regularly encountered pasty-looking, unkempt prisoners with glassy, red-rimmed eyes. Like the archetypal problem housing estate where natural surveillance is hindered, this wing, because of its architectural design of long landings with parts of each spur obscured from the central area, provided ample opportunities for crime to occur unnoticed by prison officers. An air of tension was perceptible. These individual wing milieus provide the institutional context for the nature of interpersonal relationships which unfold.

In contrast, on Medway and Weald wings, a domesticity and relative calm was observed; Samson[7] referred to the latter positively: 'it's like a family, you know…everyone gets on, everyone chats'. Power shifted with the high 'churn rate', as people were shipped in and out. In this sense, life on the wings could be relatively sedate punctured by occasional disputes, but with an underlying potential for violence to occur at any time. And while the Incentives and Earned Privileges (IEP) scheme often featured as a brake on prison violence for those concerned with gaining or not losing their enhanced status or not having days added onto their sentence, this could easily be overlooked by prisoners in a heightened state of an interpersonal conflict in which masculine dominance is of paramount importance for social status.

'Postcode Pride'[8] Across Race

Arguably one of the oldest traditions of demonstrating working-class masculinity is an aggressive, spatial territorialism, which the accounts of Rochester and Maidstone prisoners attested had significant implications for social relations inside prison. This

[7] Of black African British origin.
[8] This term is borrowed from Earle (2011b: 140).

reinforces, once again, that prisoners' identities and relations in prison are also inherently shaped by their biographies, as Irwin and Cressey's importation model purported.

Historical accounts of street gangs in late 19th-century London (Pearson 2011) and early 20th-century New York (Riis 1902) described territorial battles where collective masculine identities were formed according to bounded spatial domains. For Thrasher (1927), these formations were further constituted by their essential youthfulness, spontaneity, oppositional outlook, and predatory behaviour. As such, they bear a striking resemblance to the neighbourhood collectivities which are a feature of the contemporary urban landscape, according to Rochester and Maidstone prisoners. Many prisoners admitted that they had often been involved in stealing cars, street robbery, and drug dealing 'on road' when hanging out with friends from their local areas. Hallsworth and Young (2008) refer to these as 'volatile peer groups' rather than 'gangs', where criminality is not intrinsic to group identity. Prisoners described the positive functions of such peer groups, which included sociality, friendship, and mutual safety in conflicts over neighbourhood space (see also Ralphs et al. 2009). Samson,[9] a Maidstone prisoner, fondly recalled the independence from informal control and the strong bonds of friendship which made such peer groups attractive. Growing up together from nursery school, neighbourhood friends had played football, gone clubbing together, and been in 'the kind of area where, you know, things happen...crime and just craziness you know, your friends get stabbed or shot something like that, you know, or...oh, you know getting harassed by the police'. While crime may provide a means to accomplish masculinity (Messerschmidt 1993), its pursuit can end in incarceration which has its own emasculating effects (Sabo, 2001).

Although neighbourhood territorialism has been recently rediscovered in Kintrea et al.'s (2008) work, and dramatically described today as 'postcode wars' by journalists (for example, *Sun*, 10 May 2008), back in the late 1970s Robins and Cohen (1978: 73) had described territoriality as integral to working-class, masculine cultures. Street battles afforded participation in the symbolic process of 'magically appropriating, owning and controlling' a material

---

[9] Of black African British origin.

locality (see also Tolson 1977).[10] They suggested that this was structured through 'gangs' or 'fighting crews' which were pitted against rivals who engaged in ritualistic displays of aggression.

For the younger prisoners at Rochester and Maidstone, a central referent was localized 'postcode identities' shaped by their lives outside prison—at school, college, in parks, clubs, and foremost on the streets. They were formed according to sharply delineated spatial zones such as social housing estates, town areas (particularly for Home Counties' prisoners), or in London it was the symbol of the postcode—SE15, SW9, SE13, E15, E3—that predominated (see also Harvey 2007). The street provided a stage for a performance of masculinity[11] which demonstrated toughness, violence, strategic acumen, and fear-making dominance over non-affiliated residents. Rafael,[12] a prisoner from London E8 (Hackney), described the strictly delineated streets in East London where area boundaries (and gendered 'property') were actively policed. Rafael had been 'rushed' [beaten] by boys from London E9 (Victoria Park) 'because I went out with some girl from their area that they all wanted'. Similarly, Jason[13] spoke of a habitual 'war' between housing estates in the Kent town where he and his friends would 'go out on a weekend tooled up ... because we know we're going to bump into them [rivals from the other estates]'.

These area-based solidarities inscribed with a class-based solidarity often usurped or overlaid identities organized through race or ethnicity (see also Bosworth and Carrabine 2001; for similar findings in youth cultures see Back 1996; Alexander 2001).[14] This must be viewed alongside a convergence among many white *and* minority ethnic prisoners of the latent emptiness of ethnicity for self-identities (see Chapter 4). As Gilroy (2004: 132) has suggested, 'factors of identity and solidarity that derive from class, gender, sexuality and *region* have made a strong sense of racial difference

---

[10] See Earle's (2011b) fascinating account of the young men at Rochester which evoked comparison with masculine collectives in the early European medieval period.

[11] Butler's (1989) work has been at the forefront of ideas about the performativity of gender.

[12] Of black African British, Christian origin at Rochester.

[13] Of mixed white/Gypsy British, Christian origin at Rochester.

[14] The Keith Inquiry into the murder of Zahid Mubarek by Robert Stewart similarly found that Stewart had previously shared a cell with a mixed race prisoner with whom he had a strong geographical bond.

unthinkable to the point of absurdity' (emphasis added). This from Abdullah and Philip from Rochester:

[M]ost of the prisoners they're from Kent they're from this area. But someone who's from like say London yeah, most of the black boys on here are from London. And you can tend to talk to them about the same things that are going through, like happen in your life, and you can't really talk about Kent. (Abdullah, black East African, Muslim)

When it comes down to it, it doesn't matter about race and all that like on my estate, like. When there's people like they're trying to like fight one of us we all stick together, it doesn't matter [what] colour we are...Like for example like I could have a fight with one of my black mates yeah and then like next day I could have a fight with someone from out the ends [neighbourhood] and he would jump in for me. That's the way the estate works. (Philip, white British, Christian, Rochester)

While some scholars have emphasized globalized mobility and extensive communication networking as modes of reconfiguring and hybridizing youth cultures in disparate nations (Pilkington and Johnson 2003), young prisoners' identities clearly need to be understood through a local lens. Bauman (2004) may be right in claiming that in times of ontological insecurity territorialism provides a mode of secure being and certainty. Despite the negative depictions of their neighbourhoods (see Chapter 1), prisoners expressed sentiments of intense pride about belonging to these areas.[15] By erecting boundaries of belonging which exclude others from strictly delineated and symbolic 'area zones', these young men claim dominion, (perceptions of) power, and perhaps most importantly, status over other young men, which is central to the demands of protest masculinity. The opportunity to exclude may be one of the few means by which these young men, marked by their low social, political, and economic position in late modern society, can exercise agency, and avoid the stigma which Bauman (2004) sees as the lot of the 'underclass'.

The Seductive Imaginary of Prison Gangs

Alongside neighbourhood territorialism, the factors supporting the emergence of street gangs, according to Hagedorn (2007)—

[15] Notwithstanding, many prisoners' aspiration was to move to a 'nice middle class area' on release, to move out of the clutches of criminal associates, tempting influences, and sometimes painful memories. Without irony, prisoners talked of such areas, almost always defining them on the basis of their crime-free potential, with good facilities and schools, in which their children could grow up.

exclusion, inequality, and the neoliberal residualization of welfare—are clearly evident in the United Kingdom (see Chapter 1). Moreover, there is an increasing body of empirical work which has variously documented gangs, networks, crews, collectives, and cliques within delinquent or organized criminal groups outside prison (Phillips, C. 2012). While some scholars remain deeply sceptical of these constructions of youth delinquency and violence, particularly because of their controlling and racializing tendencies (Alexander, C. 2008; Hallsworth and Young 2008), it is not inconceivable that gang formations might be operative in prisons (Hobbs 1997). Recent newspaper headlines have raised the spectre of prison gangs in England (see, for example, 'Prison Officers Fear That Muslim Inmates are Taking Over Control', *The Times*, 26 May 2008 and 'Gang in Jail Reign of Terror', *Mirror*, 18 January 2005). These headlines discuss Her Majesty's Inspectorate of Prisons' (HMIP's) (2008, 2004) inspections of Whitemoor and Liverpool prisons, both of which contemplate 'gangland culture' being imported into prison. More broadly, these headlines and inspections raise perennial concerns about social order in prisons, but now added to the mix are new questions of racialized and religious identification.

The penetration of street gangs into the prison was a theme in Jacobs' (1974; 1977) classic study of Stateville Penitentiary. The black and Latino 'supergangs' in Stateville variously provided physical protection, material advantages often gained through bullying and extortion, information about institutional matters, psychological support, and a sense of belonging. Structured hierarchically with gang leaders, lieutenants, cell house chiefs, and soldiers, these organized gangs had 'international rules' which forbade rip-offs, interference in gangs' activities, the stealing of dealers' commission to a particular gang, and the protection of non-members. These restrictions were an attempt by gang leaders to regulate inter-gang conflict (see also Irwin 1980).

Despite Jimmy's colourful commentary below which captures the contours of the somewhat fantastical image of prison gangs and life inside, Rochester and Maidstone prisoners categorically disavowed the presence of organized prison gangs like those in Stateville:

I lived a life of crime and I've lived with criminals for 30 years…prison is a mini city…out there on the landings there, that's your streets, and the wings, the 1, 2, 3 and 4s are housing estates…you've got the people that brews hooch, you've got your drug traffickers, you've got your pimps, you've got your prostitutes, you've got your violent gangs, you've got your gangs that traffics drugs, gangs that goes and collects debts…if you see prisoners separate from the rest of society then you have a confused view…(Jimmy, white/Romany, Christian, Maidstone)

Prisoners of all ethnicities, faiths, nationalities, and those from urban, suburban, and semi-rural communities were unequivocal in denying the presence of organized gangs such as the infamous Bloods and Crips, although they were a familiar point of reference. Astutely, Varinder,[16] a Rochester prisoner, recognized the 'stereotype' of a gang as a 'group of guys causing trouble or making money by selling drugs' but instead suggested that they were no more than a group of friends. He went on, like other prisoners, to say, 'It's not really like there's a gang that runs the prison or some bullshit like that, that don't really happen in YOIs', but these groups would often protect members so that 'if you have a problem with one of them you're probably going to have a problem with all of them'.

Formed on the basis of deeply embedded postcode identities, these collective affiliations structured micro-interactions, allegiances, and disputes, particularly among younger prisoners (see also Crewe 2009). Such groupings provided the basis for sociality and companionship, and a route for exchanging goods in the informal economy to mitigate the pains of imprisonment, akin to Irwin's (2005: 93) 'cars' in Californian prisons (cf. Harvey 2007):

[A]s soon as I got on the wing I knew about a handful of people…people will say 'Oh there are gangs or whatever', but we're local guys from the same area or we know a friend of a friend and we stick together because we're all Boys, do you know what I mean? If I run out of juice I can go to him and he'll give me a bottle of juice…(Melvin, black African British, Muslim, Maidstone)

These 'postcode identities' established for prisoners an ontological attachment to a known and owned space, operating as a way of anchoring prisoners' belonging to somewhere external to the prison, and this was true even if those places were a site of family discord, personal disappointment, or violence. Prisoners' talk was of local identification as a mode through which new friendships were

---

[16] Of Indian British origin.

forged, enabling them to make meaningful connections with conversations covering mutual friends, leisure, education, or employment venues. Neal,[17] for example, talked of prisoners he had made friends with from his area and with whom he would go to parties and clubbing once released.

Arcel,[18] another prisoner at Rochester, described the 'tribal' practice of prisoners calling out their postcodes after evening lock-up, whilst, Dabir[19] noted that 'it don't matter what you're in for it's just who you know and what area you're from'. Inside, mutual defensive support in minor 'beefs' (disputes) was part of the obligation to assist those from your area, as Austin,[20] a Rochester prisoner, observed: 'if you're from someone's ends [neighbourhood] then, yeah, they are, they got a certain amount of liability to look out for you innit...you have to look out for each other'. These sentiments were echoed in many interview accounts, of prisoners of all ethnicities:

...everyone from Poplar...that is a guaranteed we are going to stick together...If anything kicks off then we are all there for each other, innit. Whoever else gets involved with a little scene then we are there for them. (Clinton, black African British, Christian, Rochester)

[To] get by [in prison] is your friends from road. Well I had here a few friends from my area in here, innit, like ones that I used to know and speak to on road....Say they see you with a bit of beef or whatever, and then they will come behind and they'll say like, I'm backing you. So that means that if you fight him they'll jump in as well. (Darren, white British, no religion, Rochester)

In practice, and as Harvey (2007) has recognized, it can be difficult to assess the extent to which prisoners actually adhere to this code but it has significant symbolic importance as a means for performing masculinity and meeting the need for support during incarceration.

Petty disagreements related to the irritants of proximal living sparked fights, but such incidents began typically as individualized, one-on-one masculine contests, and even if they involved supporters, they were not influenced by organized gang allegiances:

---

[17] Of mixed race British, Christian origin.
[18] Of black Central African, Christian origin.
[19] Of Pakistani British, Muslim origin at Rochester.
[20] Of white British origin, with no religion.

...two people had a fight it's just a fight that's all it is and it's done with...It really isn't a gang thing. But then you might see his friend getting beat up so he might then put the boot in, and he might see his friend and there's two jumpers so he might jump in, that could happen...as far as gangs for example like that gang v that gang, that doesn't happen, I've never seen that. (Matthew, white British, Christian, Maidstone)

Neither were prison pecking orders, such that existed, founded along gang lines, although this may be more a feature of maximum security prisons (see Liebling, Arnold, and Straub 2012). Crime type, length of sentence and time served, and physical prowess and presence established through a tough reputation from road or in prison were indicators of esteem. Securing financial control on the wings through the distribution of prized items (such as 'burn' (tobacco), drugs, mobile phones, food, and shower gel) was a key factor in wing dominance, just as Sykes (1958) found with 'merchants' who instrumentally responded to the institutional exigencies of imprisonment. Unlike Irwin's (1980) 'racketeers' who worked collectively, a more diffuse arrangement existed in Rochester and Maidstone prisons, with many entrepreneurial individuals operating to maximize profits as well as some small groupings using 'runners' to distribute goods and seek repayment. Simple exchanges or borrowing were also practised, but 'double bubble' rates or 'taxing' often prevailed outside an individual's friendship groups with the same mixed views on the practice voiced by the Wellingborough prisoners studied by Crewe (2009).

Occasionally the permeation of 'area beefs' into the prison occurred as (sometimes historical) conflicts between rival gangs on road were imported into the prison creating tense social relations:

...London jails or Manchester, anywhere around Manchester, where what you have got is certain gangs will come into a jail, you see from the different areas...even people in gangs will not be able to put their finger on it, why they dislike that person so much or from a different area...It's almost postcoded...because it's ran through the family and through friends' friends...(Larry, white British, no religion, Maidstone)

Views differ on the role of gangs in escalating violence and conflict 'on road' (Katz and Jackson-Jacobs 2004; Hales, Lewis, and Silverstone 2006), but in prison, security departments are often alert to gang disputes which may flow from 'road' to prison. A prison officer at Rochester described the difficulties involved in managing these locality-based tensions among 'the London Posses, or the

Faversham Boys, Essex Lads, Kent Boys, North Kent Boys' (Field-note, 17 July 2006). Detailed discussions with the governor and other prison officers also noted clashes between south London and north London collectives fuelled by the arrival of two signifi-cant 'gang members' who were transferred in from another prison. The strident refusal of another self-proclaimed street gang member to let 'street problems' become 'his business' inside Rochester prison, being 'not for in here', allowed him to identify the 'ringlead-ers' who spurred the clashes (Fieldnotes, 5 January 2007; 16 Janu-ary 2007). Antagonism between the opposing London collectives dissipated following the ringleaders' segregation and later transfer. The 'shipping out' of prisoners remained a means for distilling localized collective conflicts and was also referred to in prisoner interviews as a way of dealing with conflicts between east London- and south London-affiliated prisoners in Rochester prison.

On occasion, prison might even serve as a respite for these area beefs which could be suspended or mediated through individual interaction in prison, as this extract from Anton's interview reveals:

> But like before I came to jail and that yeah, Brixton and Peckham yeah, they're always in this mad beefing thing, yeah. Since I came to jail I met a lot of Peckham boys…I get on with them and them sort of things innit. They don't make what's on the outside bother them on the inside…(Anton, black Caribbean British, Christian, Rochester)

That the prison can act as a breathing space within which to rene-gotiate past or ongoing conflicts is significant. The unifying experi-ences of incarceration can displace animosities as protagonists accept that there are often severe disciplinary costs of pursuing grievances inside.

'Muslim gangs'

For C. Alexander (2008) the trope of 'the gang' presents a ready racializing vessel which often symbolizes a wider social angst about violence and disorder, particularly among minority ethnic groups. As Hallsworth and Young (2008: 185) have observed, 'the gang is always seen to wear a black or brown face', despite empirical evi-dence to the contrary (Mares 2001; Bennett and Holloway 2004; Bradshaw 2005; Aldridge and Medina 2008; Hallsworth and Sil-verstone 2009). Interestingly, it was uncommon for Rochester and Maidstone prisoners to associate gangs with an essential blackness, but assertions of a 'Muslim bloc'[21] within the prisoner body was among the most animated topics in the interviews with Rochester and Maidstone prisoners. This formulation of 'the gang' corresponded with what C. Alexander (2008: 13) has called the 'ghetto fabulous/threatening "Other"' where the gang is recast as a cohesive body of racialized, minority ethnic prisoners unified by their exclusive 'Muslimness'. There is a clear fit with the pathologizing imaginings of the dangerous 'Asian gang' that Alexander (2000b) has previously deconstructed as more myth than reality. Here, the threatening presence of a Muslim collectivity in prison matches the masculine depiction of the '"bad" Muslim' now associated with hypermasculine gang violence and home-grown terrorism, according to Kalra (2009) which is contrasted with the '"good" non-Muslim' of Hindu Bollywood. It is this former characterization which has reared its head in prison communities as new sensibilities concerning political and religious terrorism have marked the prison as a potential site of radicalization[22] and threat to social order (Hamm 2009; HMIP 2010; Liebling, Arnold, and Straub 2012).

In essence, what surfaced among non-Muslim prisoners was a keenly felt hostility to the seemingly universal and supreme unity of Muslim solidarity. Comments about the 'Muslim gang' in both institutions included: 'there's no gangs in Rochester it's just Muslims stick together', Muslims 'walk around the wings in tens', 'it was like all the Muslims were sticking together', and 'people will say that the only gang in here are the Muslims they always stick up for each other'.[23] Such comments were part of a narrative which hinted at an envy of the assumed solidarity of Muslim prisoners which was loosely characterized in gang terms. The mutual aid,

[21]   In part this reflects the 'regendering' of Asian masculinities, previously feminized in the private sphere, now emerged, according to Alexander, C. (2000b) in the public sphere.

[22]   References to terrorism or radicalization were rare and this was likely the result of the offending profile of prisoners at Rochester and Maidstone. Liebling, Arnold and Straub's (2012) study in Whitemoor, which held several prisoners convicted of terrorism offences, revealed a risk of political radicalization among Muslim prisoners, but also significantly a climate of fear among both staff and prisoners in a place of uncertainty and vulnerability, presenting ripe conditions for new belief systems to take hold.

[23]   From interviews with: Sacha (black African British, Christian, Rochester), Darren (white British, no religion, Rochester), Lloyd (black Caribbean British, Christian, Maidstone), and Bradley (mixed race British, Muslim, Rochester).

reciprocity, group loyalty, and protection believed to be collectively exercised by Muslim prisoners resembled the cohesive adaptations described by Sykes (1958) and Carroll (1974) (and also, to a degree, Jacobs 1974) as a means to partially neutralize the pains of imprisonment (but cf. Harvey 2007). It is not surprising that these collective modes of being are coveted, as such high-level peer solidarity is at a premium in the insecure setting of the prison (Crewe 2009; see also Liebling, Arnold, and Straub 2012). Further, it is in this regard that the alleged conversion of prisoners to Islam to secure protection rather than for spiritual motives was regarded (see Chapter 4). Viewed by many non-Muslim prisoners with contempt, it was seen as akin to 'fronting', and therefore deemed disingenuous, reflecting cowardice, personal weakness, and an inability to hold one's own in prison social relations. This is indicative of the dividend attached to the active demonstration of a physically assertive masculinity which cannot be accomplished within a fake Muslim identity.

Significantly, these elements of a cohesive brotherhood were central to positing the collective presence of Muslim prisoners as a gang, even though surrounding oneself with religious others is a key feature of many religions, particularly those with evangelical roots (Kerley and Copes 2009). Non-Muslim prisoners' racialized talk which symbolically bound together the Muslim prisoner population as 'a gang' tended to ignore its internal heterogeneity. Discussions with the Imam at Rochester prison revealed the complexity of Muslim identities which were mediated by national, regional, and local origins, as well as country of origin and generation:

[T]hey [may] share a Bengali heritage, for example, but then also it will depend on where they are from—what town or area. Most are second generation and will have some, but looser, ties to that country [of origin]. You may get an Algerian and a Moroccan, who are both Muslim, and Arab, but come from different parts of the country, or city, say London. If they come from north London or south London, or even within south London, if they come from Brixton or Peckham, then that may be important, a connection and a difference. It is complicated. (Fieldnote, 30 August 2006)

Muslim prisoners themselves acknowledged that the solidarity engendered by sharing a faith was deeply felt. The observed greetings between fellow Muslims, a chest to chest touch and handshake with the words 'As-Salaam Alaikum' ('peace be upon you'), represented an explicit recognition of a bond of brotherhood. Archer's

(2001; 2003) research suggests that considerable significance is attached to the strength of the Muslim 'brotherhood' as it acts as a counter to essentialized notions of weak Asian masculinities.[24] Certainly, in prison being Muslim presented masculine obligations in prisoner relations just as area allegiances required mutual defensive protection for prisoners. It was articulated by Dabir in this way:

> I see Muslims will stay closer together so…obviously you have to look out for your brother, help his brother, it's a Muslim's duty. And it's like whatever, whatever I want for myself I should want for my brother. (Dabir, Pakistani British, Muslim, Rochester)

This was seen as embedded in the Islamic faith, a basic tenet, which also encompassed a positive sense of interdependence. It was asserted that Muslim prisoners 'don't put themselves in a situation where they need anything from the officers at all…all that they need they get from their people',[25] including sharing burn (tobacco) and not charging 'double bubble' rates in the exchange of goods. Of course, self-reliance and cultural inwardness can be two sides of the same coin, often prompted by exclusion and ostracism from majority cultures (Phillips, D. 2006). The collective backing in prison beefs was one aspect of Muslim solidarity that was particularly despised but also desired by non-Muslims:

> [I]f someone hits on one white person, the rest of the white people aint gonna do nothing, they'll say, 'you sort it out yourself', but if you pick on one Muslim, the rest of the Muslims are going to help that person…They're very closely knit and that's how I am with my friends back home…They're together and they run together and hardly ever let anyone else in. (Abbott, white British, Christian, Rochester)

> [I]t doesn't matter what jail you go to, um if you have an argument with a Muslim brother or Muslim inmate you are guaranteed to end up fighting I don't know, a couple of them at least if not they're going to rush you. (Jed, white British, no religion, Maidstone)

Moreover, while Muslim solidarity was certainly prevalent, it was far more contingent, less assured, and less likely to make exclusive claims on an individual's sense of belonging and identity than sug-

---

[24] Kalra (2009) suggests a colonial legacy to such representations: Sikh masculinities during the British colonial period were represented as solid, strong, martial, and independent whilst Bengali (Muslims) were characterized as feeble, delicate, and effeminate.

[25] Samson (black African prisoner at Maidstone, previously a Muslim convert).

gested by many non-Muslim prisoners. Thus, prisoners would exercise their own judgment about entering into disputes, at least some of the time operating with what Crewe (2009: 229) calls a 'prudent individualism', seeking to avoid disciplinary punishments which increased the length of their sentence. Here, Paul, a recent convert to Islam, explained:

If it was um a Muslim and a Christian [fighting]…I don't think I would have started throwing punches in front of officers, but if there was chance, if he was in a different location that I would feel obligated to help the Muslim…I'm not stupid and I know I'm going home and I aint going to do anything that's going to jeopardize myself, innit. (Paul, black African British, Muslim, Maidstone)

'Cool Pose', Hypermasculinity, and Racialization in Prison

Until relatively recently the focus of minority ethnic masculinities has been almost exclusively on black hypermasculinity. According to Alexander C. (2000b), the gendered behaviour of Asian men had tended to see them subordinated in masculine hierarchies, negatively portrayed as effeminate, physically weak, viewed through the lens of (foreign) language, strong family ties, and internally cohesive communities. There was little to support such claims in Rochester and Maidstone prisons. The low numerical presence of British Indian, Pakistani, and Bangladeshi men and Asian men of foreign nationality in the study prisons (5 per cent) and nationally (7 per cent) rendered Asian prisoners largely invisible in racialized hierarchies. Alternatively, where their presence was articulated it was typically tied to a local identity, through their residence in multicultural London, along with other minority ethnic groups.

Running through much of the literature on black masculinities is a deterministic thread in that it is perceived as a reactive, subversive, and destructive positioning shaped in response to white societal racism and powerlessness, particularly in the US context (Messerschmidt 1993; Hooks 2004). Its markers are rampant homophobia, violent responses to personal slights, and sexual exploitation. According to Majors and Billson (1992), black American masculinity can be encapsulated in the term 'cool pose' which refers to an ethnicized and gendered performance used to cope with racialized humiliation and emasculation with its roots in resistance to slavery (see also O'Donnell and Sharpe 2000 in the

British context). They describe it as a 'ritualized form of masculinity that entails behaviors, scripts, physical posturing, impression management, and carefully crafted performances that deliver a single, critical message: pride, strength, and control'. Black men project an exterior of toughness, defiance, confrontation, and emotional detachment. Hustling, crime, heterosexual promiscuity, and young fatherhood are its hallmarks. Convincingly, Rios (2009) has claimed that African and Latino American hypermasculinity has developed as a coping strategy to deal with institutionalized police surveillance and harassment in the form of feminized ridicule and humiliation.

For C. Alexander (1996), black British masculinity cannot be regarded as a singular experience or set of cultural practices. Her ethnographic study of a diffuse black, male, peer group in London showed an acute awareness of negative stereotypes of the black 'folk devil'—heightened sexuality, for example, but on occasion, the men used these stereotypes to their advantage, for example, in attracting white women. In this sense black cultural practices were highly contextual, agentially produced, but also 'transiently essentialized' and constrained by structural forces (Alexander, C. 1996: 194). Similarly, Sewell's (1997) study of black boys at school indicated that they resented teachers' negative othering of them, but at the same time saw power in the fear that their appearance, style, and assertive physical presence invoked in teachers. His later work blamed black hypermasculinity for low educational attainment, pointing to its oppositional stance to learning and education.

In Rochester and Maidstone some white prisoners did engage in a process of essentializing and reifying black masculinity. Drawing on rigid stereotypes of inherent aggression, Robert, a Rochester prisoner, suggested that black prisoners 'have to have that bit of attitude' because 'it's just the way that they're brought up...just their culture'. Jack's talk draws on naturalizing sentiments in which blackness is fixed to physicality and violence:

I think some people in here, I'm not racist but I'd say mainly black people yeah, they seem to think when you've got a gun and you sell drugs that makes you a gangster, I'm the man and things like that...That don't make you a man, that makes you a mug...Handling responsibilities like and looking after people that makes you more of man than handling a gun...[at the gym] The white boys don't want to get so much bigger. But...it is mainly like the Asian boys and the black boys and the Muslim boys. (Jack, white British, Christian, Rochester)

In this way, common racialized scripts can implicitly position white masculine identities as superior to the racialized black other (Fanon 1967/2008; Barth 1969; Hughey 2011). This process can reinscribe older, entrenched, ethnic ascriptions and boundaries. Notwithstanding, Melvin, a Maidstone prisoner, admitted acting in ways which resonated with cool pose—being defensive, angry, and aggressive, and deliberately engendering fear in other prisoners. His story was of material aspirations hindered by life in an economically impoverished household with his and his friends' 'fathers away' and educated in a school with low expectations. Melvin had cultivated a violent lifestyle and had served several prison sentences. In a reflective and touching moment, he talked of men like himself entering prison 'not knowing themselves' with the 'same chip on their shoulder, same bad boy attitude...just negative, just everything that people have done [to them] is negative'. He went on:

Straight confrontation was one of my ways...If you dis[respect] me you've violated me, you've taken a liberty...this has to be sorted out and I have to teach you a lesson that you know, this can't happen again...my whole attitude, and my whole body language was a big defensive mechanism...Don't hurt me, I don't want you to come in my life to hurt me...But in prison it's like yeah, I'm fighting everyone else and then when there was no one else left to fight I realized...I was fighting myself all this time, do you know what I mean, I actually wore myself out...(Melvin, black African British, Muslim, Maidstone)

Ruhi, also at Maidstone, spoke poignantly of his path away from violence when he 'was down the block all the time, segregation unit, for getting into fights'. As his sentence had progressed he had accepted the value of adopting a more conciliatory and less aggressive persona. Jonathan, a prisoner at Rochester, talked of being in and out of prison since he was a 'little kid', having grown up in residential care, but having been 'shoved around like a yoyo, up and down the country'. After an initial overconfidence from the crimes he had committed, Jonathan had mellowed significantly after his completion of various offending behaviour courses and the respectful and concerned treatment from prison staff. This interview extract indicates his emotional vulnerability and the costs of the hegemonic masculine standard:

Because for one when you're locked in your cell you have to be like...your freedom is not there, you miss your family. And then when you come out of your cell it's a whole different ballgame. So you're lonely in your cell and then you come out and then you have to put on some big front where you're not really upset, really hurting inside...You have to hit someone, you have to do something to prove to someone that you're not an idiot...I'm a big gangster, mate. I really weren't, you know what I mean [laughs] but that's what I thought in my head...I was doing so much fighting...hitting people left, right and centre...I'd just pick a fight like. You know, just if someone looks at me wrong I'd just hit them I'd just be violent. But I've sorted myself out...I haven't had one nicking in four months. (Jonathan, white British, Christian, Rochester)

Cool pose and these kinds of redemptive narratives are most certainly evident but they did not appear to be exclusively found among black or other minority ethnic prisoners.[26] These were common, familiar stories of anger, of the pain of familial absence, desperation at being inside, challenging authority, and, over time, coming to terms with prison life. They appear to be part of a developmental path towards partial conformity (reinforced through prisoners seeking enhanced IEP status), emotional maturity, or, more instrumentally, the stoic prioritizing of release over a hard prison reputation. But they also signify the fluidity of masculinity at the individual level.

Particularly at Rochester some black prisoners did seem invested in these essentialized identities, which were deeply inscribed with a sense of the corporeal, of an aggressive, assertive bodily presence, which demonstrates physical toughness and a self-assured poise of 'cool' dominance, in which comportment, linguistic, and designer styling are key. Sacha,[27] a prisoner at Rochester, felt that black prisoners got 'slightly more respect in jail', exaggeratedly maintaining that they 'run the whole jail..., the whole jail system basically' because of their exclusive role in 'shotting burn' (dealing tobacco) on the wings. Paul,[28] a Maidstone prisoner, felt that black prisoners 'had the edge' because of their superior fighting skills and blackness equated with intimidation. Manu[29] at Rochester professed to being known as 'the dictator...they call me Bigs', at the same time,

---

[26] In 2010, black prisoners were overrepresented among those identified as assailants and fighters in prison (MOJ 2011a) and those from minority ethnic groups were also over-represented as victims. Without further analysis and contextualization, this provides little to illuminate the inter- and intra-racial nature of such conflicts in prison.

[27] Of black African British, Christian origin.

[28] Of black African British, Muslim origin.

[29] Of black Central African, Christian origin.

perhaps disingenuously, denying that if 'anything [illicit] goes on in the wing you have to see him'.[30] Rafael,[31] also at Rochester, tellingly recalled how a new black prisoner had come onto the wing seeking authority, but it was only the white boys who had feared him, suggesting a generalized white fear of black prisoners. Black boys, he suggested, were powerful inside because they were considered 'hyped and brainless', wild, even mad. Whilst not the same as claiming black domination on the wings at Rochester, these sentiments were echoed by Jackson, who suggested that the fight for supremacy on the wings at Rochester was between white and black prisoners:

The Blacks think that yeah, they're the baddest, while the Whites is thinking yeah, they're still bigger than the Blacks and the Asian comes in after that. The Chinaman comes and he sits. He gets along with everyone and there's no argument for him. (Jackson, black Caribbean, Christian)

In this sense, dominant black masculinities, echoing elements of cool pose have become culturally hegemonic on their own terms,[32] yet lacking the institutional power to claim authority in any meaningful sense, either inside or outside prison. Yet the cultural imagining of black masculinities easily slips into pathology, and rather than representing a collapse of racial hierarchy, just as in school, prison officers may tune in to these markers as indicative of problematic or illegal activity, an issue I return to in Chapter 6. We know from the recent National Offender Management Service (NOMS) *Race Review* (2008), for example, that black prisoners are still more likely to have force used against them, to experience punitive segregation, and to be on the lowest level of privilege (basic).

Moreover, whilst this popular supremacy signalled the possibilities of physical dominance by black prisoners, for example, in prison pecking orders, in securing the best opportunities and resources on the wings (access to the showers or playing pool), or as traders

[30] It was this dominant role that he disliked as it led to his reputation as someone who hurt others.

[31] Of black African British, Christian origin.

[32] At the time of writing in August 2011, academic historian, David Starkey, boldly, but erroneously, claimed that the riots across England in August 2011 were the result of white 'chavs' becoming black as a 'particular sort of violent, destructive, nihilistic gangster culture has become the fashion' with the intrusion and common use of Jamaican patois. Multiple complaints were received when these views were aired on the BBC's *Newsnight* programme ('David Starkey's *Newsnight* Race Remarks: Hundreds Complain to BBC', *Guardian*, 15 August 2011).

in the informal economy, this was mostly refuted as rumour, and little in this regard was revealed in the observational periods of the study. The few exceptions to this included a specific mention by Manu:

[Y]ou do get incidents that like two or three black boys and they will target one white guy ... I was walking past and I heard them talking about they were going move on him, meaning going to attack him ... they walked to his cell, they took his stuff and his CDs and stuff and they walked off ... I always have been against violence but I have been denying it for so long and now is the time for me to make my mark. And I did go to them, and I was, I know you done it, I heard who said it. Before the gov comes to you I think it would be better if you give the boy the stuff back because if you don't give it, I don't care if you want to call me a snitch or nothing, or a snake, I will tell the gov and the gov will take the things off you. And yes they did do it and yes they did call me names and stuff, that doesn't bother me. It gets me really angry because that's why, that's why other cultures how they look at black people, you know, they seem to think all the same ... they targeted him because he was white ... apparently he had a new Tupac [Shakur—rap artist] album ... these are the sort of things that makes me laugh when I think about it because music is music. Everyone plays music, they listen to Eminem. Elvis Presley make music, black boy listen to Elvis Presley. I know black who love Elvis Presley, you know. 50 cent plays music, white boys listens to him, Asian listens to him, black boy listens to him. (Manu, black Central African, Christian, Rochester)

There was less talk of black prisoner dominance at Maidstone prison but it was not absent. Black prisoners' attempts to secure a higher position on the gym list were referred to by a white prisoner at Maidstone, in the context of saying that 'the majority of the problems I have will be from dark skinned people'. Judging the validity of these allegations of dominance in prisoner hierarchies was tricky and it seemed that this was an area where the up-close and personal nature of ethnography is compromised in the prison setting, both by the gender of the ethnographer and the inability to observe directly the hidden areas and moments of prison life which occur behind closed doors, in cells, or during freeflow, when bullying might occur and deals are done, out of range of prison officers and prison researchers alike.

Systematic queue-jumping by black prisoners was named as a problem on Thanet wing where they were also said to dominate the cooking area. As described in Chapter 4, Barry[33] alleged that the

[33] Of white British origin, no religion.

gas rings in the self-cook area on Kent wing were out of the reach of any prisoners other than 'the West Indians' who took over and would physically challenge any prisoners who tried to use them. Anthony too bore out this claim on Weald wing, but he seemed more robust in being willing to assert his right to share this precious resource:

This is me right, this is me. I don't care who you are, I'm having that ring, you know what I mean, you're not having two rings because that's being greedy, I want that ring…They [black prisoners] respect me more for doing that than standing in the corner waiting, do you understand. Because if you let people think they can overpower you alright, then they'll do it all the time…I walk in and I go, right lads 'me chap mates' [in an attempted Caribbean accent] come on then let's work it all out…(Anthony, white British, Christian, Maidstone)

That said, Lieblin, Arnold, and Straub's (2012) extensive study of Whitemoor prison did indicate Muslim faith being used manipulatively by some black and mixed race prisoners as a resource to shore up power and enact violence against prisoners, whilst simultaneously demonstrating compliance and model behaviour to prison officers. The larger share of minority ethnic prisoners and Muslim prisoners, the older age structure of the population at Whitemoor, and its higher security categorization and longer sentences served for serious offences, compared with Rochester and Maidstone prisons, might explain these very different findings.

Prisoners' accounts at Maidstone prison revealed little to support racialized economic domination in the sale of drugs, mobile phones, or everyday items like coffee and shower gel. Drug supply proved to be extremely lucrative, with seemingly easy access routes due to the prison's town centre location and its relatively low walls (HMIP 2007b). Just like the Wellingborough prisoners studied by Crewe (2009), supplying drugs was a major source of power in an environment where demand and profits were high and sales were managed through outside bank accounts. Prisoners at Maidstone reported greater equality in drugs markets as far as supply was concerned; Pete[34] noted, 'drugs don't discriminate'. Regan[35] felt that white prisoners had the advantage and power because of their links to local Kent drug markets. Conversely, Jasper, a white pris-

---

[34] Of white British, Christian origin.
[35] Of black Caribbean British, Christian origin.

oner, perceived a threat from black prisoners who stole drugs and mobile phones brought into the prison when debts were owed to them. While he noted that white prisoners would also seek recompense for bad debts, black prisoners did this with a 'group mentality' and were 'tooled up'. By and large this was a minority view; market priorities seemed to determine the configuration of trading. As Anan observed:

[W]ith drugs it's not necessarily about race it's about the market. And you will find them really sometimes black and whites just mixing together to protect their interest. (Anan, black East African, Christian, Maidstone)

Body capital: 'hench' and prison dress

That the body represents an identity tool where the construction of a bodily presence is directly implicated in social action has been increasingly recognized theoretically (Messerschmidt 2005; Connell and Messerschmidt 2005). The embodiment of masculinity through developing upper-body muscularity in the prison gym permits the physical display of masculinity which nurtures self-esteem and the respect of one's peers, but also illustrates self-control, motivation, and discipline, and may be used to counteract the unhealthy prison diet (Sabo 2001; Shabazz 2009). The gym facility was prized for its possibilities for enhancing a physical masculinity and relieving stress, and prisoners liked the sociality of training, with friends providing guidance on how to avoid muscle strains. Sculpted upper bodies was referred to as 'hench' particularly among young black men, but it was common for prisoners to say that to look tough provided a potential cloak from masculine challenges in the public spaces of the prison. In informal conversation, a Polish prisoner, for example, acknowledged his reliance on his muscular presence before he had learned English. Rafael,[36] at Rochester, suggested that becoming big was a way of getting noticed for those with 'unknown' reputations on road, a point supported by Jack, a white prisoner at Rochester, implicitly contradicting his earlier perceptions about minority ethnic prisoners prioritizing hench appearances at the gym:

I want to be bigger by the time I get out…even like when you're on road yeah, and people see that you're skinny…Because I'm a nice person but I've got to get bigger so people can't think that they can push me around and all that.

[36] Of black African British, Christian origin.

The value of the gym and physical exercise was indicated by its regular inclusion as a feature in *Life Behind Bars*, Rochester's in-house magazine, put together by prisoner representatives from each wing and the writer-in-residence. Carrabine and Longhurst (1998) have argued that the prison institution colludes in these masculine practices by supporting physical education as a form of social control. By reducing prisoner frustration men become more compliant with state authority (see also Sabo 2001). Such a view ignores the value of this resource for the presentation of self among prisoners, although it is true that some prisoners resisted this idealized form of masculinity, subverting its more destructive hypermasculinist elements:

I go [to the gym] a couple of times a week, but it's only because I've probably got a waist since being in prison, so it's weight loss for me. But other people want to build up bigger muscles and be stronger and it's, I suppose, important to those people…to get more status on the wing. To me that's not important. That's not who I am, I don't have to show that I'm a big strong man or whatever…I'm happy in myself, I'm…I've got my child and my partner and that's all I really care about. I don't…I don't care what anyone thinks of me. (Mark, white other, Oceanian, Maidstone)

For Goffman (1961), a central element of the mortification that prisoners experience on entry to the total institution was 'personal defacement' as individuals are stripped of their own clothing. A significant emblem of self-identity, Ash (2010) claims that the wearing of cheaply tailored prison clothes provides a further physical reminder of being othered and de-individuated. To some degree this is mitigated today by prisoners conspicuously demonstrating their consumerism, making style statements through designer clothes and trainers which can communicate an individual's self-worth and social standing (Jewkes 2002). As Lennard,[37] a Rochester prisoner, quipped, if 'someone's like got £120 jeans or something…[they are] obviously doing something right'.

Maidstone prisoners tended to be sanguine about prison dress but their positions on this were not wholly passive. For some prisoners, wearing only prison clothes was not a sign of capitulating to state design and authority. It was a fatalistic decision; wearing prison clothes made pragmatic sense because in the absence of women or other important figures there was no need to impress anyone.

---

[37] Of mixed race British, Christian origin.

This, of course, underlines the relational nature of masculinity which can only be formulated in contradistinction to women (Connell and Messerschmidt 2005). Wearing a mix of prison clothes and personal items was a compromise, maintaining an element of personal identity but without bearing huge cost. Yet other prisoners felt an acute need to present a public image of themselves which was not hugely dissimilar to how they were outside prison. Samson's reflections on this linked attire with coping inside:

everyone has different ways of handling their sentence...Some, they dress up like they're on the street. Others, like I said, like myself, mid-way, half prison clothes, half you know, half casual. But then there are others that are like look I aint getting caught up in that, I'm in prison, I don't care what I look like at the end of the day. I'll fix myself up when I get out, you know...those people are the long-termers (Samson, black African British, Maidstone)

Sami,[38] at Maidstone, used his prison clothes as pyjamas and only used toiletries that his wife supplied as a way of externalizing the 'prison mentality' and maintaining his dignity, whereas Andrew,[39] a prisoner at Maidstone, wore prison clothes during the day while at work but would dress for evening association in clothes he would normally wear on road. Even where prisoners wore their own clothes there was fashion uniformity—most wore tracksuit bottoms, occasionally jeans, sports T-shirts, trainers, with only a minority wearing prison-issue denims.

Sexuality Inside

Sexuality is, of course, deeply inscribed in masculinity practices, and in its hegemonic form, the male heterosexual sex drive is regarded as powerful, uncontrollable, but above all, natural. The new sexualities literature suggests a more nuanced, de-essentialized range of scripts and options available to men in intimate relationships with women which challenges this unitary model (Plummer 2005). In outlining the contours of hegemonic masculinity, there is a valorizing of heterosexuality and contempt for homosexuality. Bosworth and Carrabine (2001) have also suggested that homosexual relationships in prison may represent a form of resistance to sexual deprivation and a means to disrupt stereotypical images of

[38] An Arab Muslim of West Asian origin.
[39] Of mixed race British, Christian origin.

heterosexuality held by prison staff. Crewe's (2006) ethnography of Wellingborough prison found that prisoners' talk around women partners either displayed a tenderness where women were positioned as assisting their redemption or an anger as women's corrupting influence was mentioned.

Samson,[40] a Maidstone prisoner, epitomized the former position, describing his partner and son as his 'saving grace'; but for their presence in his life he could imagine himself in prison at an earlier stage, or even dead. Such relationships seemed to have an emotional depth to them not in spite of but because of prison separation and in such cases, prisoners referred to these partners as their best friends. Yet, it was generally acknowledged among Maidstone prisoners that prison brought forth an emotional dependence on partners which had changed the dynamics of heterosexual relationships, providing an opportunity to cultivate, deepen, or renew romantic bonds (see also Comfort 2008b). Jonathan, a Rochester prisoner, described becoming 'proper sensitive...you become somebody you're not because your feelings, you're all wrapped up'. Matthew, similarly, put it like this:

On the out you never really sit down with your missus and have a full scale conversation or anything like that. In prison on visits and on the telephone all you've got to do is to talk so it's probably better where the girls are concerned because they feel more involved and more loved and more close when you do talk to them so when you can only talk to them it becomes that way because on the out you don't really talk. (Matthew, white British, Christian, Maidstone)

Contrastingly, Anthony,[41] another Maidstone prisoner, like others, had felt that they had attracted women who enjoyed the money and lifestyle that was possible with the rewards of crime but such women had less genuine loving feelings towards them. These relationships had left prisoners feeling bitter and distrusting of intimacy which simplified their lives inside as they avoided the 'mental torture' of uncertainty about their partner's fidelity.

Of course, men's sexuality is effectively curtailed in prison, reliant on masturbation, perhaps with the use of pornography or available through homosexual relations. Yet the latter identity is typically positioned as subordinated, along with those convicted of sexual offences (Newton 1994). The deeply threatening nature of

[40] Of black African British origin.
[41] Of white British, Christian origin.

being labelled as gay was exemplified in an overheard altercation between a prison officer and a prisoner at Rochester YOI. In barely disguised rage, the prisoner challenged the officer to come to his cell, one-on-one, in response to the 'put-down' he claims the officer engaged in, in front of other prisoners. When the officer suggested this was a homosexual invitation the prisoner's apoplectic retort was 'What?! What?! You, you fucking nonce screw, you're the one that's gay!'. This masculine face-off ended without further incident as the prisoner returned to his cell to calm down, but was all the more keenly felt because of the hierarchical relations between the two and the officer's ability to further humiliate the prisoner. According to Sim (1994: 116), it is this form of psychological domination and control by prison officers which enables the prison to reproduce 'normal men' through the 'umbilical cord of masculinity'.[42] Thus, homosexuality as a mode of male sexuality was ultimately taboo in Rochester and Maidstone prisons.[43] Such attitudes explained the challenge for Arthur[44] to hide his bisexuality and his sentence for the sexual assault of a boy.

Unsurprisingly, the longing for sex was experienced as one of the major pains of imprisonment, with sexual exploits on road more often a topic of conversation among the younger prisoners at Rochester than at Maidstone. But it was not only sexual relations that were missed, it was also the absence of affection, being cared for, nurtured by women, the opportunity to unleash their emotions, which were constantly held in check in prison for fear of being misinterpreted as weak and vulnerable and therefore a target for intimidation. Bernard[45] recognized the importance of touch, not being cuddled, not feeling needed and wanted, and as he said wistfully

[42] See Salter and Tomsen (2012: 318) for a discussion of filmed 'cage vs. cons' fights outside prison which pit ex-prisoners against police, legal, and prison staff cage fighters, contrasting the brutal violence of working-class convicts with the violent but 'civilised manhood' of law-enforcing agents of the state.

[43] There is an interesting study to be done which examines if and why homosexuality is practised to a lesser degree in prisons in England and Wales compared with the US, South Africa, and elsewhere, and how such practices are commodified in sexual and material relations between prisoners. In the South African context, for example, sexual favours elicit goods which prisoners are routinely unable to access given the more impoverished conditions both inside and outside prison (Moolman 2011). There was little indication that male rape was a feature of prison life as it has been more consistently observed in prison life in the US and South Africa (Sabo 2001; O'Donnell 2007; Shabazz 2009; Moolman 2011; but see Wolff and Shi 2011).

[44] Of white British, Christian origin.

[45] Of white British origin, no religion.

'nobody in the prison rolls over and says I love you'. Samson's[46] feelings that the research interview had been like a therapy session, and the avid interest in the study in its early stages as I moved around the wing, seem related to the unique restrictions of prison and the lack of contact with the opposite sex:

I see one of the guy[s]. [His]...attention is sexualized in a muted sort of way, the guys are flirting, greedy for her [Coretta's] attention. They are mainly Black guys. I feel a little frustrated because the intention of coming onto the wing to observe servery and the cook area has been largely de-railed by the kind of attention Coretta is getting...Coretta cannot move more than a few yards before her attention is claimed. (Fieldnote, 17 May 2007)

Crewe (2009) found that accounts of relations with female prison officers were laden with prisoners' fantasies about their own sexual attractiveness which were often rehearsed publicly, reinforcing an image of heterosexuality and promoting inner confidence about their own, recently untested, sexual appeal. An alternative representation was of chivalrous protection against sexualization and the risk of violence, and a likening to cherished female relatives. Similarly, in Maidstone prison, Sandy[47] said that he was 'gentle to the females', offering to 'deck' anyone who assaulted a female prison officer. Female prison officers were often regarded as more understanding, showing greater generosity in assisting prisoners ('that woman heart' was how Jan[48]described it), and more easily conversed with. Alan[49] referred to the women governors at Rochester as 'softer...they'll pretend they're your Mum'. However, Crewe's study found interpreted challenges to (masculine) authority by female officers were angrily resented and elicited gendered condemnation in a way which did not occur with male officers. One such example in Maidstone was the ruckus caused by an angry prisoner blaming a female prison officer for not allowing him to make a phone call. The vitriol that followed—'that bitch cunt says "I can't do nothing for you"'—clearly expressed such feelings. Other prisoners struggled with their tempting sexual presence as 'eye candy' but ultimately untouchable. Regardless of whether female officers were subject to a chivalrous, professional, sexualized,

[46] Of black African British origin.
[47] Of white British, Christian origin.
[48] Of black Caribbean Western European, Christian origin.
[49] Of white British, Christian origin.

or feminized discourse, which were sometimes overlapping, they were nonetheless gendered and positioned relationally to assert masculine credibility and self-esteem. Male prisoners may also use gendered talk in repartee aimed at goading prison officers, winding them up, and resisting their control, as this observed interaction at Rochester shows:

One of the cleaning orderlies in the wing comes and rattles the bars at the wing exit gate and says 'Come, let me in there, I want some air'. The PO asks if he wants to go on exercise and the guy says no, just into the 'foyer' zone. He's half asking, half demanding, half serious, half just trying for some sport…[In] a faltering, semi-serious attempt at an argument…the PO [prison officer] isn't really wanting to play the game. The prisoner makes another attempt to get a bit of a rise…'Yeah, yeah and I know your girlfriend, I'm going to see your girlfriend in the car park' [implying a sexual liaison]. The PO gives it back without much enthusiasm, like it is a stock, ready, response. 'Yeah, that's right, and you are going to get HIV!' [implying promiscuity]. (Fieldnote, 11 September 2006)

The prison social world provides a further relational take on masculinity inside which provides possibilities for prisoners to project stigma and shame onto others positioned lower than them in the prison hierarchy (Thurston 1996). The 'nonce', the sexual monster predator, is cast as non-human, a deviant among deviants, an object of violent revulsion, an aberration. As Anan,[50] a Maidstone prisoner, remarked, from personal experience, being a sex offender was worse than being a murderer, hence some may make efforts to pass as non-sex offenders (Schwaebe 2005). Prisoners feared the forced social relationship with 'undesirable fellow-inmates' that Goffman (1961: 34) saw as a key mortifying feature of the total institution. Where they are not segregated, as at Rochester prison, there is ever the uncertainty among 'normal' prisoners of contamination by sex offenders. As Jason[51] observed, 'I'm not too keen about talking to people I don't know because you could be standing there talking to someone and for all you know he could be a rapist or a nonce'. Other prisoners were uneasy about exposing their children to the bogeyman sexual predator in visits whilst in prison, or in the hostels to which they would subsequently be released.

There is, of course, no reason to assume that prisoners would be immune from the fear-making, dehumanizing media discourses

---

[50] Of black East African, Christian origin.
[51] Of mixed white/Gypsy, Christian origin.

which position sex offenders as below humanity (Cowburn and Dominelli 2001; Hudson 2005), but this positioning also makes available, in its mirror image, the ordinary prisoner as a putative, heroic male protector of women and children. This can operate to uphold hegemonic masculinity in a not dissimilar way to cussing.

Within Thanet wing itself there was a further fine-grained hierarchy of othering which reflected 'acceptable' and 'unacceptable offences', a finding in other research on sex offenders (Hudson 2005). Arthur, a Maidstone prisoner, explained:

When sex offenders look at things, raping a woman is…is probably the least bad thing to do, because they say well she really wanted it, you know, she never said no. And then people say well there's always that doubt. You know what rape's like in court, you know, how difficult to prove it…So you know, it's not so bad as in the way they look at things here. Then sex with a girl is obviously the next thing, 'well she's a bit underage, she was 15 or whatever', you know. Then it's toddlers and then it tends to be boys afterwards, you know…I mean when I first came in I said it was a girl of 15, she uh she knew what she wanted and all that sort of rubbish, you know, to cover up. (Arthur, white British, Christian, Maidstone)

Even some sex offenders, such as Rufus and Larry from Thanet wing, who had been sentenced respectively for indecent assault and sexual assault, expressed such views and often advocated extreme punishments, including castration and hanging for child sex offenders. Larry put it like this:

I'm not undermining my offence, but there's some people in here who are in for some horrific things. And me as an individual I would find it very hard associating myself with some people like that, you know. (Larry, white British, no religion, Maidstone)

Despite the stigmatizing gaze cast on Thanet wing, this did not seem to have automatically engendered prisoner solidarity. Prisoners' accounts pointed to a more atomized experience of prison than in the main prison despite their collective vulnerability. Notwithstanding, echoing the findings of Carroll (1974) in the United States, Rufus observed that at Friday prayers, the paedophile or nonce tag of abuse was completely dropped and he was greeted according to Islamic custom.

It is interesting, although hardly surprising, that sex offenders on Thanet wing were far more preoccupied with the reasons for their incarceration than other prisoners at Maidstone. Some prisoners, like Sami,[52] were at various stages of appealing their convictions. His master status as appellant led to an all-consuming mindset in which he was mentally divorced from prison life—'I'm just a body in prison, but my mind is not in prison'—was how he described it. Sami's resistance to his sex offender status was activated through a refusal to be absorbed, 'sucked in' by the 'whirlpool of mentality' of the prison experience, enjoying being 'behind doors' where he could more easily disavow the prison world and his stigmatized status. Similarly, Rufus refused to class himself as a sex offender, instead protesting his innocence, just like the total deniers in Hudson's (2005) study of sex offender identities:

even though I've been convicted of a sex offence I'm not a sex offender, I'm innocent…if I did something I'd say I did it, you know what I mean, like all my other um previous convictions I could show them to you, whatever I've done I've put my hands up to, you know what I mean. Because at the end of the day I'm not lying to no one else except from God. I'm lying to Allah and Allah knows that I'd be lying, you know what I mean, it's a sin. (Rufus, black Caribbean British, Muslim origin)

Aspirational Masculinities: Fathering and Being Fathered

Connell's (1987) concept of hegemonic masculinity was not meant to be viewed in binary terms, but rather as a contested ideal. Her more recent work has been concerned with uncovering the 'mismatches, the tensions, and the resistances' to hegemonic masculinity, but also recognizing positive elements of hegemonic masculinity, such as being a wage earner and maintaining a sexual relationship (Connell and Messerschmidt, 2005: 841). Similarly, even in the closed world of the prison, I would argue that the hypermasculine discourse is too limiting as a one-dimensional imagining of how men accomplish gender inside, without recognizing the agential possibilities of men to construct and occupy alternative masculine formulations (see also Collier 1998; Bosworth and Carrabine 2001). 'Doing fatherhood inside' is one such masculine project (Clarke, L. et al. 2005), but as Evans and Wallace's (2008) narrative interviews in a Category B prison indicate experiences of being *fathered* are central to men's sequential accounts of their masculinity.

---

[52] Of Arab Muslim, West Asian origin.

In wider society the constructive elements of positive fathering—financial support, physical care, and nurturing—have increasingly become cultural expectations, reinforced by public and policy discourses (but see Lewis 2002). It is estimated that 25 per cent of prisoners in YOIs are fathers (Ministry of Justice (MOJ) 2009)[53] and 59 per cent of adult prisoners have dependent children (Prison Reform Trust 2007). Of course, being a 'good parent' presents unique challenges for male prisoners, but it can offer a means of accomplishing hegemonic masculinity. While Meeks' (2011) study of young prisoners found that fatherhood was a significant element of hoped-for selves, it is important to recognize that long periods of time spent in solitude may put a gloss on the demanding challenges of parenting, at a time when prisoners are engaged in reflection and have aspirations of following a positive and constructive path post-prison. As a prisoner surveyed by Nandi (2005/2002: 413) noted, 'Many never take the time on the street to sit and reflect. There's nothing like steel and concrete to slow you down and give you that time'. Moreover, as Uggen et al. (2004) have observed, prisoners may imagine a conformist paternal identity in prison, but lack the training and socialization to sustain this identity actively on release. However, these imaginings should not be seen solely as examples of optimistic storytelling for they may be rehearsals for substantive internal change.

Some older prisoners at Maidstone revealed creative ways in which they sought to be actively engaged in their children's welfare and upbringing. Anthony had deliberately got a 'nicking' for using a mobile phone in his cell at Maidstone so as to get an audience with the governor. He wanted to challenge the time it was taking to get his D-Cat status,[54] which would have enabled him to have a town visit with his son whom he had not seen for the duration of his sentence. Of the imagined town visit, Anthony said:

That's my day and it's not, it's not going out there, going down the pub and have a meal with your family, I want to be with my little boy ...That's more important to me than anything else in whatever. I don't care what they do to me in here, but that is the most important thing. (Anthony, white British, Christian, Maidstone)

[53] Reynolds (2009) also argues that young fatherhood can present a public statement of black men's virility and heterosexuality, achieving aspects of the hegemonic ideal which might be denied through, for example, success in the labour market.

[54] Signifying a low risk prisoner unlikely to escape.

These kinds of narratives about prisoners' parenting practices or even their hopes and dreams make clear that masculinities are not solely inscribed with violence and patriarchy. Like those outside prison who aspire to domestic conformity and performing masculinity through paid work (McDowell 2002; Nayak 2006; Hopkins 2006), prisoners talked of taking their place within the family and of being the provider for children as well as their guide and adviser. They aspired to a traditional breadwinner role, meeting all financial commitments, including the economic dependence of a girlfriend or wife; as Sim (1994) asserted long ago, the prison reproduces 'normal men'. Clinton explained it in this way:

Being there for your kids. That is being a man. Full stop. Providing for your family. Giving them a better life so they don't lead the life that you lead. That is being a man. (Clinton, black African British, Christian, Rochester)

Being a man was also associated with personal responsibility for your own actions, not being involved in crime, being able to walk away from trouble, and showing humility, often referred to as 'being humble'. This from Nazir:

…a man and a boy would have two different attitudes. I know for a fact like when I first came in someone come up to me and said to me, oh you're this—I'd snap like that. But if he come up to me now I'd say, I'd just repeat it back to them or I'd just laugh at them, you know what I mean…I don't need to be showing off to someone…I don't need to impress no one…if you want to be a man about things you need to conquer them sort of backgrounds and the attitude, you need to have a solid attitude…(Nazir, black East African, Muslim, Rochester)

Maturity was linked to being wise, sensible, calm, self-aware, showing respect for others, particularly family members, taking advice as opposed to ignoring it, showing mental and emotional strength and independence, and acting selflessly. This was an ongoing project of self-actualization for some of the younger prisoners. Bradley,[55] at Rochester, for example, felt that he was 'still getting there' and was self-critical enough to recognize that platitudes about caring for his children were easily compromised by his activities on road which risked his freedom and therefore his time with them. Gary[56] admitted feeling lost, without purpose, unanchored biographically because of growing up in care without family love and support, and thus unsure

[55] Of mixed race British, Muslim origin.
[56] Of black Southern African, Muslim origin.

of what constituted happiness. The contrast with the strong familial and paternal identifications of many older prisoners underlines the fluidities and contingencies of masculine subjectivities generally, but also how these are conditioned by the prison as a specifically gendered cultural environment. Nandi's (2005/2002) small-scale qualitative study of black masculinity in prison found that prisoners often described becoming 'real men' inside; they attached importance to morality, education, self-belief, purpose, direction, honesty, not being materialistic, positive thinking, and gender equality. Being fathers within a family setting was also part of the change hoped for after prison among many prisoners in this study.

Yet as far as black fatherhood is concerned Reynolds (2009) has noted that public discourses in Britain have defined it by its physical, financial, and emotional absence and its inherent fecklessness. Her study of working- and middle-class, non-resident black fathers found that 'being there' represented a key strategy in maintaining paternal relationships for them, and importantly this did not depend on a regular, physical presence. This was certainly the case for some black prisoners like Lawrence who referred to 'being there' for his children, signifying a deep emotional commitment in his approach to 'fathering from prison'. During his interview and at other times on the wing, Lawrence's talk was peppered with references to the positive relationships he had with his two teenage children. I have chosen to read his account at face value, rather than as a gendered performance, because he did not hide his failings to support his 'baby mother', having served several sentences which included a medium term when his children were babies. In urging her to move on and do the best for herself, but maintaining contact with his children, Lawrence appeared to have created what Clarke et al. (2005: 229) refer to as his 'own personalized fathering role script' in which he positioned himself in comparison to his peers inside, as someone with a good, strong, loving, and respectful relationship with his children. During his time in prison, visits had been maintained even though the relationship with his 'baby mother' had 'crashed'. Upcoming was Lawrence's release on licence and he was hoping to negotiate different hostel conditions which would allow him to be in shared accommodation which his children could safely visit. As this (necessarily long) extract demonstrates, 'being there' for Lawrence involved regular, sometimes daily, phone contact with his children in which emotional support, guidance, and homework and gendered behaviour monitoring, as well as admonishment, was dispensed, as he pursued his parental responsibilities at a distance:

My son said to me the other day, 'Dad you don't phone me as much as Alicia' [Lawrence's daughter], yeah. So he might be feeling that he's being left out, right. Now I knew I was going to come across that situation with my kids. So I said to him, I said, 'I'll tell you how it is. You see you, you're not my problem, you aint a problem…I don't really need to speak to you all the time, but she's my problem'…And he took that to bed with him, because the next day yeah, I could tell by his voice, yeah dad's right you know…I had to reassure him…You see Alicia yeah, my daughter yeah, she can't breathe with that phone that she's got…Like if it rings it's dad [laughs]…She won't mug me off…I know every movement she makes, I'm on her like a rash. Do you understand?…When it comes to my kids I don't hesitate. My son's always wrapped round his mum, so he's alright, he aint my problem. My daughter, yeah we'll she's 15, and I know that boys are sniffing, yeah…Remember I'm in prison, so I have to give and take yeah, I can't always be like on their case. I give them their room to breathe, yeah, but don't take the piss. And I honestly believe I've come up trumps with my daughter and with my son…even though I'm in prison yeah, that doesn't stop me from communicating with my kids and making my kids know that listen, yeah, dad, yeah, you know I love you innit. I tell my kids. (Lawrence, black Caribbean British, Christian, Maidstone)

Aside from the prisoners who presented as committed fathers or expectant fathers, there were other familiar stories in which prisoners were estranged from their children. These fractured relationships were the source of considerable pain, guilt, and shame for prisoners and these emotions sometimes foreclosed full discussion in interview. 'Not being there' was the key characteristic of fathering experiences among prisoners in Clarke et al.'s (2005) research where prisoners developed a '"behind bars" fathering identity' (see also Meeks 2007). Dimitri,[57] a young prisoner at Rochester, said ruefully of his son, 'he calls me daddy and that, he knows who I am, I think, but to him I'm just the sweetie man in the big bright orange bib'. Shane[58] similarly described himself as a 'long distance dad' fighting for his daughter to avoid adoption outside his family. Some, like Jed,[59] talked about the difficulties of 'building bridges' with his daughter; others, like Pete,[60] struggled with the knowledge that

[57] Of white other, Christian origin.
[58] Of white British, Christian origin, Maidstone.
[59] Of white British origin, no religion, Maidstone.
[60] Of white British, Christian origin, Maidstone.

they did not have their children's trust. Matthew,[61] a prisoner also at Maidstone prison, in a matter-of-fact way, admitted an abstract love for his children but accepted he had yet to form a bond with them. However, children also served as a spur to a redemptive mindset, where prisoners described their children being the sustenance they needed to get through their sentences, to survive imprisonment, and to have hopes and dreams for a crime-free future. Rufus,[62] for example, felt that his children were the 'ones that's keeping me going'.

Meeks' (2007) research on prisoners' 'possible selves' brought up intergenerational fears about poor parenting based on prisoners' own experiences as children. Rochester and Maidstone prisoners also produced narrative accounts which showed desperate familial relationships, particularly with fathers, which were often highly abusive, neglectful, unloving, or modelling negative and criminal behaviour. These painful accounts were constructed in ways in which prisoners' aspirations were to be 'proper dads' or at the very least to parent in opposite ways to how they had been parented. Tellingly, Larry,[63] a prisoner convicted of indecent assault, described wanting his hoped-for children to confide in him and seek advice about their emerging sexuality in a way that he had not. Leon[64] talked of missing having his own father around, saying 'I don't want to just run off and do the same cos it's not fair. So every time I think about my son…I need to do something better'. Others like Colin[65] saw his father's drug dealing, violence, and spells in prison as inimical to the stability that children need as they are growing up. Arnold,[66] another Rochester prisoner, reflected that he would be in prison when his first child was born, just as his father had been when he was born. Lawrence is worth quoting here again at length to illustrate this kind of perspective, but it was one shared with many other prisoners in the study:

[M]y mum used to feed us, wash us, and then put us in bed. So when he [father] comes in from work we're sleeping, so he aint going to wake us up to beat us, but that belt still stays there…I sat them [his parents] down one

---

[61] Of white British, Christian origin, Maidstone.
[62] Of black Caribbean British, Muslim origin, Maidstone.
[63] Of white British origin, no religion, Maidstone.
[64] Of white British, Muslim origin, Rochester.
[65] Of white British origin, no religion, Maidstone.
[66] Of white British origin, no religion, Rochester.

day and I told him. You know, I said, 'Dad I don't find it hard to say it to you, I don't love you [laughs], you might be my dad, but I'll never love you'. Do you understand? 'I'll never forget them beatings that you gave me, never, yeah'…I said what froze me, yeah, is what kind of love's that, if you marry a woman, you have kids with her through love, yeah, and you have kids, you don't put up to love your kids. I can't grow up to hate my kids… I don't want to get old and have my kids hating me…I might go to prison, that I might take drugs, that I do this, but you see my love for my kids and my kids know it. They take that to bed with them…I never had that bond with my dad. (Lawrence, black Caribbean British, Christian, Maidstone)

For others, like Paul,[67] their childhood was one of paternal absence, which unsurprisingly created a dislocation, an uncertainty, which was often left unresolved, with vacillating feelings of confusion, anger, painful rejection, and sometimes fatalistic acceptance and fantasizing about a closer relationship in the future.

As was true with other intimate relationships, there was often a recalibrating of father–son relationships as introspection and reflection brought a renewed sense of the value of these paternal relationships. Manu,[68] for example, a Rochester prisoner, had been visited by his father unexpectedly and had experienced a renewal of their familial bond, as his father had reminded him how to be a man again, by accepting his criminal past and recognizing his mistakes. Similarly, for Abbott[69] at Rochester, his father had renounced his criminality and had qualified as a highly skilled manual worker in his thirties, serving as an aspirational role model for Abbott.

Discussion

The motif of prison masculinities in the literature is one of violent domination. Whilst far from absent in social relations among Rochester and Maidstone prisoners, it seems more productive to reflect on the range of masculine behaviours revealed in prisoners' narratives. In the late modern context Crewe (2009) has argued convincingly that the structural and institutional determinants of power relations among prisoners have been altered such that prisoner prestige is now less dependent on overt exploitation of prisoners by other prisoners, as depicted in studies like Sykes' (1958) which generated the indigenous model of prisoner identities. Yet in

[67] Of black African British, Muslim origin, Maidstone.
[68] Of black Central African, Christian origin, Rochester.
[69] Of white British, Christian origin, Rochester.

prison as much as on road there is still a need for men to accomplish masculinity, to do gender in ways that affirm social status and self-esteem. Sim's (1994) invitation to see prisoners *as men* requires that we recognize that men's behaviour, their sense of themselves, and their constructions of other men's actions are not wholly determined by the institutional exigencies of the prison or the demands of the inmate code. Just as Irwin and Cressey's (1962) importation model acknowledged the permeation of criminal identities into the prison, so too can we see the demonstration of masculine identities which might similarly be forged outside. A clear example of this is in the collective manifestations of 'postcode pride' which provide an important vehicle for the long-established symbolic and often ritualized, territorial aggression seen in outside communities. This asserts a collective physical strength, mutual protection, fervent loyalty, and a vital sense of deep-rooted security in vulnerable times. These features also make it an attractive mode of being in the stark and fear-making environs of the prison. However, this is only one way to understand these deeply embedded local affiliations. Just as importantly, spatialized identities demonstrate a vehement yet affective attachment to place and a sense of belonging external to the prison which is cherished, perhaps even more so from the contemplative space in which liberty, leisure, and routine pleasures are affectionately recalled.

Arguing for a more variegated, multidimensional understanding of prison masculinities does not mean disregarding the long-observed fact that presenting a (hyper)masculine facade is crucial in the peculiar gendered order of the prison. But it is worth remembering that some prisoners disavow a prison-defining identity and this can be seen as an individual act of agency, an assertion of autonomy, a resistant stance which refuses to accept the institutional imperatives of the prison which can easily coalesce in a violent disruption of the self. Instead, a self-assured persona is adopted and performed, warding off the more damaging assaults on the masculine self. There are, of course, the other faces of masculinity which can be discerned in prisoners' narratives. Unpacking men's gender projects inside reveals their variability, albeit typically set against a hegemonic standard, but not one which is solely reducible to hypermasculine and aggressive posturing. For some of the older prisoners the promise of good fathering presents another masculine option, and while for some this is purely aspirational, other prisoners could be said to be 'doing' fatherhood from inside prison.

For younger prisoners their aspirations to become traditional men held up the ideal of hegemonic masculinity but without the tendency of aggressive violence.

The question as to what degree, if any, such masculine selves are racialized is not easily answered. In Chapter 4 the disavowal of ethnic identities would seem to preface a fluid conception of masculinity, and race was certainly not a feature of the postcoded identities of prisoners. At the same time, black masculinities have a purchase in the prison social world and not only among those white prisoners whose ambivalence indicates a troubled or uneasy relationship with minority ethnic prisoners. That the representation of black masculinity, enacted through a sense of control, confidence, and cultural dominance is envied—(albeit also contested) by some white prisoners whilst also being upheld and revelled in by some black prisoners—is testimony to its essentializing features. I do not wish to make too much of this, however, not least because assertions about black prisoners' commanding presence and their domination of public space inside were far from universally claimed. Moreover, separating out the dimensions of a black hypermasculinity is all the more difficult when its presumed core characteristics—heterosexuality and patriarchal dominance—are precisely those which also frame social relations in male prisons.

The relational positioning of sex offenders versus 'normal' prisoners on the main wings at Maidstone prison reinforces the relational hierarchy of stigmatized identities and the othering of the othered. The required performance of heterosexuality infuses prisoners' talk about women, but for some also reveals changed intimate relationships in which the terms of patriarchy are suspended, even up-ended while men are incarcerated. A time of renewal of intimate relationships is often a lifeline for prisoners struggling with the myriad pains of imprisonment.

Nor is the behaviour of men inside best understood as unchanging, static representations of prison masculinities in social action. Even if prisoners' reflections on their masculinity do represent a somewhat staged performance to impress researchers, it is also clear that prison masculinities cannot be regarded in any sense as a fixed state. Masculinities in prison, like outside, are subject to flux, and should not be seen as finished performances, but rather as contingent states which shift and are influenced by a range of factors, some biographical and some institutional (see also Banyopadhyay 2006). For example, Clinton's air of manly confidence of centring himself to avoid peer pressure inside was at the end point of a process of adapting to prison life. In interview he recounted how initially he had not been able to 'hack' prison. His sense of self on entry to prison was fragile, he was missing his mother, and struggling to cope with the pressures of feeling enclosed and crowded because of a lack of personal space. Clinton described feeling alone, acutely stressed and anxious, and he had sought regular support from prison Listeners.[70] Anthony, a white prisoner at Maidstone, largely resisted participating in fights as, for him, at the forefront of his masculine sense of self was the absolute determination to be reunited with his son and to develop this paternal relationship. Yet this had not prevented him from breaking the arm and fracturing the jaw of a prisoner who had attacked him after complaining about the food portion he had been served by Anthony.

Prisoners, like men outside prison, are not confined by a unitary masculinity. Male subjectivities inside are complex, multiple, and involve self-conscious and unconscious constructions of the self, which are variable and contingent. In prison, the typical portrayal, centre stage, is of men impassively coping with the dynamics of insecurity, fear, dominance, threats, and violence. But on the sidelines, in the mundane reality of prison life, other masculinities are performed; indeed, the prison cultivates the possibilities of introspection, self-reflection, and character analysis, perhaps in a way which is impossible on road, with the heady distractions of crime, and the immediate structures of patriarchy to contend with. That prison is a place where men can find themselves sounds trite, but it may be there that men have the opportunity to deconstruct, reevaluate, and reinvigorate the part of themselves which may still closely reveal their hegemonic influences, but also their aspirations and hopes of becoming better men. As Richard, a black Caribbean prisoner at Maidstone put it, prison 'is where a man's got to start fixing up, innit?'

---

[70] These are Samaritan-trained prisoner volunteers who provide 24-hour cover to assist distressed prisoners.

6

The Pains of Racism

[W]ith regards to almost all aspects of prison life, the perceptions of BME prisoners are still more negative than those of their White counterparts. Both MQPL [Measuring the Quality of Prison Life] data and HMCIP [Her Majesty's Chief Inspector of Prisons] surveys indicate that the most significant differences between BME and White prisoners are in perceptions of their relationships with staff, with BME prisoners having more negative perceptions than White prisoners. (National Offender Management Service (NOMS) *Race Review* 2008: 15)

…racist implications linger, silenced but assumed, always already returned and haunting. Buried, but alive. (Goldberg 2009: 152)

It was during my stint as race relations orderly a few years ago that I first discovered a weird affect that can come from management paying attention to race relations; it pisses off the white guys. 'Why should they get everything?' was a question I spent a lot of time answering, sometimes without effect. (Ben Gunn, Her Majesty's Prison (HMP) Shepton Mallet, from *insidetime* (January 2009))

This first quote is suggestive of a core consensus about the racialized nature of imprisonment among those of minority ethnic origin, laying open the possibility of the prison as a site of endemic racism which mediates minority ethnic experiences. Goldberg's (2009) quote, although not made with specific reference to institutional environments, alludes to the pervasive nature of racism and its fluid ability to permeate aspects of everyday life. It also points to the submerged possibilities of racism and its power to seep into the fissures of our postcolonial social fabric, to remain a dormant presence. This seems to me to be a useful way of understanding the 'now you see now you don't' dynamic of racism in prison, its hidden presence, its covert manifestations, but also its absence, which I describe in the first part of this chapter. Is it too far-fetched to equate prison racism with the pains of imprisonment (Sykes 1958)? These deprivations are inherent to incarceration, albeit reconstituted in new forms in late modernity as eminent and upcoming prison scholars have suggested in a recent journal special issue (Crewe and Jewkes 2011). But is it correct to see the painful consequences of racist practices inside, by individual prison officers, and collectively through the regime, as an essence intrinsic to captivity, a by-product of societal punishment? And yet the experience of racism inside can also be painful, humiliating, and a diminution of the self, as famously captured in Fanon's (1967/2008) conceptualization of colonial racism. In Fanon's work the weight of oppression is evident, producing feelings of fury, bitterness, alienation, and, above all, a desire to be one's self without interference, or being made to feel and then internalize inferiority. This chapter applies these reactions to racism in a similar but different system of state domination of the individual.

The third quote from prison blogger Ben Gunn appears to challenge the binary picture of white racism, signalling once again the vexed nature of race and ethnicity in prison social relations. Building on Chapters 4 and 5, I aim to further unpack some of the complexities of this area. I try to interpret and make sense of the plaintive resentment of race equality measures among some white prisoners where whiteness is depicted as a position of institutional weakness and political disadvantage. Colloquially, this is often referred to as 'reverse racism'. In an environment where emotional degradation is a common currency, racialized powerlessness, inferiorization, subordination, and inequality, these pains of racism, variously understood and experienced by prisoners of different ethnicities, faiths, and nationalities seem to be etched into the walls of the late modern prison.

A study examining prisoners' race relations can never be fully divorced from wider prison race relations (Jacobs 1979). Contrasting narratives which, on the one hand, underline the painful and devaluing experience of racialized discrimination which frames the front-stage experience of some minority ethnic prisoners, coexist with accounts which deny the continued relevance of race markers in relationships between prison officers and prisoners. In between are those that point to vestiges of a partially hidden, covertly performed, backstage racism (Picca and Feagin 2007). The limited range of responses to these experiences are nonetheless illustrative of the agency of prisoners to defend against the ultimate power of the prison institution.

The Prison Service, of course, has a chequered history when it comes to the institutional treatment of minority ethnic prisoners, as Chapter 2 outlined. While at the forefront of developments in ethnic monitoring[1] among the criminal justice agencies, its murky past included documented accounts of racist brutality, discriminatory practices in work allocations and disciplinary treatment informed by pejorative racialized stereotyping, and an acceptance that some prison officers were card-carrying members of racist, ultra-right-wing nationalist parties. The multicultural prison of the 21st century (based on the research from the current study and larger, more representative studies, reviewed in Chapter 2) *is* undoubtedly different.

In its response to the damning criticisms of the Commission for Racial Equality's (CRE's) (2003a, b) formal investigation, the Prison Service has established comprehensive ethnic monitoring and Measuring the Quality of Prison Life (MQPL) measures of different aspects of prison life for assessing unequal outcomes at the level of individual prisons and nationally (NOMS 2008; but see Liebling's (2004) critique of the art of performance management in prisons). While invaluable for service delivery, here I instead use observational fieldnotes and interview data to understand more fully prisoners' *perceptions* of their treatment. In this way more detailed commentary is available on the mundane interactions of prison officers and prisoners which are not captured by, and indeed go beyond, the outcome measures of access to Home Detention Curfew and the like. I have assumed that what constitutes the nature of prison officer/prisoner dynamics is not simply that which can be measured using survey-based techniques, important though they are. Seeking to elaborate more fully the snubs, undercurrents, flashpoints, feelings, viewpoints—both positive, negative, and mixed—about living race and diversity is ultimately more revealing of the racial temperature of the late modern prison. Significantly, this also provides the possibility of exploring the dimensions of racialized institutional treatment from the perspectives of the white majority prisoners. Analytically there may be a problem here in

---

[1] Gordon (1983) has argued that the original push for ethnic monitoring was not to detect discrimination by criminal justice agencies but rather to show the increasing problems of black solidarity in prison and the issue of racial disproportionality.

that not heard, of course, are the perspectives of prison officers.[2] From other work, like HMIP's thematic inspection report, *Parallel Worlds* (2005), we see that white prison officers were sensitive to the risks of being falsely labelled as racists by prisoners. Lacking understanding of the principles of diversity, there was also a fear of ignorance, of saying or doing the wrong thing in working with minority ethnic prisoners. Similar themes emerged in Crewe's (2009) ethnography of Wellingborough prison. Some prison officers were also resistant to supporting minority ethnic festivals, demonstrating a similar reticence for equalities policies mentioned by Ben Gunn at the beginning of the chapter.

In view of the more limited primary material available then, the first part of this chapter is deliberately shorter, and necessarily presents a partial insight into prison officer/prisoner relations. It is unable to present officers' perspectives on the issues raised in the *Parallel Worlds* inspection, nor can it take account of the racialized aggression shown by some minority ethnic prisoners towards prison officers which is unlikely to be absent. One such example was provided to Rod while he was making a cup of tea in the health centre kitchen. He was shown a medical report form which had 'two diagrams of the human body and a red biro mark...drawn around the ankle of one. They [healthcare staff, both white, one male and one female] point to the remark at the top: "I ain't gonna be examined by no white cunt nurse"' (Fieldnotes, 27 September 2007). Yet the purpose of this chapter, and indeed the book as a whole, is to appreciate the dimensions and boundaries of how race is experienced among *prisoners* at this particular moment in time, not strictly or only in an objective sense, but as subjectively felt and lived through. This means laying out the contours of these various positions without focusing exclusively on their 'truth', instead recognizing their value as elements of prisoners' social realities and appreciating that, as Hewitt (2005: 75, 77) maintains, they may indeed be 'true to the teller'.

The (Hidden) Presence and Absence of Prison Officer Racism: Prisoner Perspectives

Our understanding of the essence of positive relationships between prison officers and prisoners has been significantly enhanced by

---

[2] The reasons for the decision not to interview prison officers in this study are discussed more fully in Chapter 3.

Liebling's (2004) study of prisons' moral performance. Respectful and trusting interpersonal treatment is key from the prisoners' point of view. Being treated as an individual, with humanity, support, and fairness in the delivery of prison regimes, is what counts. Fair and equal treatment is also at the heart of penal legitimacy, and this is just as true in the prison setting even though prison officers have at their disposal coercive and violent mechanisms of control (Sparks et al. 1996; Tyler 2010). Routinely, prison officers must act in authoritative ways, exercising power, but according to what is acceptable to prisoners and with which they are therefore willing to comply. As Bottoms and Tankebe (2012) assert, in this regard, legitimacy is best seen as an ongoing dialogic sequence in which legitimacy has to be perpetually cultivated. Yet it is the unfair treatment of minority ethnic prisons by largely white prison officers which has plagued race relations in prisons for more than three decades.

Therefore, it is important to note at the outset that there was nothing in prisoners' accounts or in our observations of prison life which portrayed prison life as primarily determined by the racist practices of prison officers. It was immediately evident that much has changed in prison officer/prisoner relationships, for the better, with many prisoners recognizing improvements in their treatment. Present institutional treatment was often perceived in a far more positive light for those who had experienced imprisonment before the implementation of the CRE Action Plan (2003). This is how Ruhi referred to the changes:

I've been in a long time . . . But you don't tend to get it [racism]. Early days in prison you did, earlier days you did. You did get comment[s] from members of staff and you got comments from prisoners, but that's died down a lot. (Ruhi, Pakistani British, Muslim, Maidstone)

Notwithstanding, the interviews revealed an array of perspectives: from the less common but determined accusations of blatant racism by a few prisoners to more tentative suggestions about the potentially racialized sources of differential treatment, and even flat denials of the incidence of prison officer racism. As such, these were not the defensive outpourings of victimization by vengeful prisoners; instead they were (mostly) careful assessments and reflections on the dynamics of race in the multicultural prison of late modernity.

Some white and non-Muslim prisoners claimed to have witnessed or suspected prison officer racism against exclusively minority ethnic prisoners, sometimes because of their ethnicity, but on other occasions because of their religious faith or nationality. These accounts, from a small minority of prisoners in Maidstone and Rochester prisons, are particularly important if we accept Picca and Feagin's (2007) claim that white people's sensitivity to racist discrimination is partial, non-existent, or limited in depth and understanding. Expletives peppered with racist overtones, pointed asides, and mumbled comments said under the breath but within earshot of white (or sometimes non-Muslim) prisoners were included in these examples. So too were resentments and disgruntlement at the prison making 'special provisions' for Muslim prisoners, such as serving halal food or the early delivery of canteen items[3] so that Muslim prisoners could attend Friday prayers. As will be clear as the chapter unfolds, such opinions were by no means solely the preserve of prison officers. Significantly, this is the (semi-)backstage arena where racial performances are socially situated within the broader context of racialized oppression, where the outgroup is demonized, and, importantly, through agreement, laughter, or silent collusion, validated by the audience (Picca and Feagin 2007). This may be regarded as an arena where the 'idealized forms of the white male self' are actively performed (Hughey 2011: 133). Without being stymied by the discussion about prejudiced attitudes and their likely translation, or not, into racist behaviour, it is telling that some white prison officers rightly assume that their remarks are likely to go unchallenged by subordinated prisoners who may overhear them, but also that there may be a receptive audience for their invectives among their colleagues. Below, two instances of this were remembered by Anthony at Maidstone[4] and Michael at Rochester prisons:

Now I've been down there [wing office] untold times right when I'm waiting to go to work or I'm doing something out the office waiting, you know, trying to get something out of the officer and something...some black geezer's shouting something [in the background]. That officer's the first one up, 'fucking bastard blacks', you know what I mean, 'fucking why

---

[3] This refers to the weekly shopping which prisoners have ordered in advance from a list of approved items such as stamps, writing paper, toiletries, and confectionery.

[4] Later in the interview, Anthony discussed a conversation with a black prisoner who suspected that he had been discriminated against by a white prison officer in Anthony's presence. Anthony had promised to back up the claim if his friend wished to pursue a complaint of racism.

don't they get rid of them', you know what I mean. At the end of the day I'm thinking, phew, you know, should I really be hearing this?...I see that a lot in here. (Anthony, white British, Christian, Maidstone)

The only thing you see really is like you see like with all the food and things like that where the govs have to stand there and serve up the food, they get pissed off and say things. Like you should all have the same food. Or on a canteen day when all the Muslims have to come out first and they get pissed off with that don't they? (Michael, white British, Christian, Rochester)

The patience of prison officers can easily reach its limits in the sea of demands and duties that have to be performed, particularly at crunch times, such as getting prisoners off the wings and to various parts of the prison. In Rochester prison, where our research office was next to the wing office, we regularly observed the queue of prisoners in the morning, handing in applications for visiting orders or trying to sort out work schedules; voices were sometimes raised in frustration and anger by both prisoners and prison officers. Our fieldnotes noted similar pressures at Maidstone: one fieldnote on Medway wing recorded 'one or two officers in there [wing office] looking harassed'. It is, however, the collective admonishment of black prisoners and the references to *them*, rather than blame being attached to a single individual, which is emblematic and archetypal of racism (Fanon 1967/2008). As Goldberg (2009: 343) clearly states, even if it is dismissed as a joke or denied the:

particular targeting at this time reinforces the accumulated targeting (both historically and contemporarily), exacerbates the vulnerability, reiterates the charge of inferiorization, of exclusion and excludability, concretizes and cements in place again and again the targeted group's or individual's marginalization.

At the other end of the spectrum to racist name-calling but rarely observed in the current sentences served by prisoners in the study were instances of extreme brutality which were perceived to be motivated by racism. Here, Darren describes a shockingly violent incident that he witnessed involving a black prisoner and a white prison officer:

I remember one black boy, he was alright, he was a good boy as well...it was lunch like, they bust your doors and you go downstairs, get your lunch and that. And his jug, he'd [the black prisoner] just washed it yeah, and a little tiny drop of water, yeah, and he was swinging it around, bam, bam and it hit, like the water hit this [white] gov's face...and the gov ran up to

him and punched him, proper like, just like that, bam, and he hit the floor
then he was jumping on him, punching him and that, pushing his bell. And
they [other prison officers] all come and they beat him up and that, it was
bad...(Darren, white British, no religion, Rochester)

In between were the racist epithets which prisoners said had been
occasionally directed at minority ethnic prisoners. A variety of the
usual classics were easily recalled—'nigger', 'monkey', 'black bastard', but 'why don't you fuck off back to your own country' was
now reserved for foreign national prisoners.[5] Pearce, an Irish traveller, had felt insulted when a governor called him a Gypsy; spitting
at the governor had led to time on the segregation unit. In an early
observation of association on B wing in Rochester prison, I recalled
this conversation with a mixed race prisoner:

J tells me that a gov has told him about a nursery rhyme which refers to
niggers and God not having time to make them white. He tells me that
white prisoners tell them [minority ethnic prisoners] about how racist govs
are, and they don't like it either. He tells me that it's because they're from
Kent—'They're not from London—they don't know miss that it's all unity
and love in our communities...Miss, they don't like niggers.' He tells of
how his mother (black) had to wait 30 mins to get into the visits room but
his white father didn't. (Fieldnote, 26 July 2006)

In contrast, even then, some minority ethnic prisoners, like Aaron,[6]
were relaxed about such abuse: 'they're old school...and it's just
slipped out...they ain't meant what they're saying'. Conor[7] also
recognized that there were 'redneck' prison officers, but also that
they were some 'black lovers' too.

Elsewhere, racism was perceived in routine actions and petty
humiliations between prison officers and minority ethnic prisoners
which left them disadvantaged in some way. In the absence of
racially abusive language—'they don't [always] say Muslim cunt',
as Frankie[8] observed—prison officers' antagonistic views could
nevertheless be discerned by particular actions. Typically, this was
inferred from an evident unwillingness among prison officers to be
helpful or to assist minority ethnic prisoners in ways which would
occur more often immediately or automatically in the case of white

---

[5] This kind of racist abuse was first prohibited in Prison Service Circular Instruction 56/1983.
[6] Of black Caribbean British, Muslim origin at Maidstone.
[7] Of white Irish, Christian origin at Maidstone.
[8] Of white British, Christian origin at Maidstone.

prisoners (see also Edgar and Martin 2004). An example from Jack at Rochester:

Like if we went in there like into the office and asked them for a form like, or to sign a form for us, like they would say, alright and they'll sign it straight away. But if it's a black boy like they'll say, oh no I can't get you the form now, or I'll sign it tomorrow or something like that. (Jack, white British, Christian)

Not locking or unlocking a prisoner's cell door, allowing an extra phone call, providing a larger, different, or additional food serving for lunch, and allowing cell moves outside of specified regulations, could all be regarded as common prisoner frustrations (Liebling 2011). However, in light of the above, these were often interpreted through the lens of racism. It is significant that such informal aspects of prison practice are not captured in the SMART[9] ethnic monitoring data used to flag up possible discrimination. Nevertheless, as Liebling (2011) has noted, it is precisely these kinds of interactions which lie at the heart of interpersonal relationships in prison and the absence of respectful engagement causes psychological pain, distress, and damage to the human self. Illustrating one such suspicious exchange, Asad said:

Me, I was going to play pool...I come to the desk and then I was queuing there, yeah, put my name down. So a few people they come and they were behind me and...he [prison officer] was putting their name down and then he put my name after also right at the end and then that pissed me off...and all of these boys were white boys as well...(Asad, Bangladeshi British, Muslim, Rochester)

Similarly, another black prisoner recalled how he had been initially told that he could not have rice and potatoes for his Christmas meal. Accepting this initially he later saw a white prisoner with both on his plate; when he challenged this the prison officer allowed him both too (Fieldnotes, 3 January 2007). Such incidents present the possibility of upsetting ongoing attempts to establish and sustain what Bottoms and Tankebe (2012: 132) have referred to as 'audience legitimacy' (among prisoners) by 'power holders' (prison officers) which prevents social disorder.

[9] This is the Systematic Monitoring and Analysing of Race Equality Template used by NOMS to monitor outcomes by ethnicity to ascertain any disproportionate impact of policies and processes.

Given this, it is not altogether surprising that personal slights (such as not acknowledging a greeting before a cell door is slammed) can easily be perceived in the same way. Similarly, offhand comments by prison officers could be quickly ratcheted up to mean something more significant if disrespect was assumed. Time and time again in informal discussions and interviews with prisoners at Rochester, reference was made to a prison officer who clumsily announced the arrival of food for observant Muslims who were breaking their fast during Ramadhan. His appeal on the tannoy system for 'all you hungry Muslims to come and get your food' was interpreted as implicitly denigrating this religious practice. The per-haps tenuous connection to racism was fully recognized but still left some prisoners feeling deeply uncomfortable. As Lennard,[10] a Rochester prisoner, explained: 'I thought it was racist, personally . . . if a Muslim person would have come in and went "Oh, all you starving Catholics, hurry up and get your lunch," someone might have said, "hold on, you can't say, that" . . . [but] someone [else] might say what he said was fully legitimate'. Other comments sug-gested that some black prisoners had a heightened sensitivity to what they regarded as veiled deprecation with racist overtones in the way prison officers spoke to them in comparison with their white counterparts, referencing their greater involvement in gangs, violence, or drug-related offences. Individuals who are stigmatized in society because of their ethnicity and their criminality may be hyper-vigilant to further rejection through discriminatory actions (Barnett-Page 2010; see also Berjot and Gillet 2011).

Minority ethnic prisoners sometimes seemed to draw on their 'racedar'[11]—an intuitive sense or belief about an individual's rac-ism even if it was not articulated through the use of racist language. Comments such as 'you always have a feeling', 'you can see it in their eyes', 'he's talk to white people like, different', and 'you can just tell . . . it's not brain science' attested to this method, although it was recognized that this was hardly infallible. Ianos,[12] a prisoner at Rochester, believed that prison officers were xenophobic: 'if you're not from their country they don't care about you'. This articulated a view among some prisoners that blatant racism had 'gone

[10] Of mixed race British, Christian origin.
[11] This replicates the portmanteau of 'gay' (but replaced with 'race') and radar which refers to a suspicion that racist beliefs are present in an individual's actions, expressions, or non-verbal expressions.
[12] Of white Eastern European, Christian origin.

underground'—it had simply migrated to the backstage, to private areas of white-only audiences. Today, racism is more covert, less obvious, less said, but still imagined in the minds of minority ethnic prisoners like Alex;[13] racism was done 'in a lot more intelligent way' by prison officers these days, he suggested. This sense of racism being camouflaged was aptly captured by Dale reflecting on the 2007 airing of the TV show *Celebrity Big Brother* where accusations were made about the racism of some contestants:

[W]hat's going on in *Big Brother* [the racist comments by English contestants directed at Indian contestant Shilpa Shetty sometimes made only to the camera and therefore the audience] is exactly the same as, as prison life, like, the girls, they'll be seen to be bullying the Indian girl Shilpa...but the racism aspect to it, it's indirect, they're keeping it, like between themselves. We're only seeing it because there's cameras there. She doesn't know that they're being racist towards her...that's just like prison...if someone, if someone is being racist, I don't think you'd, you would know unless, you can probably suspect it, but I don't think you will have any evidence or proof, but it will be indirect innit. (Dale, black West African, Christian, Rochester)

This did not mean that prisoners jumped to assume racist motivation in conflictual or problematic interactions between prison officers and prisoners. Typically, they were deduced by a process of elimination, but often reluctantly, with most prisoners erring on the cautious side of generosity. Many prisoners in interview seemed to be what might be termed 'reflective agnostics'; they were willing to consider whether a particular officer's actions might be motivated by a genuine, as opposed to racist, dislike of the prisoner, or because of a personality clash or previous negative interaction. Comments such as those by Salif,[14] at Rochester, were frequently heard: 'it looked like racism to me yeah, but it could be because he don't like the guy'. An extract from Melvin's interview further illuminates this kind of thinking:

I mean you go to certain officers and you say, 'look guv, you know, I've had a bad phone call and that, is there any chance you can kind of help me get a phone call?' And this officer might have, I don't know, might have judged you from a later [earlier] date or whatever and he says no. But then a white guy will come along, same problem and he says yes...And then I might come along and he says yes. But if you stop it then and you go back a step

13 Of black African British, Christian origin.
14 Of Pakistani British, Muslim origin.

now, he's said no to a black guy, he's said yes to a white guy, you get me, then it suggests to me, why is Melvin different? Melvin's different because I have already interacted with them, I'm going past the stages where you judge me and that, I mean I've grown with you, you know who I am now. So when I'm speaking to you it's the respect you give to your fellow colleague you will give to me. But maybe this guy's come along, a bit arrogant, a little bit ignorant or something like that and, do you know what I mean. (Melvin, black African British, Muslim, Maidstone)

There was also generally an acceptance that prison officers had off days when their mood might be affected by something happening in their personal lives. A further counterpoint was the recognition that perceptions of racism by prison officers were often restricted to a small number of named officers. Deeply respectful and positive relationships between prisoners and prison officers were also mentioned. Unsurprisingly, the showing of kindness, encouragement, and humanity had considerable significance in the evaluations of these officers by prisoners (Liebling 2004, 2011); as Bottoms and Tankebe (2012: 149) note, 'true audience legitimacy is sometimes accorded by prisoners to certain prison regimes and to individual prison officers who carry out their duties in certain ways'.

Further, there were generalized accusations of pervasive discriminatory treatment made by minority ethnic prisoners. They claimed that, for example, black prisoners were rarely granted access to open prison conditions, able to gain parole, be released on Home Detention Curfew, or access particular work placements, and so on (see also Edgar and Martin 2004). Paul explained it in this way, and a further illustration was recounted by Ainsley:

...the system and whereas parole and um D-cat, there's definitely a lot of racism in there...If you're black you don't get nothing in this prison. You don't get things you're entitled to in this prison...Yeah, in all prisons in fact. If you're black it's more harder to get a D-cat, it's more harder to get your parole, it's more harder to get home leave, it's more harder to get enhanced, it's more harder to get your things you're entitled to basically. (Paul, black African British, Muslim, Maidstone)

[T]here's some boy called Vinny on the wing, white boy...he was here about two months ago. He got released and he come back after about a month and a half. Within a week he got put on enhanced [highest level of privilege in IEP], he had a cleaning job, then he got onto serving within a week...I remember one time I went about five months without getting a single red entry, still never got my enhanced, still never got a cleaning job, nothing. (Ainsley, black Caribbean British, Christian, Rochester)

The national picture using SMART ethnic monitoring data for 2010–11 provides some support for such claims. Accessing Release on Temporary Licence (ROTL), security re-categorization upwards,[15] the rate of adjudications and the use of segregation (for cellular confinement, good order and discipline, and awaiting adjudication) did show comparatively black prisoner disadvantage. Significantly, the use of force was also markedly higher for black prisoners, double the rate used against white prisoners. But there were proportionate or more advantageous outcomes for black prisoners' security re-categorization downwards,[16] and contrary to some of the allegations of prisoners like Paul, for Home Detention Curfew and enhanced IEP status (Ministry of Justice (MOJ) 2011b).[17]

Linked to this, a further category of discriminatory treatment by prison officers related to a less generous or flexible use of discretion in incidents where prisoners were at fault. Minority ethnic prisoners believed with some certainty that white prisoners were more often the recipients of institutional or disciplinary leniency than themselves. This was articulated by Alex in the following way, but similar examples of red entries[18] for negative behaviour given to

---

[15] Where prisoners are placed in a higher security category based on their risk of escape, causing harm to other prisoners and staff, and risk to the public if they were to escape.

[16] Where prisoners are placed in a lower security category based on their risk of escape, causing harm to other prisoners and staff, and risk to the public if they were to escape.

[17] MQPL data for Rochester for May 2006 produced a mean score slightly above other Young Offenders' Institution (YOI) scores and above those for the whole estate: 59% strongly agreed/agreed that Rochester YOI encouraged good race relations (HM 2006). Shortly before the fieldwork started in Maidstone prison, HMIP (2007b) had carried out an inspection which included data on race equality from January 2007. Apart from being more positive than white prisoners when asked about education, employment, and vocational skills training, minority ethnic prisoners were typically less positive about their experiences across a range of aspects of prison life: 26% of the random sample surveyed claimed to have been victimized by staff because of their ethnicity compared with 1% of white prisoners. SMART ethnic monitoring data were not made available at the two prisons because of the small numbers in certain categories which prohibited data release due to the risk of identifying individual prisoners. These exclusions also prevented the meaningful use of the range-setting used to statistically identify differential outcomes.

[18] This refers to a written entry on a prisoner's file which indicates poor behaviour or performance.

minority ethnic prisoners for minor infringements peppered prisoners' accounts:

I had a work warning and I know that for example if the white boy I serve with as well, he's had three work warnings, seven red entries and I've only got three, and then he was on suspension and he got his job back, but they put me off my job instantly. . . . I didn't get no second chance like it was just strictly first warning and then they took me off my job, so I start thinking like, he's white, he got dealt with differently and why are they treating me different. (Alex, black African British, Christian, Rochester)

This extract from an interview with Samson shows a reasoned assessment of prison officers' behaviour before a claim of prison officer racism is made:

There was an argument between a Muslim guy and a white guy, you know, just the other day . . . So at this point the officers have come and pulled the Muslim guy away and he's screaming 'what about that guy, what about that guy, you know, why are you just locking me up?' And I thought about it and I thought one way to look at is because obviously you're the one shouting and he's suddenly gone quiet, you know, he's trying to act calm. But at the same time, it's true, I mean they saw both individuals. Do you know what I mean? About to fight. So therefore both individuals should be going back to their cell. And that's the problem here, whenever there's an incident, the [minority] ethnic individual always seems to get locked up while the other individual's left on the wing or to roam about, you know. (Samson, black African British, Maidstone)

Some prisoners described the aggressive policing of black prisoners on the wings which was felt as a pervasive and stereotyped rejection of black cultural practices, ranging from challenging the exuberance of black prisoners loudly and competitively slamming down dominoes to disallowing particular dress styles or use of accessories which were more commonly worn by black or Asian prisoners. The heightened risk of cell spins—searches for prohibited items—also fell into this category, as did assertions that black prisoners were more vulnerable to high levels of violence and force or harsher treatment by prison officers:

[L]ike say on association on the landing there will be a group of black boys in one cell and a few outside the cell. Certain govs will come down like, rushing around, what's going on. And like we think, what you doing like, what's wrong, what's wrong boss? And they go oh nothing, just looking, just looking. Then when, when there's all the white guys down there taking their drugs and all that like they don't want to know, they're just interested in what the black people are doing more or less really, because they think we're up to no good all the time. (Lloyd, black Caribbean, British, Christian, Maidstone)

It is the informal nature of many of these interactions which struck Edgar and Martin (2004) in their study of racial conflict. For them, informal partiality, a form of discrimination in which minority ethnic prisoners were frequently disadvantaged in routine interactions with prison officers, resulted from negative racialized stereotyping. The power associated with prison officers' use and misuse of discretion in mundane actions explained the adverse perceptions of institutional treatment among minority ethnic prisoners. Its effects were profound, pervasive, and destructive of good prison officer/ prisoner relationships.

Reactions and adaptations to prison racism

In describing the unique pains of imprisonment, Sykes (1958) saw the deprivations of liberty, goods and services, heterosexual relations, autonomy, and security as inflicted on those individuals who traverse society's moral boundaries and who, through their actions, become subject to state control at its most coercive and painful. Such deprivations and the concomitant frustrations were regarded as part and parcel of modern punishment. While not harming the body through sadistic beatings and other corporal punishments, Sykes (1958) recognized that the inherent psychological pain of incarceration could be just as immense for the individual prisoner. These state-endorsed deprivations can fundamentally harm the self. For Crewe (2011a) the pains of late modern imprisonment render different pains to those identified by Sykes, creating oppressive burdens and neo-paternal pressures to perform appropriately, while Liebling (2011) identifies psychological damage when unfairness and arbitrary actions by prison officers are experienced by prisoners. But there is little in these works to indicate the impact of prison racism. Fanon (1967/2008), for example, talks powerfully of the systematic negation of the native self during colonialism. The denial of humanity, of existence, Fanon reckons, provokes powerful emotions of shame, rejection, and self-contempt, creating defensiveness, rage, and mental pathology. These are the psychological reactions to the internalization of violent racial hatred, the destruction of native culture, and the 'crushing objecthood' of white racism.

The racialized practices that I have discussed remind minority ethnic prisoners that in the prison domain the regime may be delivered sometimes equally but also sometimes unequally by majority white prison officers. As such, nothing is certain or assured. Here the 'white world' of the prison is hegemonic, although this hegemony is contested, and in unpredictable ways, as the last section of this chapter reveals.

The most common individual response to these practices where racism was suspected was fatalistic acceptance. This seemed to connect with the position of prisoners in two key ways. First, prisoners often regarded themselves as the 'lowest of the low', 'the scum' of society, the stigmatized 'Others' who 'didn't count', who were undeserving of basic humanity. Being the victims of racism inside was all part of this painful experience of imprisonment and societal excision. Secondly, the broader experience of racial discrimination in society meant that prison was simply regarded as an extension of these processes of inequality and discrimination. For many prisoners these interactions were not politically or experientially challenged, simply normalized and accepted. 'It's the same on the outside in jobs and the system, but that's just how it is', was how Paul[19] put it. Aaron[20] professed to have known since he was a child, 'like being black and being from London you've got to sort of like stand out a little bit, you can't just be like run of the mill, you're not going to get nowhere' in accessing equal opportunities anywhere in society, including prison. There is little here that seemed to challenge the unfairness of racial discrimination; prisoners were sanguine about the possibilities of experiencing racism inside with little to indicate any threat to penal legitimacy because of perceptions of unfairness. Some minority ethnic prisoners themselves were complicit in this, effectively endorsing a lesser eligibility notion of equality and fairness despite these being the bulwarks of procedural justice (Tyler 2010). Prisoners' fatalism may have been partly to do with the recognition that proving racial discrimination was often near-impossible and therefore voicing such claims was futile. Disturbingly reminiscent of the enforced passivity of slavery, Samson,[21] at Maidstone, talked of prisoners being 'housebroken',

---

[19] Of black African British, Muslim origin, Maidstone.
[20] Of black Caribbean British, Muslim origin, Maidstone.
[21] Of black African British origin, Maidstone.

with resistance muted because of a feeling that 'this is prison, after all', this is simply what prisoners deserve.

Often it was believed that there were few options for challenging discriminatory behaviour by prison officers; complaining or confronting officers was likely to lead to being unfairly targeted at a later stage. Thus, as Jan[22] noted, 'the best thing you just have to take it'. Coming up against 'the system', through complaints or directly questioning the practices of officers on the wings or further up the occupational hierarchy, was typically deemed a waste of time or as provoking further trouble. For Anton,[23] a prisoner at Rochester, a retreatist response could be seen, not wholly dissimilar to what Sykes (1958) defined as psychological withdrawal, as apathy and resignation prevail. Based on extensive periods of block time[24] for alleged but then later withdrawn charges of bullying, which he interpreted as racially motivated, Anton withdrew from complaining about his experiences inside, ruefully accepting that 'that's what the system's like for me'. The pained submission of not attempting to buck but rather to 'just go along with the system' was palpable. A defeatist withdrawal marked the means for Anton to avoid further pain. Such retreatist positions were not unlike Crewe's (2009) *stoics* in Wellingborough prison, whose responses to incarceration were characterized by the suppression of their frustrations with prison life so as not to challenge prison authority and risk their release from prison being delayed. Their compliance then was instrumental, akin to what Bottoms and Tankebe (2012: 165) call 'pragmatic acquiescence';[25] dissent was seen as counter-productive underlining the extreme powerlessness they felt (see also Crewe 2011a).

Only occasionally did prisoners respond collectively to perceived racism. Monifa,[26] at Maidstone, recalled a prison officer who had been informally identified as racist by a number of prisoners. He had issued several IEP warnings to black prisoners for 'nothing, just because you drop something on the floor or you smoke on the landing, or you are cooking, you came like to the door'. A collective racist complaint from eight prisoners was formally submitted and

---

[22] Of black Caribbean Western European, Christian origin, Rochester.

[23] Of black Caribbean British, Christian origin.

[24] Prisoners' term for punishment in the prison's segregation unit where privileges such as association and TV are withheld.

[25] This is akin to Carrabine's (2004) concept of 'dull compulsion'.

[26] Of black West African, Christian origin.

the officer was moved on to another unit within the prison. Monifa and other minority ethnic prisoners had allegedly been told that 'he want to see all the Africans in basic [the lowest level in the IEP scheme]'.

The hurt and humiliation of discriminatory practices in prison, over which prisoners have little or no control, represents another layer of the diminution of the self (see also Liebling 2011; Crewe 2011b). Manu[27] talked of being called a 'monkey' in the prison he was held in before he arrived at Rochester. He emotionally recalled it 'getting to him', the being 'treated as an animal'. These comments were evocative of Fanon's (1963/2001: 200) depiction of the harms of colonialism, the 'systematic negation of the other person and a furious determination to deny the other person all attributes of humanity', in which the essence of bestiality is at the forefront of the colonizer's mind. For Manu these hurtful comments had a wider significance, highlighting how his blackness marked him out as forever vulnerable, unlike those whose white skins guaranteed privilege and 'being wanted'. Sometimes these stories of racist snubs or belittling were told in an abstract way, narrated almost as if occurring to someone else, or simply presented as statements of fact, rather than as victimizing or discriminatory experiences which were qualitatively different for white prisoners. They could also produce feelings of confusion, self-doubt, and alienation, further unsettling prisoners in their quest to survive and cope in prison. As Asad noted:

if you see many people get a lot of things and you see yourself you don't get it, you're odd innit, so you think to yourself yeah, what have I done wrong... I haven't done nothing wrong, I'm sure I've done nothing wrong, is it my colour? (Asad, Bangladeshi British, Muslim, Rochester)

Such onslaughts on identity do not automatically lead to low self-esteem, but they do present an extra stress added to the other multiple stressors associated with the pains of imprisonment (for a brief review of some of the social-psychological literature on discrimination, see Berjot and Gillet 2011). Perceptively, the additional emotional burden associated with discrimination was not lost on some sympathetic white prisoners. As Anthony[28] said, 'fucking hell we're all in here in the same boat... you've got your problems you

[27] Of black Central African, Christian origin.
[28] Of white British, Christian origin, Maidstone.

don't need the fucking shit from these idiots down here'. How prisoners actually cope with these negative stressors and what characteristics assist emotional resilience in the face of racial discrimination
is a task for future research.[29]

A minority of other prisoners in this study seemed to adopt a
more defiant, rebellious, oppositional attitude to perceived discrimination by prison officers, and such actions may be empower-
ing (Ziersch et al. 2011). Although not necessarily articulated in
this way by prisoners themselves, they were effectively more willing
to claim and assert a political equality in the context of equal citizenship rights (Kymlicka 2007). Resisting discrimination as an
assault on the self, sometimes a literal, physical micro-aggression,
and sometimes a more subtle devaluation or mistreatment, these
prisoners were prepared to submit racist complaint forms even
where sceptical of the outcome of internal investigations. More
rarely these altercations became part of an ongoing interaction in
which cooperation was violently resisted, although rarely collectively. Regan,[30] at Maidstone prison, for example, described being
racially abused by a prison officer in his cell. His response was to
loudly and continuously identify the prison officer as a racist and to
assume that his complaint would lead to a 'cover up'. On one occasion, his pre-emptive attempt to protect himself from retaliatory
violence when cornered by prison officers added to the list of 'nick-
ings' he got. The following week, provoked by the original officer
coming to his cell and making monkey faces at him, and again creating a scene, he was transferred to another wing, with 21 days
added to his sentence. Regardless of the validity of Regan's claims,
his open and persistent defiance was at the opposite end of the spectrum to the fatalistic acceptance of racial discrimination by other
minority ethnic prisoners. Jack, a white prisoner at Rochester prison, perceived these kinds of negative interactions to lead black

[29] A particularly interesting line of inquiry will be to see whether Folkman and
Lazarus' (1980) claim that emotion-focused coping (managing the associated emotional stress) where there is a perception that discrimination is unchangeable is
more common among prisoners than problem-focused coping where there is belief
that elements of the discrimination can be changed. The psychosocial subjectivity
of suffering and wounding wrought by capitalist economic and political domination and exclusion, now receiving greater scholarly attention, could also be relevant to this field, seeing to what degree racist experience is emotionally internalized
(see, eg Frost and Hoggett 2008).
[30] Of black Caribbean British, Christian origin.

prisoners to 'not care anymore' and an ongoing mutual lack of respect, itself fuelling a negative spiral of aggressive challenges and inevitable red entries and then punishment on the block (segregation unit) for black prisoners.

The absence of prison officer racism

Goldberg (2009) has claimed that institutional reforms which follow in the wake of high-profile racialized events (such as urban riots) typically dissolve into modest anti-racist absolutions subsequently inscribed in law. This position may be somewhat pessimistic (but see Bourne 2001). The major overhaul of the management of race equality in the Prison Service has prompted a cultural shift in which blatant racism has been reduced significantly, although not completely excised from prison officer/prisoner interactions (NOMS 2008). The late modern, multicultural prison is most certainly different to that of the pre-CRE prison world, as was regularly confirmed by prisoners like Douglas who had experienced incarceration in both periods:

Um, I mean years ago it weren't like, you know, the officers didn't like it, you know what I mean, they were really prejudiced and I had hard times, you know...and they call me Micky the Muslim...the officers will beat the Muslim out of you, you know what I mean. (Douglas, white British, Muslim, Maidstone)

Nowhere was this more evident than in the comments of minority ethnic prisoners at both Rochester and Maidstone prisons who clearly articulated the absence of racism in their experiences of imprisonment. Even taking account of variation in the ability of individuals to recognize or detect discrimination in their environment—the discussion of the 'racedar' makes clear that it is far from an exact science—a significant proportion of prisoners whom we might imagine would be most vulnerable to prison officer racism categorically denied its presence in their prison lives. Some prisoners of black Caribbean, black African, Pakistani, Bangladeshi, white Muslim, and mixed race and foreign national origins, explicitly stated that prison officer racism was not a regular feature of life inside; many had never even witnessed it. These accounts epitomized this view:

Since I've been here I've had not one racist comment. (Glen, mixed race British, Christian, Rochester)

They're not going to hate us because we are foreign national or because we are Muslim I don't think so… (Amjad, Arab Muslim, West Asian, Rochester)

Never experienced it, never, never, personally. Never, never seen it either. I've been, as I say, four different prisons. (Gamal, white North African, Muslim, Maidstone)

I haven't really seen any pure racism in jail since I've been in jail. Probably a gov won't like you but it don't mean he don't like you because of your colour. (Rafael, black African British, Christian, Rochester)

This perspective was more often voiced among the younger prisoners of Rochester, who, as was seen in Chapter 4, were generally more comfortable in the multicultural prison. In contrast, the historical imprint of prejudice, discrimination, racism for minority ethnic prisoners who experienced life in the decades after the post-war mass migration might have been sensitized to its presence in the contemporary period. As Picca and Feagin (2007: 13) have suggested, racial performances can represent an acting-out of past behaviours as 'racial events tend[s] to generate collective memories of times past'. Discussed in Chapter 4, just as there was a tendency for some white prisoners to fall back on traditional processes of racial othering, it may be just as easy to situate oneself in familiar narratives as a minority ethnic individual, consciously or unconsciously. In the hierarchical order of the prison, it is not inconceivable that, on occasion, minority ethnic prisoners might assume a racist framing to encounters based on past negative experiences; after all, the 'racedar' is imperfect. This is not a suggestion of over-sensitivity, of prisoners seeing racism everywhere—the large number of claims made by minority ethnic prisoners across a range of ages, ethnicities, and nationalities, indicates that this is not the whole picture, but it may certainly be part of it—particularly if we accept that current experience is frequently processed through the frame of previous experience.

It was testimony to the permeation of a race equality agenda in prison that most prisoners were fully aware of the punitive response which could accompany racial abuse and discrimination in prison. Tellingly, Colin, a white British prisoner at Maidstone prison recalled abusive comments made by prison officers regarding sexual offenders but said pointedly, 'I swear to god that every officer that I have spoken to and they've heard a racial comment they go fucking mad about it, genuine, they go mad'. Officially, then, the climate of the prison was opposed to racism and this message had been clearly received by many prisoners and prison officers.

Among some prisoners, it was recognized that officer laziness or intransigence might easily be misinterpreted as racial discrimination. An officer who is asked to perform a simple action to assist a minority ethnic prisoner may refuse and then be assumed to have refused because of the race or ethnicity of the prisoner. At the same time the officer's unhelpful behaviour might be a feature of his personality and he may be equally inclined to deny help to a white prisoner. That prisoners might cast aspersions about an officer's conduct simply because they had not been able to get what they wanted was also openly acknowledged among some prisoners. Obsessive claims about an officer's racism could also be used to mask a prisoner's failings, according to Dominic:

I do have to say that a lot of the times that negative thing is just paranoia and it's something to moan about...especially on this wing, I wouldn't agree with anyone who said that they thought that any of the officers in here was racist or done anything because they was racist...it's frustrating subject because I'm black myself...I wouldn't condone racism to any race and or bullying...I think if they just pulled their finger out and went the right way about certain things then they will get what they want...it's not racism but it's definitely a problem that a lot of staff do have...they forget that like we are here as prisoners and our liberties have all been taken away so therefore when we're speaking to you like have some professionalism when you're answering us. But then at the same time you've got some people that aint got no respect either, so when they speak to staff they will make staff want to not want to give you back any respect because you're not giving them none. (Dominic, black Caribbean British, Christian, Maidstone)

Understanding the multicultural prison, then, requires recognizing that its space is contested and conflicted and the vicissitudes of racialization are experienced daily but not in a singular sense. A range of perspectives reveal how race shapes the dynamics of the prison, but this is not a static, fixed picture, and for some prisoners, traditional racial boundaries based on a white (prison officer)/minority ethnic (prisoner) binary are less frequently invoked. While arguing previously that this was a feature of younger prisoner/prisoner relationships inside (Phillips, C. 2008), it also appears significant in prison officer/prisoner relationships in the post-CRE prison where overt racism has become highly stigmatized. One final example of the variegated manifestation of race inside talks to the flip side of minority ethnic prisoners' assertion of their citizenship rights to be treated with fairness and equality. Such notions are increasingly being utilized by some white prisoners who are 'pissed off'—to quote Gunn at the beginning of this chapter—that equalities policies place them at a disadvantage.

'Everything is Curried Out':[31] Political Correctness and the 'Forgotten Majority'

Multicultural influences are now recognized throughout society, from the sporting achievements of athletes such as Mo Farah, to the crowning of the anglicized invention chicken tikka masala as the nation's favourite food.[32] The late modern prison has not escaped these effects and, in many ways, as the previous chapters have shown, it has at least partially, embraced them. Sensitive to the needs of prisoners from minority ethnic groups, it is now possible to get curry and halal chicken from the prison servery and to get black hair products and Muslim prayer mats on the canteen list.[33]

However, just as John Alexander and Claude Johnson[34] had their legal claims for injury to their feelings upheld as a result of their systematic racial discrimination in prison, there is also evidence of a pained discontent among some primarily white and non-Muslim prisoners who feel aggrieved about, and disadvantaged by, equalities and diversity policies in prison. These claims bear many of the hallmarks of, but are not necessarily equivalent to, the pains of racism and discrimination, previously only the preserve of minority ethnic prisoners. Now added to this mix is an indignant victimhood carried on a current of 'backlash' against multiculturalism in prison. In this sense, for a significant minority of white prisoners the white hegemony of the prison is breaking down, destabilized by the political demands of minority ethnic prisoners and the politics of equalities policies.

'Backlash' has a long history in Britain which Hewitt (2005) has traced back to parts of Enoch Powell's 'Rivers of Blood' speech in

---

[31] Quote from a white female prisoner in Kruttschnitt and Hussemann's study (2008: 722) in which she claims that the prison primarily caters for Jamaican prisoners in the food served.

[32] In 2011 it appears that chicken tikka masala has been displaced by a new minority cuisine, Italian food.

[33] See fn 3.

[34] Respectively, the black prisoner who first challenged his treatment in trying to access a job in the kitchens in 1987, and the black prison auxiliary who was successful at three separate employment tribunals in 1995, 1996, and 2000 in proving racial discrimination, victimization, and discrimination (see Ch 2).

1968[35] in which he recalled a conversation with a 'decent, ordinary fellow Englishman', a middle-aged constituent who felt that 'in 15 or 20 years' time the black man will have the whip hand over the white man'. His view, however, was not an isolated one, according to Powell; this was what 'thousands and hundreds of thousands are saying and thinking'. As white British citizens struggled to find hospital beds and school places, they saw their neigbourhoods changed and at work 'found that employers hesitated to apply to the immigrant worker the standards of discipline and competence required of the native-born worker; they began to hear, as time went by, more and more voices which told them that they were now the unwanted'. More recently, impassioned claims for equal *white* access to social housing have again picked up this theme, illustrating how claims for scarce resources are easily racialized (Dench, Gavron, and Young 2006; Garner 2009). In the Citizenship Survey of 2008–9, 26 per cent of white respondents who had had contact with social housing providers in the previous five years believed that they would be treated worse than other racial groups. No other ethnic group felt as strongly in relation to social housing; the closest was half this figure at 13 per cent of black respondents who believed that they would fare worse than members of other racial groups (Department for Communities and Local Government 2011). Negative reactions to positive action, equality, and diversity policies in public sector employment pre- and post-Macpherson (1999) are also well documented (Carter 2000; Creegan et al. 2003; Foster, Newburn, and Souhami 2005; Loftus 2008). In discussing these counter-narratives of race and inequality in the late modern prison I hope to avoid the danger of what Back (2009: 210) calls being 'racism's accomplice', but by the same token I hope to be able to navigate a path away from wholesale demonization of these primarily white perspectives among prisoners at Rochester and Maidstone prisons (Macdonald 1989; Keith, M. 2008).[36]

[35] This was a speech to the Conservative Association on 20 April 1968, reproduced in full in the *Telegraph*, 6 November 2007.

[36] The inquiry into the racist murder of Ahmed Ullah in 1986 in a Manchester school concluded that the failure of the school authorities to accept that the white murderer was not part of the same camp as other white students (who were not allowed to attend Ullah's funeral) was no less racist than ignoring the racism of the murder itself. Shortly after there were racialized disorders between white and Asian students which later led to some white pupils being transferred from the school for their own safety. The Macdonald Inquiry questioned the way anti-racist policies were introduced and maintained largely without consultation, which had created a climate of fear, polarization, and distrust.

Some prisoners' talk in Maidstone (and to a far lesser extent, Rochester) prison represented a criticism of both the reach and content of equalities and diversities policies. It was troubling to some white prisoners that race equality issues were 'pushed in your face', rather than being 'done on the quiet'. The explicit focus on diversity, it was argued, brings the corresponding problem of highlighting prisoners' differences instead of underlining prisoners' inherent similarities. Bernard, a white prisoner at Maidstone, for example, recalled how a Muslim child at his primary school, without explanation or warning, regularly left the classroom. For Bernard it was sufficient for this child's absence to pray and observe his Muslim faith to go unremarked upon. In contrast, he felt that the prison brought attention to cultural difference by employing diversity staff who then made 'too big a point of it' with 'constant reminders that there are different races, there are different colours, there are different religions'. He concluded by stating clearly, 'race has become an issue because the prison has made it an issue'. Barry's perspective on this was similar:

Well you have it jammed down your throat all the time don't you ... Diversity is always a great thing. Uh it's enriching for everybody who's in the melting pot ... [but] it has to be tempered with reason. (Barry, white British, no religion, Maidstone)

This is a variation on the theme of a politically naive, colour-blind policy approach in which difference is airbrushed out of social relations with the assumed concomitant disappearance of racial discrimination of its own accord. This occurs as individuals, not reminded by their markedly different phenotypical features, and their differences in first language, religious participation, and faith, and their various national and cultural practices and modes of being, concentrate instead on their inherent likenesses as human beings, or specifically, as human prisoners. This feeling is indeed one at least partially shared by some minority ethnic prisoners who disavowed their ethnic identity, eschewing it in favour of a common humanity (see Chapter 4). It was believed by prisoners such as Bernard and Barry that it is the 'overdoing' of race in prison which is its downfall, bringing feelings of resentment among prisoners who feel pressure to notice and acknowledge difference. Prisoners feel unhelpfully and unwillingly preached to. There is the slightest hint here that the prison which has historically sought to manipulate and reform the souls of the prisoners, redirecting them to the correct and righteous path through solitude and religious doctrine, is now seeking to mould their racially suspect minds (see Chapter 4).

This 'overdoing' of race inside is linked to a broader complaint about political correctness, an example of which is remembered by one prisoner as the 'gollywog on the marmalade'.[37] 'All this racial this that and the other' was how Max, another white prisoner at Maidstone, referred to it. This is the context for prisoners' recall of preposterous edicts about what can and cannot be said or done in the field of race relations, far beyond any semblance of common sense. Even Adam, at Maidstone, who lived in an urban area of London with a large concentration of minority ethnic groups, admitted to being confused about the appropriate nomenclature. He recognized that black people preferred to be referred to as 'black' rather than 'brown' or 'coloured' but was unsure about whether he could use the term 'black' in the prison environment.

The use of language can become particularly fractious in prison social relations. White prisoners are understandably upset that minority ethnic prisoners can call them 'white wankers' or 'white cunts' seemingly without such abuse being named as racist and without fear of punishment or despite the weight it carried in an environment when black prisoners were perceived as culturally dominant. It presupposes that racism can travel in only one direction and that protagonists can only be white. White prisoners' sharply felt grievance was that their experience of racist victimization in these encounters was overlooked by the prison administration. This from Stuart at Rochester:

Black people always say white people racist, I tell you what the black people are the most racist…they are more racist than anyone else and yet if something goes…to court…But if we're sitting there going, 'yeah that little Paki cunt,' or 'big black prick', then all of a sudden, we're, we're labelled as a racist. (Stuart, white British, no religion)

Just as confusing was the white prisoners' sense that they could not use the word 'nigger' or 'Paki' even though the terms were sometimes used by minority ethnic prisoners themselves (Earle 2011b). How could these terms be racist when they were used by their supposed victims? This is baffling and fear-making. Being labelled racist in the 21st century is particularly abhorrent, morally stigmatizing

---

[37] This concerned the appropriateness of having golli*wogs* on Robertsons' jam jars. As an aside, it was a common racial taunt to 'get back on your jam jar' in the playground where I attended primary school.

(Gadd 2009), but also dangerous inside when violent reprisals are common or disciplinary sanctions certain (see Chapter 4). This infuriates white prisoners, as they see it as a prime example of 'reverse racism'. White identities can be ridiculed, humiliated, and criticized, but the use of race equality measures to challenge and punish such abuse is an option effectively closed to white prisoners. The unfairness of this inequality is intensely felt and fuels a sense of grievance that there are no corresponding 'rights for whites', an idea which has proved extremely fertile in the political campaigns of the British National Party (Rhodes 2010).

Just as in discourses circulating outside prison, the perceived absence of a cultural recognition of whiteness or 'Englishness' was also resented (see Chapter 4). Bearing this in mind it is hardly surprising that minority ethnic groups are then represented as a cultural threat. Although this strand of the 'white resentment' discourse was far less clearly articulated in prison, there was a feeling that minority ethnic identities were in a superior cultural position whereas majority whiteness was being forgotten, left behind in the cultural politics of late modernity. Such claims-making should not be rejected out of hand, particularly if we accept Taylor's (2003) argument that cultural recognition is a vital human need; but it is nonsensical to argue that whiteness is anything other than hegemonic in British society. October may be Black History Month[38] in the prison, but every month is white history month in that 'white culture' is transmitted in all its variations through cultural outlets in society, and in prison through education, the use of the library, and television. Nonetheless, these fears of cultural threat are real even if the foundations on which they are based are largely groundless. They are also pervasive, not just to be found in prison, but also, of course, in the post-industrial heartlands and the leafy suburbs of middle England (Mann and Fenton 2009; Clarke, S. and Garner 2010; Rhodes 2010b).

Inscribed within these counter-narratives are perverse notions that minority ethnic prisoners have an unfair entitlement to scarce prison resources, creating a form of inverted privilege. In this way minority ethnic groups are positioned as a material threat to the white majority. Outside prison, tales of migrants arriving at Heathrow, immediately

---

[38] This is an annual commitment to promote knowledge of black history, culture, and heritage, to increase awareness and confidence among black people, and to celebrate positive black contributions to society.

going to the front of the queue at a local housing office, and moving quickly with their large, state-dependent family into the most sought-after house with a garden, courtesy of social housing, are frequently churned out by the tabloids (see, for example, 'Immigrants Blag One Out Of Eight Council Houses', *Daily Star*, 28 October 2010; cf. Rutter and Latorre (2009)). In prison there are similar apocryphal stories which feed white and non-Muslim prisoner resentment, but there are also specific examples that prisoners recalled in interview. Such claims go to the heart of debates about entitlement, most often framed in the context of welfare benefits, but just as easily transposed to the prison environment, where psychological wounds and the injuries of class are nursed (Ware 2008).

The vitriol saved for Muslim converts was related to the use of a fake or casual observance of Islam to secure certain concessions from the prison administration. Non-Muslim prisoners were particularly upset by what they regarded as the flagrant abuse of faith to secure concessions from the prison administration—be that extra time out of cell to attend Friday prayers or extra food portions to break the fast during Ramadhan. Cynics were particularly troubled by the perceived increased rate of conversions shortly before Ramadhan which represented a despicable manoeuvring by some minority ethnic prisoners. Seemingly such allegations were not solely the result of envy; the Imam at Rochester prison had taken the congregation to task for a number of Muslim prisoners eating meals allocated to non-Muslim prisoners while they were meant to be fasting. Prisoners were given a long ticking-off at one Friday prayers session where the Imam reminded prisoners about the reputational damage to the 'Muslim prisoner cause' which he had fought hard to promote at the prison. 'We don't need another reason for people to hate us' was the message forcefully delivered after the sermon (Fieldnotes, 6 October 2006). In response, rather incongruously, Mark, a mixed race, foreign national prisoner at Maidstone, proposed that any prisoner should be able to fill out an application and claim Ramadhan food; it should not be a privilege only accessible to Muslim prisoners. Similarly bizarrely, Jonathan, a white British prisoner at Rochester, bemoaned his inability to buy Muslim toothpaste while Muslims were able to—although it was unclear why they might want to—purchase Catholic rosary beads:

On the canteen yeah, like you've got a list of things you can buy yeah and you've got rosary beads yeah, you've got a Muslim prayer mat, you've got a Buddhist what are they called, incense sticks…they have Muslim tooth-paste and all this, it says Muslims only. So why can I not buy that, but a Muslim can buy a Roman Catholic cross…Muslims go to their church yeah, like say Christmas yeah and they was giving out free gifts. Any Muslim went to the church, but we can't go to the what's it called, the mosque (Jonathan, white British, Christian, Rochester)

Along similar lines were the instances where prison practices in the name of equal treatment somehow led to white prisoners losing out. Nathan, for example, described as 'reverse discrimination' the preferential allocation of places to minority ethnic prisoners on a bricklaying course at Maidstone prison. It was alleged that the course leader ('a blinding geezer', so the fault clearly did not lie with him) had to ensure that a percentage of places went to black prisoners. This left a larger (although proportionate) number of white prisoners competing for the remaining places. This was interpreted by Nathan as a form of favouritism as the black prisoners—in his example interest was only shown by exactly the number of black prisoners who could be allocated places—'know as long as they just say certain things yeah, they're on the course'. This meant that all the black people who wanted places on the bricklaying course were guaranteed those places, whereas the competition was numerically, but not proportionately, much greater for white prisoners. That access was proportional to the representation of ethnic groups in Maidstone was not understood by Nathan nor explained by prison staff.

Similarly, it was felt that meeting the religious needs and entitlements of Muslim prisoners, including their avoidance of haram (forbidden) foods, should have no place in the prison; after all, as Max stated emphatically, 'it's bullshit, we're in prison'. No one should be seen as getting a leg-up from the prison administration in doing their time. Matthew's views were that the prison system worked in favour of black prisoners while white prisoners 'haven't got that card we can throw in'. In this respect race equality policies are seen as violating the inmate code that prisoners should do their own time without fear or favour. Instead, as Max suggested, prisoners should be united by the 'only thing that matters…the common thing with all of us, every night we are put into a cell and that door is locked…we're all behind the door'. This is a powerful register of the commonality in the prison experience—the deprivation of liberty, equally shared. Prisoners need to feel that they are all in the same boat (to use Anthony's phrase), equally rocked by the waves without anyone sitting on a raised seat where their feet are not getting wet.

Yet there is something disingenuous in perceiving these wrongs perpetrated so egregiously by the prison administration. After all, as M. Keith (2008) has observed, ethnic competition is always about rational self-interest and nowhere is that more true than in prison, where survival is dependent on making the best of it and alleviating the pains of imprisonment, individually or collectively. However, in these expressive narratives there was a clear sense that minority ethnic prisoners were being assisted to renege on the unspoken contract that no one or everyone should be able to access the 'good life' in prison without preference to ethnicity or religion. And while, as already discussed, there is minimal evidence that minority ethnic groups experience advantages compared to their white counterparts (MOJ 2011b), account must also be taken of the mundane interactions between white prison officers and minority ethnic prisoners, which are observed by white prisoners and come to act as self-evident truths.

Playing Cards: Minority Ethnic Privilege/White Disadvantage

Continuing the theme of the cards being unfairly stacked against white prisoners in favour of minority ethnic groups, this alleged privilege was more explicitly furthered by the perversion of protections against racial discrimination and inequality as minority ethnic prisoners falsely claimed racism (see also Edgar and Martin 2004). This provoked the most vehement sense of outrage and contributed hugely to a smouldering resentment among aggrieved white prisoners. The playing of the 'race card' or the 'religion card' was a source of deep-seated rage and it was regularly asserted that minority ethnic prisoners availed themselves of this protection to ensure that they had the freedom to do exactly as they pleased in prison. Matthew's views were that black prisoners specifically had a 'persecution complex' which white people did not have; in this regard claiming racism was special pleading which was exaggerated by black and Asian people. A recurrent example of using the race card mentioned by several prisoners is discussed here by Don:

a lot of people play race cards...I'll give you an example. There was a person pushing in the dinner queue, um and he was a black guy and one of the staff saw him, it was a white member of staff and said, look you've got to go to the back because you pushed in and he said, that's because I'm black and I'm putting a racist complaint in and he did, and got away with it. So I mean it's classed... pushing in is classed as bullying in here, and...that's what they class it as, they class that as bullying, so um...because he's black he got away with it because he put a racist complaint in. (Don, white British, Christian, Maidstone)

Other arguments were made in a general, non-specific way but similarly referenced the abuse of the system by minority ethnic prisoners, the culpability of the prison administration, and the fear associated with 'political correctness'. In the area of equalities, the prison administration was often viewed contemptuously. According to Mark, a mixed race, foreign national prisoner, the failure of the Prison Service to ensure fairness to white prisoners was because they were 'walking on eggshells' in their treatment of minority ethnic prisoners, allowing them advantage in doing their time, and not wishing to fall foul of equalities policies and face complaints of racial discrimination. Jasper described a 'jumping through hoops' when a complaint of racial discrimination was received because the prison administration 'shit themselves when it comes to the blacks'. Prison officers, however, did 'fuck all' when there was a white complainant. From Pete, another white prisoner at Maidstone, there was an evident confusion and scepticism about current equalities policies:

It's fucking unbelievable because the prison is not run properly. I mean the thing is they talk about the old days and all that, it's not to do about the old school and the old days, it's just fucking people knew where they were. These people are frightened to... listen, they're even frightened to raise their voice in case they get racially discriminated against or some bollocks like that, do you understand. It's all like a, I don't know, PC [political correctness] shit, they don't... and it don't work, the Human Rights, it don't work, people abuse it. (Pete, white British, Christian, Maidstone)

The instrumental abuse and corruption of race equality was the source of much rancour in prison. Such feelings of victimization, of being wronged and mistreated, often created profound feelings of anger and frustration that had no legitimate outlet in prison. This was part of a discourse, powerfully expressed, painfully felt, of a corrupting, aberrant state of affairs in which the forgotten white majority were victims of inequality and racism in prison. Cowlishaw's (2004) ethnography of an Australian town where

similar antagonistic social relations were present between 'whitefellas' and 'blackfellas' argued that this potent, 'hidden white injury'
is a source of political and psychological strength, although also a
site of psychic anxiety (see also Gadd and Dixon 2011).

Dean, a Maidstone prisoner, believed that minority ethnic 'elders'
who had suffered 'real racism' would be appalled by the cowardly
and inappropriate uses to which equalities policies were being put.
Some prisoners extended their sympathy to prison officers who
they believed were held hostage to such practices as the prison's
enforcers of political correctness. Liebling, Arnold, and Straub
(2012) found that staff fears of this kind led to withdrawal and
disengagement from interaction with prisoners and was linked to a
lack of support from senior staff in working with radical 'extremist'
prisoners which flowed into their work with less-politicized Muslim prisoners and reduced staff morale. Here, Mark outlines his
experience of minority ethnic prisoner–prison officer relations at
Maidstone:

The majority of racism I would say from my point of view, from what I've
seen, is prisoners against officers...Like for instance I think there was
three or four of us...waiting at the window at the desk office on the wing.
Um there was a dark skinned chap came up and started barking orders at
the um at the officer. Um and then he must have turned round and said oh
it's cos I was black, you're not, you know, you're ignoring me. And the
officer turned round, rightfully so, I have to agree with him, it's not because
you're black, it's because you're ignorant. As you can see, I've got these
four people that have been queuing up, I've got to see them first, and then
I will deal with your problem. Um but I find that the black people generally they try and use it as a leverage, oh it's cos I was black. And I see that
probably, without exaggerating, probably five times a week. (Mark white,
Oceanian, no religion, Maidstone)

Since these stories comprise the social realities of prisoners, it is not
necessary—even were it possible—to quantify the number or proportion of false claims made by minority ethnic prisoners to assess
the validity of white prisoners' accounts. It is important to note,
however, that such views were sometimes supported by minority
ethnic prisoners:

I mean the thing about what you've got to realise about prisoners, if something doesn't go their way and if it's a white officer, they tend to say it's
racism. And it's not down to racism, it's just a member of staff's trying to
do their job...I've been in a long time and I know it's not because I've been
on race relation boards and I've been on wing committees and things like

that...it's not racism, it's just the fact that the prisoner can't get his own way, therefore he's saying it's racism. (Ruhi, Bangladeshi British, Muslim, Maidstone)

There may be an instrumental use of ethnic identities to make claims on the prison administration and it is a hard call to determine which of these are genuine or reasonable. In an environment where simple advantage can be everything and individuals are primed to do anything they can, legitimately or illegitimately, to reduce the pains of imprisonment, it is certainly more than possible that some such abuse does occur. One example already mentioned was the admonishment of Muslim prisoners by the Imam at Rochester prison, after he had been advised that some had taken ordinary prison meals as well as those they were entitled to have during Ramadhan.

Notwithstanding, these narratives rest on the assumption that racism can only be objectively understood, that it is either present, blatant or not, that there are no grey areas in which minority ethnic prisoners' claims can be considered. They are simply spurious, instrumental, and immoral, with no possibility of error. Implicitly, and by extension, these white counter-narratives challenge the entitlement of minority ethnic prisoners to claim racial inequality, since this is now a thing of the past, a legacy of slavery or empire, and an irrelevance in the 21st century (Goldberg 2009). It is not possible from this standpoint to acknowledge the history of race relations in prison. The typically upheld tribunal cases of both prisoners and prison officers with proven racial discrimination, and the need for the CRE to mount a formal investigation into the Prison Service and then to lay 17 findings of unlawful racial discrimination against it, are not part of this mindset. As Rhodes (2010) notes, this is a white victimhood which conveniently forgets the past, ignoring the political and economic hegemony of white privilege historically and in the contemporary period (see also Knowles 2003), although such privilege is mediated by class and less available to the likes of prisoners in their classed position (see Chapters 1 and 2). At the same time these narratives seem to act as a reminder that traditional hierarchies of privilege are being contested in the prison environment, are no longer assured, and that somehow white prisoners instead of minority ethnic prisoners are now the disadvantaged.

There is a strong hint of melancholia expressed in the troubles of white prisoners, and Gilroy's (2004) ideas about post-imperial melancholia are apt here. The stage for Gilroy's work is a global one, whereas I use his arguments in the institutional and political context of the prisoner experience. From these accounts of white prisoners the late modern prison appears disorientating, confusing, bewildering, and not as it should be. Minority ethnic prisoners are in the ascendancy in the stakes of cultural dominance in the social world of the prison, as Chapters 4 and 5 outlined. Now they also have institutional means at their disposal to further cement their objective position, or so it is imagined by white prisoners. There seems little possibility in returning to the moment when it was not so. There is a reluctant acceptance that multiculture is a permanent feature of the prison, but a frustration that this is so. Gilroy (2004: 98) talks of the national shock and resultant anxiety as Britain has had to recognize the absence of a distinct and coherent national culture in the aftermath of empire. In prison this seems to be true in two senses. First, many white prisoners' identities seem shorn of any value or cultural content, and this in itself can be a source of shame (Ray, Smith, and Wastell 2004; Earle 2011a), contrasted with what are seen as 'culture-rich' black and Asian identities. Secondly, long gone (if it ever existed) is the notion of a prisoner collective, united by the inhumane pains of incarceration, state coercion, and injustice, collectively felt, and spawning a united identity and oppositional force against prison officers (Sykes 1958; Crewe 2009). This ethnic and prisoner solidarity is sorely missed and hankered after; indeed, there is somewhat of an ironic sadness that this element of the old days of prison life are gone even though they were brutalizing times.

There may be others ways in which to interpret these narratives of white disadvantage, loss, and of being forgotten. One promising lead has been explored by Ware (2008), using German philosopher, Scheler's, concept of *ressentiment* which can accommodate some of the psychological import of the 'politics of resentment' as Ware refers to them (see also Loftus (2008) in the context of policing). Scheler (1913/1994: 25), following Nietzsche's lead, characterized *ressentiment* as a 'self-poisoning of the mind...a lasting mental attitude' associated with the emotions of 'revenge, hatred, malice, envy, the impulse to detract, and spite'. *Ressentiment* is likely to be present in situations where individuals feel proud but they are in a subordinate and powerless position, while the other—in this case minority ethnic prisoners—are perceived as being in a powerful position (see also Meltzer and Musolf 2002). It will fester in conditions where there is formal equality but where it can rarely be achieved in practice; of course, for Merton this created anomie. *Ressentiment* is more than this, however; it can only be said to exist when these precipitating feelings cannot be acted upon and must remain hidden, creating a strong sense of impotence. This is true in the climate of fear of the prison where to disparage the actions of minority ethnic prisoners or to disbelieve their perspectives may be tantamount to racism, an abhorrent identity for anyone these days, but especially in the proximal living conditions of the late modern prison which holds large concentrations of minority ethnic prisoners. Perhaps most worryingly of all, Scheler (1913/1994: 29) believed that the restoration of equal rights (or in the case of white prisoners their *perception of this*) does little to change *ressentiment* because there is a 'growing pleasure afforded by invective and negation'. It could therefore be speculated that the envy and spite which littered a minority of white prisoners' talk cannot easily be recalibrated since this is its very purpose, ensuring its continual perpetuation.

Similar ideas have been used by Jock Young (2009) with regard to public and political reactions to criminals, picking up a thread in Cohen's (1965) ideas of moral indignation and the punitiveness that follows. Applied to white prisoners' plaintive narratives, there is an irate voice questioning the morality of minority ethnic prisoners' abuse of ethnic and religious protections against discrimination and inequality. And as Young (2009) observes, individuals can operate an attitude of 'sour grapes'—in the prison context, white prisoners can lambast, reject, but also understandably lament and covet the extra food portions, time out of cell, queue-jumping, and brotherly solidarity that is perceived to be variously available to black, Asian, and Muslim prisoners.

There is one final issue I consider before concluding this chapter, and that is the problem of penal legitimacy. Applying Bottoms and Tankebe's (2012) conceptual analysis of 'audience legitimacy' it is clear that there may be more than one prisoner audience to consider when thinking about how power-holders can maintain their authority legitimately. And as this chapter has indicated, in the context of what constitutes racism and racial equality in prison, this is clearly contested by different prisoner groups identified according to their race, ethnicity, faith, and nationality, who may have competing or divergent priorities. Tyler's (2010) procedural justice model fundamentally rests on the idea of fairness—a concept which is purportedly unambiguous. Members of the public are law-abiding and compliant because they have a faith and a belief in the inherent fairness of the criminal justice system to dispense justice. In prison, Tyler argues that prisoners give their consent to be controlled by prison officers because they accept that the rules of the prison are fair. But this raises important questions in the context of race equality. Is there a legitimacy deficit when minority ethnic prisoners experience subtle forms of discrimination? How can there be justice inside when some groups are perceived to unfairly claim concessions and dishonestly gain privileges? If these conditions impede the development of penal legitimacy, how can social order be guaranteed? Are the politics of resentment a prequel to a breakdown in prison order? It is anticipated that future work in this area will shed further light on this (Jackson et al. 2010; Taylor, D. 2010). There are some useful pointers in Tyler's (2010) outline which can translate to giving a voice to *all* prisoners in developing and implementing equalities policies and ensuring the neutral, respectful, and robust application of rules on equality to *all* groups of prisoners as a means of achieving genuine compliance or 'true audience legitimacy' (Bottoms and Tankebe 2012: 149; but see Crewe 2011a).

Discussion

This chapter has described the contorted inflections of racism in the late modern prison which defy a simplistic binary. They have provided a lens with which to explore the meanings of racism in late modern Britain within a specific institutional site. Present are the familiar tales of racial discrimination perpetrated by white prison officers; but the racist brutality of past times is pleasingly rare, although not necessarily non-existent. Prisoners themselves often remarked on improvements in this regard in the post-CRE equalities climate, and for some, particularly younger prisoners at Rochester, racism had not framed their prison experiences. For those alleging racist victimization, however, the hurt, humiliation, and anxieties of these discriminatory practices, over which one has little or no control, represents another layer of the diminution of the self in prison. But it is a pain which is stoically shrugged off in the spirit of fatalism, accepting the racialized status quo which exists inside and outside the prison walls. This carrying of additional painful and emotional baggage has largely escaped research attention despite its undoubted significance. Whilst these sharply felt inequalities resemble the deprivations, frustrations, and anxieties that have always marked the experience of imprisonment, they are only inherent to it in that they are inherent to any social relations in postcolonial societies where vestiges of racism forever linger (Goldberg 2009).

This picture of painful prison social relations marked by racist practices sometimes hidden but present in backstage and sometimes front-stage arenas, had its parallel. This featured the perceived injuries of reverse racism, identified by disgruntled white prisoners, whose political assertions, although not yet loud, could be regarded fittingly as a 'sullen movement' (Hewitt 2005: 34). This indignant camp visualized the victory of minority ethnic prisoners and the defeat of white majority prisoners in the politically correct world of race equality in prison. The pendulum has swung too far in the opposite direction of white racism (Rhodes 2010). At its core this narrative sees a zero-sum game where racial equality for long-discriminated-against minority ethnic groups cannot be attained without the equivalent disadvantage of the white majority. The rules of the game have changed and the white majority are now the beleaguered, to use Clarke and Garner's term, and no longer top of racial hierarchies, or so it is perceived. Like Clarke et al.'s (2009: 150) English respondents, some white prisoners also saw being white British as a 'social location of relative weakness that now has to be defended'. The forgotten white majority have to defend against equalities and diversities policies which are a sop to political correctness.

That the terrain of racialized prison social relations was so uneven with regard to prison officer–prisoner relationships should not really come as a surprise given the similar analyses found in Chapters 4 and 5. I turn now to consider the implications of these variegated research findings in order comprehensively to understand the racial temperature and nature of prisoner identities and social relations in the late modern multicultural prison.

7
Conclusion

Outside prison, scholars and pundits have earnestly discussed, in the wake of the 7/7 bombings in London, the retreat, even the end, of multiculturalism. And whilst this may represent little more than 'wishful thinking' (Gilroy 2004: 1), in the prison such debates are redundant. Prisoners with diverse identities are brought together in strained and pained circumstances and they have no option but to live together. It is true that the composition of prison populations in England and Wales does vary, and the dynamics described in this book may have relevance only for those prisons which are multicultural, but given the links between criminality, urban locales, and race, Rochester and Maidstone prisons will be like many others in the prison estate of England and Wales. However, far from being blind to difference, the Prison Service has implemented a major reform of its policies which recognizes diverse ethnic, religious, and national identities. The prison is not an environment where identities, or anything else for that matter, can be privatized, which is the traditional call of opponents of liberal multiculturalism wishing to maintain the neutrality of the state (Barry 2001). Multiculturalism is both alive and kicking in the late modern prison. That multiculturalism is alive is meant in both its literal senses. It is a fact of life in prison that an ethnic monitoring system exists because of both the potential and actuality of ethnically disproportionate outcomes in prisoner treatment, access to goods, services, and facilities, with measures also in place to respond to complaints and racist incidents.[1] Prison managers, officers, other staff, and prisoners are sensitized to the potential implications of multicultural difference in the social world of the prison.

But multiculturalism is also alive in another sense. In a recent article Les Back (2009) describes his conversation with a white

---

[1] Now Discrimination Incidents covering discrimination, harassment, and victimization for all protected characteristics.

fishmonger in a market in south-east London who is lamenting the changed multicultural landscape of his community; he now sells red snapper and monkfish for the 'black and ethnic people' rather than plaice and haddock for the indigenous white majority. In his interrogation of these narratives which speak poignantly of cultural loss there is another remarkable story to be told. This is one where the fishmonger and his 'ethnic' customers engage in 'rituals of sociality and banter' in real time, haggling over prices, sharing recipes, and multicultural London is a place where 'people within this diverse social fabric, regardless of the repeated pronouncements to the contrary, simply get along, acknowledge each other, live alongside each other intimately, and even learn to love each other' (Back 2009: 209).

The picture is, of course, more complicated in the multicultural prison. Surviving 'doing time' is paramount in the wake of a variety of emotional, mental, and (at least threatened) physical assaults on the self. Few prisoners are looking for intimacy or love inside and fewer still want to 'belong' to the prison in any meaningful sense (Clemmer 1958; Phillips, C. 2007). But within these constrained conditions prisoners *are* engaging in a lively, vibrant, and dynamic multiculture in which racial difference is not always foregrounded. White prisoners learning about the tribal histories and culture of the Congolese, Muslim prisoners respecting the right of non-Muslim prisoners' to cook bacon, Bangladeshi prisoners cooking and exchanging food with Turkish prisoners, and white prisoners blasting grime beats from their cells are all emblematic of this multicultural backdrop. This is all the more radical because of its location. Prosaic encounters between prisoners on the wings, in education classes, and in workshops were often ordinary, mundane, and routine, demonstrating a sociality without incident. Communication across ethnic, religious, and national boundaries did not necessarily present insurmountable difficulties among prisoners and, where problems did arise, like in the self-cook areas at Maidstone prison, they could often be resolved through cooperation and compromise. And while the typical aphorism that when America sneezes Britain catches a cold is increasingly rejected across the criminal justice terrain, the absence of fine-grained accounts of the role of race in *prisoner* social relations in England and Wales is all too easily occupied by an imaginary of an American racial dystopia. However, far from visions of racially segregated factions underwritten by gang politics, this study has shown the multicultural

English prison to be less fraught, less violent, and less racially divided than its American counterpart (but see Liebling, Arnold, and Straub 2012). These positive indicators should not be dismissed in the political pessimism which portrays Britain as divided.

Multicultural conviviality inside is partially imported from outside communities where diversity is lived 'on road' in the urban locales of London and beyond. Ethnic, racial, and religious identities have been shaped in outside communities but are often overlaid with local identities of the postcode, housing estate, or neighbourhood, and this is also a feature of the suburban and semi-rural areas of Kent from where many white prisoners hailed. Spatial solidarities provide for a collective mode of being inside, a basis for sociality and companionship, and when required in the context of prisoner disputes, protection, with these localized identities a vehicle for the active demonstration of a young working-class masculinity. But masculinity inside prison needs to be understood in its plural forms—violent domination is one manifestation but it is not the only expression of manhood. Male prisoners utilize positive, agential behaviours to uphold a sense of masculine self-esteem through their use of body capital in the gym, for example, or by 'doing fatherhood inside'.

These lives of both white and minority ethnic prisoners can also be understood through the lens of macro-sociological accounts of penality in late modernity. Brought into sharp focus by these analyses are the 'wretched' who occupy an inferior position in the social structure as well as comprising the main constituents of prison populations in England and Wales and elsewhere. Without denying agency there is something of an irrevocability of the endgame of prison among many of those deeply affected by socio-economic marginality in post-Fordist societies. This is a feature which can transcend or be compounded by race and ethnicity, but indisputably affecting many if not most of the white, black, Asian, and other prisoners who shared their stories in this book. Their narratives fill the outlines of human faces and experiences only sketched in the macro-level theses (Hannah-Moffat and Lynch 2012). In addition to having a low social position in common, these prisoners share the inherent (and new) pains of imprisonment although the ties between them are much more loosely drawn than suggested in Sykes' (1958) seminal work. The deprivations created by the indigeneity of the carceral experience suggest an essential quality to the prison experience which is shared by prisoners regardless of their social identities and biographical histories. But importantly they are not reducible to material circumstances alone and it would be an error to assume that race can simply be subsumed by class. Prisoners' identities are complexly constituted in the round and are not fixed.

The everyday rhythm of multicultural conviviality is often punctuated by an edginess which pervades some encounters between prisoners. In the underbelly of prisoner society, racialized tensions often bubble just below the surface. There is an unsettling of traditional hierarchies of race in social relations with blackness a marker of prestige in the cultural politics of the prison. This new dominance is disorientating for white prisoners who find themselves unsure of these new politics in which they are not necessarily dominant, and may themselves face a denigration of their white identities. There may be a reversion to a boundary-making which posits black inferiority, but in the political context, when being labelled as racist carries such negative cachet and risks disciplinary attention from prison authorities, such views often seek private expression behind doors.

The textured story told in this book highlights the absence of a singular picture of race and identity inside. Manifestations of racism in the two prisons in this study seem to be all of these at once: distant, absent even, yet familiarly present, albeit rather hazy. I return again to the issue of racism in football which I referred to in the Preface to this book. The saga of the alleged racist abuse of England player and Chelsea football club captain, John Terry, is still unfolding at the time of writing. Usefully I think, it has begun to open up discussions about what is meant by and counts as racism, what harms it can do and under what circumstances, what the role of the criminal justice system should be in responding to racist abuse, as well as highlighting the consensus that racism, which has long been associated with English football, can no longer harbour there. Equally telling, however, is the backlash to these claims of racism; the alleged victim Anton Ferdinand has received anonymous death threats and a bullet in the post. Defenders of racist practices still have a voice, albeit a marginal one. There is not as much distance between the football field and the prison wing as might be imagined and while this incident will undoubtedly blow over eventually, it serves to illustrate the tangles and ambiguities of race and racism in the early 21st century. These bear a striking resemblance to the complex dimensions of race in the prison social world.

Inside the prison, multicultural conviviality waxes and wanes, significant numbers of prisoners do not assert their identity through their ethnicity, yet blackness is culturally dominant while whiteness seems devoid of meaning, and racism is either avidly disavowed or claimed to have been erased, while for others it is now just better concealed, less blatant, perhaps migrating to covert forms and backstage arenas among both prisoners and prison officers. A new element of prison social relations reproduces familiar fault lines of exclusion/inclusion but there has been a repositioning in the sides taken. Entitlement, inequality, and discrimination framed within a discourse of equalities policies have opened up a seething white resentment of perceived minority ethnic advantage. Whether this 'sullen movement' as described by Hewitt (2005: 34) gains political wings in the future remains to be seen.

The portrait of prisoner identities painted in this book has been made possible by looking for interpretative analyses outside the discipline of criminology, in the sociologies of race, ethnicity, gender, and masculinities, to make sense of the complex meanings of identity and identification, individually and collectively, and for making explicit the frames with which they are interpreted at the micro, meso, and macro levels of the social structure (Bloch and Solomos 2010). These should not be peripheral issues within criminology given the core interest of the discipline in questions of social order, social justice, and in acknowledging how punishment is inextricably linked with inequality, and the particular forms it takes when it involves men from a low social position who are often racialized. As prison scholars have long observed, the prison walls are porous and there is much to be learned from other disciplines to explicate what goes on inside.

From a policy perspective there is now an onus on prisons as public authorities to prohibit discrimination, harassment, and victimization and to remove disadvantage. Additionally in the Equalities Act 2010 there is a public sector duty to 'foster good relations between persons who share a relevant protected characteristic (for example race, ethnicity, nationality, religion) and persons who do not share it'. Inevitably this means confronting the claims of the 'sullen movement'. Assuming that they form a reactionary wedge in the prisoner population will do more to inflame than constructively inform prison social relations. In PSI 32/2011, the recent directive to prison staff, it is suggested that prison managers look to ways of tackling prejudice and increasing understanding. This is challenging work and unlikely to be seen as core prison business, but it offers a potential means to stave off potential racialized disorder. The fragility of racialized social relations in prison will not alter without non-blaming and frank intervention which unpacks the realities of racisms inside, acknowledging their multiple manifestations from the perspectives of all constituent groups including the white majority of prisoners and prison staff. Future research should seek to shed light on whether institutional practices can play a part in fermenting or moderating white opposition to achieving equality in prison. Haney (2006: 326) argues that it 'is unrealistic and unfair to expect prisons to become engines for broader social reform, or to insist on a level of racial harmony and cooperation in correctional institutions that has proven difficult to attain elsewhere in society'. And yet this is probably the most effective way to protect against large-scale racialized disturbances or racist violence inside. The prison can be seen as an unsteady space of cultural displacement where there is the possibility of disrupting existing stereotypes and transgressing fixed notions of identity to create a positive sociality.[2] This book has illustrated moments and encounters where this has occurred and there are undoubtedly ways of facilitating positive interactions between prisoners of diverse ethnic, religious, national, and cultural origins. Cultivating and encouraging the vibrant dynamism, rather than the melancholic cynicism, of multicultural diversity must be in the forefront of future work in prisons.

---

[2] Amin's (2002: 970) examples of 'threshold spaces' include further education colleges which students attend outside their residential area and night-time/weekend leisure spaces where individuals may be more receptive to establishing new friendships. Participatory theatre may provide a platform for such work in prisons (see, eg Yuval-Davis and Kaptani 2009).

References

Abu-Lughod, J. (2008) 'The Challenge of Comparative Case Studies', *City* 11(3): 399–404.

Aldridge, J. and Medina, J. (2008) *Youth Gangs in an English City: Social Exclusion, Drugs and Violence. End of Award Report* (Res-000-23-0615) (Swindon: Economic and Social Research Council).

Alexander, C. (1996) *The Art of Being Black* (Oxford: Oxford University Press).

——, (2000a) '(Dis)Entangling the "Asian Gang": Ethnicity, Identity, Masculinity', in B. Hesse (ed.), *Un/Settled Multiculturalisms; Diasporas, Entanglements, Transruptions* (London: Zed Books).

——, (2000b) *The Asian Gang: Ethnicity, Identity, Masculinity* (Oxford: Berg).

——, (2008) *(Re)Thinking Gangs* (London: Runnymede Trust).

Alexander, M. (2010) *The New Jim Crow: Mass Incarceration in the Age of Colorblindness* (New York, NY: The New Press).

Alford, R.G. (1909) *Notes on the Buildings of English Prisons. Volume I: London Prisons, and Aylesbury to Borstal*.

Ali, S. (2003) *Mixed-Race, Post-Race: Gender, New Ethnicities and Cultural Practices* (Oxford: Berg).

——, (2006) 'Racializing Research: Managing Power and Politics?', *Ethnic and Racial Studies* 29(3): 471–86.

Allport, G.W. (1954) *The Nature of Prejudice* (Reading, MA: Addison-Wesley).

Amin, A. (2002) 'Ethnicity and the Multicultural City: Living with Diversity', *Environment and Planning* A 34(6): 959–80.

Anderson, E. (1999/2006) 'The Code of the Streets', in F.T. Cullen and R. Agnew (eds), *Criminological Theory Past to Present: Essential Readings* (3rd edn) (Los Angeles, CA: Roxbury).

Archer, L. (2001) '"Muslim Brothers, Black Lads, Traditional Asians": British Muslim Young Men's Constructions of Race, Religion and Masculinity', *Feminism & Psychology* 11(1): 79–105.

——, (2003) *Race, Masculinity and Schooling* (Maidenhead: Open University Press).

——, and Yamashita, H. (2003) 'Theorising Inner-City Masculinities: "Race", Class, Gender and Education', *Gender and Education* 15(2): 115–32.

Ash, J. (2010) *Dress Behind Bars: Prison Clothing as Criminality* (London: I.B. Tauris).

Aull Davies, C. (1999) *Reflexive Ethnography* (London: Routledge).

Back, L. (1996) *New Ethnicities and Urban Culture: Racisms and Multi-culture in Young Lives* (London: UCL Press).

——, (2007) *The Art of Listening* (Oxford: Berg).

——, (2009) 'Researching Community and Its Moral Projects', *21st Century Society* 4(2): 201–14.

Bandyopadhyay, M. (2006) 'Competing Masculinities in a Prison', *Men and Masculinities* 9(2): 186–203.

Barker, M. (1981) *The New Racism: Conservatives and the Ideology of the Tribe* (London: Junction Books).

Barnett-Page, C. (2010) 'Structured Communications in Prison: A Project to Achieve More Consistent Performance and Fairer Outcomes for Staff and Prisoners', *Prison Service Journal* 191: 18–23.

Barry, B. (2001) *Culture and Equality* (Oxford: Polity Press).

Barth, F. (1969) *Ethnic Groups and Boundaries: The Social Organisation of Culture Difference* (Long Grove, IL: Waveland Press).

Bartollas, C., Miller, S.J., and Dinitz, S. (1976) *Juvenile Victimization: The Institutional Paradox* (New York, NY: Sage).

Bauman, Z. (2004) *Identity* (Cambridge: Polity).

Becker, A.J. and Harrison, P.M. (2001) *Prisoners in 2000.* NCJ 188207 (Washington, DC: Bureau of Justice Statistics).

Beckford, J.A., Joly, D., and Khosrokhavar, F. (2005) *Muslims in Prison—Challenge and Change in Britain and France* (Basingstoke: Palgrave).

Bennett, T. and Holloway, K. (2004) 'Gang Membership, Drugs and Crime in the UK', *British Journal of Criminology* 44(3): 305–23.

Berg, M.T. and DeLisi, M. (2006) 'The Correctional Melting Pot: Race, Ethnicity, Citizenship, and Prison Violence', *Journal of Criminal Justice* 34(6): 631–42.

Berjot, S. and Gillet, N. (2011) 'Stress and Coping with Discrimination and Stigmatization', *Frontiers in Psychology* 2(33): 1–13.

Berman, G. (2010) *Prison Population Statistics.* SN/SG/4334 (London: House of Commons Library).

——, (2012) *Prison Population Statistics.* SN/SG/4334 (London: House of Commons Library).

Bernasco, W. (ed.) (2010) *Offenders on Offending: Learning about Crime from Criminals* (Cullompton: Willan Publishing).

Bhattacharyya, G., Gabriel, J., and Small, S. (2002) *Race and Power: Global Racism in the Twenty-First Century* (London: Routledge).

Bhui, H.S. (2007) 'Alien Experience: Foreign National Prisoners after the Deportation Crisis', *Probation Journal* 54(4): 368–82.

Biddiss, M. (1999) 'Gobineau and the Origins of European Racism', in M. Bulmer and J. Solomos (eds), *Racism* (Oxford: Oxford University Press).

Blagden, N. and Pemberton, S. (2010) 'The Challenge in Conducting Qualitative Research with Convicted Sex Offenders', *The Howard Journal of Criminal Justice* 49(3): 269–81.

Bloch, A. and Solomos, J. (2010) 'Key Questions in the Sociology of Race and Ethnicity', in A. Bloch and J. Solomos (eds), *Race and Ethnicity in the 21st Century* (Basingstoke: Palgrave).

Bohrman, R. and Murakawa, N. (2005) 'Remaking Big Government: Immigration and Crime Control in the United States', in J. Sudbury (ed.), *Global Lockdown: Race, Gender, and the Prison-Industrial Complex* (London: Routledge).

Bosworth, M. (1999) *Engendering Resistance: Agency and Power in Women's Prisons* (Aldershot: Dartmouth Publishing Company Limited).

——, (2011) 'Deportation, Detention and Foreign-National Prisoners in England and Wales', *Citizenship Studies* 15(5): 583–95.

——, and Carrabine, E. (2001) 'Reassessing Resistance: Race, Gender and Sexuality in Prison', *Punishment & Society* 3(4): 501–15.

——, and Guil, M. (2008) 'Governing through Migration Control: Security and Citizenship in Britain', *British Journal of Criminology* 48(6): 703–19.

——, Campbell, D., Demby, B., Ferranti, S., and Santos, M. (2005) 'Doing Prison Research: Views from Inside', *Qualitative Inquiry* 11(2): 249–64.

Bottoms, A. and Tankebe, J. (2012) 'Beyond Procedural Justice: A Dialogic Approach to Legitimacy in Criminal Justice', *The Journal of Criminal Law and Criminology* 102(1): 119–70.

Bourgois, P.I. (1995) *In Search of Respect: Selling Crack in El Barrio* (Cambridge: Cambridge University Press).

Bourne, J. (2001) 'The Life and Times of Institutional Racism', *Race and Class* 43(2): 7–22.

Bowling, B. and Phillips, C. (2002) *Racism, Crime and Justice* (Harlow: Pearson Education).

Bradshaw, P. (2005) 'Terrors and Young Teams: Youth Gangs and Delinquency in Edinburgh', in S.H. Decker and F.M. Weerman (eds), *European Street Gangs and Troublesome Youth Groups* (Lanham, MD: Altamira Press).

Brah, A. (1996) *Cartographies of Diaspora* (London: Routledge).

——, and Phoenix, A. (2009) 'Ain't I a Woman? Revisiting Intersectionality', in E. Taylor, D. Gillborn and G. Ladson-Billings (eds), *Foundations of Critical Race Theory in Education* (New York, NY: Routledge).

Buchanan, D., Boddy, D., and McCalman, J. (1988) 'Getting in, Getting on, Getting out and Getting Back', in A. Bryman (ed.), *Doing Research in Organizations* (London: Routledge).

Butler, J. (1989) *Gender Trouble: Feminism and the Subversion of Identity* (London: Routledge).

Camp, S.D., Gaes, G., Langan, N.P., and Saylor, W.G. (2003) 'The Influence of Prisons on Inmate Misconduct: A Multilevel Investigation', *Justice Quarterly* 20(3): 501–34.

Cantle, T. (2001) *Community Cohesion: A Report of the Independent Review Team* (London: Home Office).

Carlen, P. (2010) 'Book Review of the Prisoner Society: Power, Adaptation and Social Life in an English Prison', *British Journal of Criminology* 50(5): 977–80.

Carrabine, E. (2004) *Power, Discourse and Resistance: A Genealogy of the Strangeways Prison Riot* (Aldershot: Ashgate).

——, and Longhurst, B. (1998) 'Gender and Prison Organisation: Some Comments on Masculinities and Prison Management', *Howard Journal of Criminal Justice* 37(2): 161–76.

Carroll, L. (1974) *Hacks, Blacks and Cons: Race Relations in a Maximum Security Prison* (London: DC Heath).

Carroll, L. (1982) 'Race, Ethnicity and the Social Order of the Prison', in R. Johnson and H. Toch (eds), *The Pains of Imprisonment* (Beverly Hills, CA: Sage).

Carter, J. (2000) 'New Public Management and Equal Opportunities in the NHS', *Critical Social Policy* 20(1): 61–83.

Castles, S. and Miller, M.J. (2003) *The Age of Migration: International Population Movements in the Modern World* (3rd edn) (New York, NY: Guilford Press).

Cheliotis, L.K. and Liebling, A. (2006) 'Race Matters in British Prisons: Towards a Research Agenda', *British Journal of Criminology* 46(2): 286–317.

——, and Xenakis, S. (2010) 'What's Neoliberalism Got to Do with It? Towards a Political Economy of Punishment in Greece', *Criminology and Criminal Justice* 10(4): 353–73.

Cheney, D. (1993) *Into the Dark Tunnel: Foreign Prisoners in the British Prison System* (London: The Prison Reform Trust).

Clarke, L., O'Brien, M., Day, R.D., Godwin, H., Connolly, J., Hemmings, J., and van Leeson, T. (2005) 'Fathering behind Bars in English Prisons: Imprisoned Fathers' Identity and Contact with Their Children', *Fathering* 3(3): 221–42.

Clarke, S. and Garner, S. (2010) *White Identities: A Critical Sociological Approach* (London: Pluto).

Clear, T.R., Hardyman, P.L., Stout, B., Lucken, K., and Dammer, H.R. (2000) 'The Value of Religion in Prison: An Inmate Perspective', *Journal of Contemporary Criminal Justice* 16(1): 53–74.

Cleaver, E. (1968) *Soul on Ice* (New York, NY: Dell Publishing Co).

Clemmer, D. (1958/1940) *The Prison Community* (New York, NY: Rinehart & Company).

Cohen, A. (1965) 'The Sociology of the Deviant Act: Anomie Theory and Beyond', *American Sociological Review* 30(1): 5–14.

Collier, R. (1998) *Masculinities, Crime and Criminology: Men, Heterosexuality and the Criminal(Ised) Other* (London: Sage).

Comfort, M. (2008a) '"The Best Seven Year I Could'a Done": The Reconstruction of Imprisonment as Rehabilitation', in P. Carlen (ed.), *Imaginary Penalties* (Cullompton: Willan Publishing).

——, (2008b) *Doing Time Together: Love and Family in the Shadow of the Prison* (Chicago, IL: University of Chicago Press).

Commission for Racial Equality (2003a) *A Formal Investigation by the Commission for Racial Equality into HM Prison Service of England and Wales—Part 2: Racial Equality in Prisons* (London: Commission for Racial Equality).

——, (2003b) *A Formal Investigation by the Commission for Racial Equality into HM Prison Service of England and Wales—Part 1: The Murder of Zahid Mubarek* (London: Commission for Racial Equality).

Connell, R.W. (1987) *Gender and Power: Society, the Person, and Sexual Politics* (Standford, CA: Stanford University Press).

——, (1995) *Masculinities* (Berkeley, CA: University of California Press).

——, (2005) *Masculinities* (2nd edn) (Berkeley, CA: University of California Press).

——, and Messerschmidt, J.W. (2005) 'Hegemonic Masculinity: Rethinking the Concept', *Gender and Society* 19(6): 829–59.

Copes, H. and Hochstetler, A. (2010) 'Interviewing the Incarcerated: Pitfalls and Promises', in W. Bernasco (ed.), *Offenders on Offending: Learning about Crime from Criminals* (Cullompton: Willan Publishing).

Copsey, N. (2011) 'Introduction: Contemporary Perspectives on the British National Party', in N. Copsey and G. Macklin (eds), *British National Party: Contemporary Perspectives* (London: Routledge).

Cowburn, M. and Dominelli, L. (2001) 'Masking Hegemonic Masculinity: Reconstructing the Paedophile as the Dangerous Stranger', *British Journal of Social Work* 31(3): 399–415.

——, and Lavis, V. (2009) 'Race Relations in Prison: Managing Performance and Developing Engagement', *British Journal of Community Justice* 7(3): 77–89.

Cowlishaw, G. (2004) *Blackfellas, Whitefellas, and the Hidden Injuries of Race* (Oxford: Blackwell).

Creegan, C., Colgan, F., Charlesworth, R., and Robinson, G. (2003) 'Race Equality Policies at Work: Employee Perceptions of the "Implementation Gap" in a UK Local Authority', *Work, Employment and Society* 17(4): 617–40.

Crenshaw, K. (1989) 'Demarginalizing the Intersection of Race and Sex: A Black Feminist Critique of Antidiscrimination Doctrine, Feminist Theory, and Antiracist Politics', University of Chicago Legal Forum: 139–67.

Crenshaw, K. (1993) 'Mapping the Margins: Intersectionality, Identity Politics, and Violence against Women of Color', *Stanford Law Review* 43(6): 1241–99.

Crewe, B. (2005) 'Prisoner Society in the Era of Hard Drugs', *Punishment and Society* 7(4): 457–81.

——, (2006) 'Male Prisoners' Orientations towards Female Officers in an English Prison', *Punishment and Society* 8(4): 395–421.

——, (2009) *The Prisoner Society: Power, Adaptation and Social Life in an English Prison* (Oxford: Oxford University Press).

——, (2011a) 'Depth, Weight, Tightness: Revisiting the Pains of Imprisonment', *Punishment and Society* 13(5): 509–29.

——, and Jewkes, Y. (2011) 'Introduction', *Punishment and Society* 13(5): 507–8.

Daems, T. (2008) *Making Sense of Penal Change* (Oxford: Oxford University Press).

Davis, A.Y. (2003) *Are Prisons Obsolete?* (New York, NY: Seven Stories Press).

——, (2005) *Abolition Democracy: Beyond Empire, Prisons, and Torture* (New York, NY: Seven Stories Press).

De Giorgi, A. (2006) *Re-Thinking the Political Economy of Punishment: Perspectives on Post-Fordism and Penal Politics* (Aldershot: Ashgate).

Dench, G., Gavron, K., and Young, M. (2006) *The New East End: Kinship, Race and Conflict* (London: Profile Books).

Department for Communities and Local Government (2011) *Race, Religion and Equalities: A Report on the 2009–10 Citizenship Survey* (London: DCLG).

Diaz-Cotto, J. (1996) *Gender, Ethnicity and the State: Latina and Latino Prison Politics* (Albany, NY: State University of New York Press).

Dobbs, J., Green, H., and Zealey, L. (2006) *Focus on Ethnicity and Religion* (2006 edn) (London: National Statistics).

Du Bois, W.E.B. (1901/2007) 'The Spawn of Slavery: The Convict-Lease System in the South (1901)', in S.L. Gabbidon (ed.), *W.E.B. Du Bois on Crime and Justice: Laying the Foundations of Sociological Criminology* (Aldershot: Ashgate).

Duneier, M. (2004) 'Three Rules I Go by in My Ethnographic Research on Race and Racism', in M. Bulmer and J. Solomos (eds), *Researching Race and Racism* (Basingstoke: Palgrave).

Dwyer, P. (2005) 'Governance, Forced Migration and Welfare', *Social Policy and Administration* 39(6): 622–39.

Earle, R. (2011a) 'Boys' Zone Stories: Perspectives from a Young Men's Prison', *Criminology and Criminal Justice* 11(2): 129–43.

——, (2011b) 'Ethnicity, Multiculture and Racism in a Young Offenders' Institution', *Prison Service Journal* 197: 32–8.

Earle, R. and Phillips, C. (2012) 'Digesting Men: Punishment, Gender and Food—Perspectives from a Prison Ethnography', *Theoretical Criminology* 16(2) 140–155.

Edgar, K. and Martin, C. (2004) *Perceptions of Race and Conflict: Perspectives of Minority Ethnic Prisoners and of Prison Officers. RDS Online Report 11/04* (London: Home Office).

——, O'Donnell, I., and Martin, C. (2003) *Prison Violence: The Dynamics of Conflict, Fear and Power* (Cullompton: Willan Publishing).

Edley, N. and Wetherell, M. (1997) 'Jockeying for Position: The Construction of Masculine Identities', *Discourse and Society* 8(2): 203–17.

Elam Jr, H.J. and Elam, M. (2010) 'Race and Racial Formations', in M. Wetherell and C.T. Mohanty (eds), *The Sage Handbook of Identities* (London: Sage).

Ellis, D., Grasmick, H.G., and Gilman, B. (1974) 'Violence in Prisons: A Sociological Analysis', *American Journal of Sociology* 80(1): 16–43.

Ellis, T., Tedstone, C., and Curry, D. (2004) *Improving Race Relations in Prison: What Works?* (London: Home Office).

Evans, T. and Wallace, P. (2008) 'A Prison within a Prison?: The Masculinity Narratives of Male Prisoners', *Men and Masculinities* 10(4): 484–507.

Eze, E. (1997) *Race and the Enlightenment: A Reader* (Oxford: Blackwell).

Falcous, M. and Silk, M.L. (2010) 'Olympic Bidding, Multicultural Nationalism, Terror, and the Epistemological Violence of "Making Britain Proud"', *Studies in Ethnicity and Nationalism* 10(2): 167–86.

Fanon, F. (1963/2001) *The Wretched of the Earth* (London: Penguin Books).

——, (1967/2008) *Black Skin, White Masks* (London: Pluto Press).

Fekete, L. (2009) *A Suitable Enemy: Racism, Migration and Islamophobia in Europe* (London: Pluto Press).

——, and Webber, F. (2010) 'Foreign Nationals, Enemy Penology and the Criminal Justice System', *Race and Class* 51(4): 1–25.

Fenton, S. (2003) *Ethnicity* (Cambridge: Polity).

Ferguson, C. and Hussey, D. (2010) *2008–09 Citizenship Survey Race, Religion and Equalities Topic Report* (London: Communities and Local Government).

Finney, N. and Simpson, L. (2009) *'Sleepwalking to Segregation'? Challenging Myths about Race and Migration* (Bristol: Policy Press).

Folkman, S. and Lazarus, R.S. (1980) 'An Analysis of Coping in a Middle Aged Community Sample', *Journal of Health and Social Behaviour* 21(3): 219–39.

Ford, R. (2008) 'Is Racial Prejudice Declining in Britain?', *British Journal of Sociology* 59(4): 609–36.

Forsythe, W.J. (1990) *Penal Discipline, Reformatory Projects and the English Prison Commission 1895–1939* (Exeter: University of Exeter Press).

Foster, J., Newburn, T., and Souhami, A. (2005) *Assessing the Impact of the Stephen Lawrence Inquiry. Home Office Research Study 294* (London: Home Office).

Foucault, M. (1975) *Discipline and Punish: The Birth of the Prison* (Harmondsworth: Penguin Books Ltd).

Fox, R. (1977) 'The Inherent Rules of Violence', in P. Collett (ed.), *Social Rules and Social Behaviour* (Oxford: Basil Blackwell).

Frankenberg, R. (1993) *White Women, Race Matters* (Minneapolis, MN: University of Minnesota Press).

Frosh, S., Phoenix, A., and Pattman, R. (2002) *Young Masculinities* (Basingstoke: Palgrave).

Frost, L. and Hoggett, P. (2008) 'Human Agency and Social Suffering', *Critical Social Policy* 28(4): 438–60.

Fuller, D.A. and Orsagh, T. (1977) 'Violence and Victimization within State Prisons', *Criminal Justice Review* 2(2): 35–55.

Gabbidon, S.L., Greene, H.T., and Young, V. (2001) *African American Classics in Criminology and Criminal Justice* (Thousand Oaks, CA: Sage).

Gadd, D. (2009) 'Aggravating Racism and Elusive Motivation', *British Journal of Criminology* 49(6): 755–71.

——, and Dixon, B. (2011) *Losing the Race: Thinking Psychosocially about Racially Motivated Crime* (London: Karnac).

Garland, D. (1990) *Punishment and Modern Society: A Study in Social Theory* (Oxford: Clarendon Press).

——, (2001) *The Culture of Control* (Oxford: Oxford University Press).

Garner, S. (2006) 'The Uses of Whiteness: What Sociologists Working on Europe Can Draw from US Research on Whiteness', *Sociology* 40(2): 257–75.

——, (2007) *Whiteness: An Introduction* (London: Routledge).

——, (2009) 'Home Truths: The White Working Class and the Racialization of Social Housing', in K.P. Sveinsson (ed.), *Who Cares About the White Working Class?* (London: Runnymede Trust).

Genders, E. and Player, E. (1989) *Race Relations in Prison* (Oxford: Clarendon Press).

Gibson, R.K. (2002) *The Growth of Anti-Immigrant Parties in Western Europe* (Lewiston, NY: Edwin Mellen Press).

Gilroy, P. (2004) *After Empire: Melancholia or Convivial Culture?* (London: Routledge).

——, (2005) 'Multiculture, Double Consciousness and the "War on Terror"', *Patterns of Prejudice* 39(4): 431–43.

Gilroy, P. (2006) 'Multiculture in Times of War: An Inaugural Lecture Given at the London School of Economics', *Critical Quarterly* 48(4): 27–45.

Goffman, E. (1961) 'On the Characteristics of Total Institutions: The Inmate World', in D. Cressey (ed.), *The Prison: Studies in Institutional Organization and Change* (New York, NY: Holt, Rinehart, and Winston).

——, (1961) *Asylums: Essays on the Social Situation of Mental Patients and Other Inmates* (Garden City, NY: Anchor Books).

Goldberg, D.T. (2000) 'Surplus Value: The Political Economy of Prisons and Policing', in J. James (ed.), *States of Confinement: Policing, Detention and Prisons* (New York, NY: St Martin's Press).

——, (2002) *The Racial State* (Oxford: Wiley-Blackwell).

——, (2009) *The Threat of Race: Reflections on Racial Neoliberalism* (Oxford: Wiley-Blackwell).

Goldson, B. (ed.) (2011) *Youth in Crisis?: 'Gangs', Territoriality and Violence* (London: Routledge).

Goodman, P. (2008) '"It's Just Black, White, or Hispanic": An Observational Study of Racializing Moves in California's Segregated Prison Reception Centers', *Law and Society Review* 42(4): 735–70.

Gordon, P. (1983) *White Law: Racism in the Police, Courts and Prisons* (London: Pluto).

Gottschalk, M. (2006) *The Prisons and the Gallows: The Politics of Mass Incarceration in America* (Cambridge: Cambridge University Press).

——, (2011) 'The Past, Present, and Future of Mass Incarceration in the United States', *Criminology and Public Policy* 10(3): 483–504.

Grapendaal, M. (1990) 'The Inmate Subculture in Dutch Prisons', *British Journal of Criminology* 30(3): 341–57.

Gunaratnam, Y. (2003) *Researching 'Race' and Ethnicity: Methods, Knowledge and Power* (London: Sage).

Hagedorn, J.M. (2007) 'Introduction: Globalization, Gangs and Traditional Criminology', in J. Hagedorn (ed.), *Gangs in the Global City: Alternatives to Traditional Criminology* (Urbana, IL: University of Illinois Press).

Hales, G., Lewis, C., and Silverstone, D. (2006) *Gun Crime: The Market in and Use of Illegal Firearms. Home Office Research Study 298* (London: Home Office).

Hall, S. (1991/2000) 'Old and New Identities, Old and New Ethnicities', in L. Back and J. Solomos (eds), *Theories of Race and Racism* (London: Routledge).

——, Critcher, C., Jefferson, T., Clarke, J., and Roberts, B. (1978) *Policing the Crisis: Mugging, the State and Law and Order* (London: Macmillan).

Hallsworth, S. (2005) *Street Crime* (Cullompton: Willan Publishing).

——, and Silverstone, D. (2009) '"That's Life Innit": A British Perspective on Guns, Crime and Social Order', *Criminology and Criminal Justice* 9(3): 359–77.

——, and Young, T. (2008) 'Gang Talk and Gang Talkers: A Critique', *Crime, Media, Culture* 4(2): 175–95.

Hamm, M.S. (2009) 'Prison Islam in the Age of Sacred Terror', *British Journal of Criminology* 49(5): 667–85.

Haney, C. (2006) *Reforming Punishment: Psychological Limits to the Pains of Imprisonment* (Washington, DC: American Psychological Association).

Hannah-Moffat, K. and Lynch, M. (2012) 'Theorizing Punishment's Boundaries: An Introduction', *Theoretical Criminology* 16(2): 119–121.

Harding, S. (1987) *Feminism and Methodology* (Bloomington, IN: Indiana University Press).

Harris, R. (2006) *New Ethnicities and Language Use* (Basingstoke: Palgrave).

Harrison, M., Law, I., and Phillips, D. (2005) *Migrants, Minorities and Housing: Exclusion, Discrimination and Anti-Discrimination in 15 Member States of the European Union* (Vienna, Austria: European Monitoring Centre on Racism and Xenophobia).

Harvey, J. (2007) *Young Men in Prison* (Cullompton: Willan Publishing).

Haylett, C. (2001) 'Illegitimate Subjects? Abject Whites, Neoliberal Modernisation and Middle-Class Multiculturalism', *Environment and Planning D: Society and Space* 19: 351–70.

Heath, A. and Cheung, S.Y. (2006) *Ethnic Penalties in the Labour Market: Employers and Discrimination. Research Report No 341* (London: Department for Work and Pensions).

——, Rothon, C., and Ali, S. (2010) 'Identity and Public Opinion', in A. Bloch and J. Solomos (eds), *Race and Ethnicity in the 21st Century* (Basingstoke: Palgrave Macmillan).

Henderson, M., Cullen, F., and Carroll, L. (2000) 'Race, Rights, and Order in Prison: A National Survey of Wardens on the Racial Integration of Prison Cells', *Prison Journal* 80(3): 295–308.

Hertz, R. (1997) 'Introduction: Reflexivity and Voice', in R. Hertz (ed.), *Reflexivity and Voice* (Thousand Oaks, CA: Sage).

Hewitt, R. (2005) *White Backlash and the Politics of Multiculturalism* (Cambridge: Cambridge University Press).

Hill Collins, P. (2006) 'New Commodities, New Consumers: Selling Blackness in a Global Marketplace', *Ethnicities* 6(3): 297–317.

Hills, J., Brewer, M., Jenkins, S., Lister, R., Lupton, R., Machin, S., Mills, C., Modood, T., Rees, T., and Riddell, S. (2010) *An Anatomy of Economic Inequality in the UK: Report of the National Equality Panel* (London: Government Equalities Office).

HMIP (2004) *Report on a Full Unannounced Inspection of HMP Liverpool 6–10 September 2004* (London: HMIP).

——, (2005) *Parallel Worlds: A Thematic Review of Race Relations in Prisons* (London: HMIP).

——, (2006) *Foreign National Prisoners: A Thematic Review* (London: HMIP).

——, (2007a) *Foreign National Prisoners: A Follow-up Report* (London: HMIP).

——, (2007b) *Report on an Announced Inspection of HMP Maidstone 19–23 February 2001* (London: HMIP).

——, (2008) *Report on an Unannounced Full Follow-up Inspection of HMP Whitemoor 7–11 April 2008* (London: HMIP).

——, (2009) *Race Relations in Prisons: Responding to Adult Women from Black and Minority Ethnic Backgrounds* (London: HMIP).

——, (2010) *Muslim Prisoners' Experiences: A Thematic Review* (London: HMIP).

HMP Maidstone (2009) *Within the Walls: A History of Maidstone Prison, 1819–2009* (Brochure to Accompany an Exhibition at Maidstone Museum and Bentlif Art Gallery, 28 May to 26 July 2009) (Maidstone: Maidstone Prison).

HMPS (2001) *Annual Report and Accounts April 2000 to March 2001*, HC 29 (London: TSO).

——, (2006) *MQPL Survey Research Carried out at HMP Rochester between 15 & 18 May 2006.*

Hobbs, D. (1993) 'Peers, Careers, and Academic Fears: Writing as Field-Work', in D. Hobbs and T. May (eds), *Interpreting the Field: Accounts of Ethnography* (Oxford: Clarendon Press).

——, (1997) 'Criminal Collaboration: Youth Gangs, Subcultures, Professional Criminals and Organized Crime', in M. Maguire, R. Morgan, and R. Reiner (eds), *The Oxford Handbook of Criminology* (2nd edn) (Oxford: Oxford University Press).

Hollway, W. and Jefferson, T. (2000) *Doing Qualitative Research Differently: Free Association, Narrative and the Interview Method* (London: Sage).

Home Office (1986) *The Ethnic Origins of Prisoners: The Prison Population on 30 June 1985 and Persons Received, July 1984–March 1985. HOSB 17/86* (London: Home Office).

——, (2000) *Prison Statistics England and Wales 1999* (London: Home Office).

Hooks, B. (2004) *We Real Cool: Black Men and Masculinity* (London: Routledge).

Hopkins, P.E. (2006) 'Youthful Muslim Masculinities: Gender and Generational Relations', *Transactions—Institute of British Geographers* 31(3): 337–52.

Howarth, C. (2002) '"So You're from Brixton?" The Struggle for Recognition and Esteem in a Stigmatized Community', *Ethnicities* 2(2): 237–60.

Hudson, K. (2005) *Offending Identities: Sex Offenders' Perspectives of Their Treatment and Management* (Cullompton: Willan Publishing).

Huebner, B.M. (2003) 'Administrative Determinants of Inmate Violence: A Multilevel Analysis', *Journal of Criminal Justice* 31(2): 107–17.

Hughey, M.W. (2011) 'Backstage Discourse and the Reproduction of White Masculinities', *The Sociological Quarterly* 52(1): 132–53.

Ignatieff, M. (1989) *A Just Measure of Pain: The Penitentiary in the Industrial Revolution, 1750–1850* (Harmondsworth: Penguin).

IPSOS MORI (2006) CRE Race Relations Survey 2006 Topline Results <http://www.ipsos-mori.com/Assets/Docs/Archive/Polls/cre2.pdf:>

Irwin, J. (1970) *The Felon* (Berkeley, CA: University of California Press).

——, (1980) *Prisons in Turmoil* (Boston, MA: Little, Brown, and Company).

——, (2005) *The Warehouse Prison: Disposal of the New Dangerous Class* (Los Angeles, CA: Roxbury Publishing Co).

——, and Cressey, D.R. (1962) 'Thieves, Convicts and the Inmate Culture', *Social Problems* 10(2): 142–55.

Jackson, J., Tyler, T.R., Bradford, B., Taylor, D., and Shiner, M. (2010) 'Legitimacy and Procedural Justice in Prisons', *Prison Service Journal* 191: 4–10.

Jacobs, J.B. (1974) 'Street Gangs behind Bars', *Social Problems* 21(3): 395–409.

——, (1975) 'Stratification and Conflict among Prison Inmates', *Journal of Criminal Law & Criminology* 66(4): 476–82.

——, (1977) *Stateville: The Penitentiary in Mass Society* (Chicago, IL: The University of Chicago Press).

——, (1979) 'Race Relations and the Prisoner Subculture', in N. Morris and M. Tonry (eds), *Crime and Justice* (Chicago, IL: The University of Chicago Press).

Jacobson, J. (1997) 'Religion and Ethnicity: Dual and Alternative Sources of Identity among Young British Pakistanis', *Ethnic and Racial Studies* 20(2): 238–56.

Jean, W. (2002) 'Message to the Streets', *Masquerade*.

Jewkes, Y. (2002) *Captive Audience: Media, Masculinity and Power in Prisons* (Cullompton: Willan Publishing).

——, (2005) 'Men behind Bars: "Doing" Masculinity as an Adaptation to Imprisonment', *Men and Masculinities* 8(1): 44–63.

——, (2006) 'Creating a Stir? Prisons, Popular Media and the Power to Reform', in P. Mason (ed.), *Captured by the Media: Prison Discourse in Popular Culture* (Cullompton: Willan Publishing).

Johnston, H. (2012) 'Porridge: "A Night In"', *Prison Service Journal* 199: 10–12.

Johnston, R., Forrest, J., and Poulsen, M. (2002) 'The Ethnic Geography of Ethnicities: The "American Model" and Residential Concentration in London', *Ethnicities* 2(2): 209–35.

Joly, D. (2007) 'Race Relations and Islam in the Prison Service', *International Journal of Human Rights* 11(3): 307–26.

Jones, M. (2010) '"Impedimenta State" Anatomies of Neoliberal Penality', *Criminology and Criminal Justice* 10(4): 393–404.

Joppke, C. (2004) 'The Retreat of Multiculturalism in the Liberal State: Theory and Policy', *British Journal of Sociology* 55(2): 237–57.

Kalra, V.S. (2006) 'Ethnography as Politics: A Critical Review of British Studies of Racialized Minorities', *Ethnic and Racial Studies* 29(3): 452–70.

——, (2009) 'Between Emasculation and Hypermasculinity: Theorizing British South Asian Masculinities', *South Asian Popular Culture* 7(2): 113–25.

Katz, J. and Jackson-Jacobs, C. (2004) 'The Criminologists' Gang', in C. Sumner (ed.), *The Blackwell Companion to Criminology* (Oxford: Blackwell Publishing).

Kehily, M.J. and Nayak, A. (1997) '"Lads and Laughter": Humour and the Production of Heterosexual Hierarchies', *Gender and Education* 9(1): 69–88.

Keith, B. (2006) *Report of the Zahid Mubarek Inquiry*. HC 1082-I (London: HMSO).

Keith, M.J. (2008) 'Between Being and Becoming? Rights, Responsibilities and the Politics of Multiculture in the New East End', *Sociological Research Online* 13(5): 11.

Kent County Council (2011) *2009 Ethnic Population Estimates: MYEE/11–May 2011* (Maidstone: Kent County Council).

Kerley, K.R. and Copes, H. (2009) '"Keepin' My Mind Right": Identity Maintenance and Religious Social Support in the Prison Context', *International Journal of Offender Therapy and Comparative Criminology* 53(2): 228–44.

——, Matthews, T.L., and Blanchard, T.C. (2005) 'Religiosity, Religious Participation, and Negative Prison Behaviors', *Journal for the Scientific Study of Religion* 44(4): 443–57.

King, R.D. and Liebling, A. (2008) 'Doing Research in Prisons', in R.D. King and E. Wincup (eds), *Doing Research on Crime and Justice* (2nd edn) (Oxford: Oxford University Press).

Kintrea, K., Bannister, J., Pickering, J., Reid, M., and Suzuki, N. (2008) *Young People and Territoriality in British Cities* (York: Joseph Rowntree Foundation).

Klare, H.J. (1960) *Anatomy of Prison* (Harmondsworth: Penguin).

Knowles, C. (2003) *Race and Social Analysis* (London: Sage).

Krumer-Nevo, M. and Mirit, S. (2012) 'Writing against Othering', *Qualitative Inquiry* 18(4): 299–309.

Kruttschnitt, C. (1983) 'Race Relations and the Federal Inmate', *Crime and Delinquency* 294: 577–92.

——, and Hussemann, J. (2008) 'Micropolitics of Race and Ethnicity in Women's Prisons in Two Political Contexts', *The British Journal of Sociology* 59(4): 709–28.

Kymlicka, W. (1995) *Multicultural Citizenship* (Oxford: Clarendon Press).

——, (2007) *Multicultural Odysseys: Navigating the New International Politics of Diversity* (Oxford: Oxford University Press).

Kyriakides, C., Virdee, S., and Modood, T. (2009) 'Racism, Muslims and the National Imagination', *Journal of Ethnic and Migration Studies* 35(2): 289–308.

Lacey, N. (2008) *The Prisoners' Dilemma: Political Economy and Punishment in Contemporary Democracies* (Cambridge: Cambridge University Press).

——, (2010) 'Differentiating among Penal States', *British Journal of Sociology* 61(4): 778–94.

Lewis, J. (2002) 'The Problem of Fathers: Policy and Behaviour in Britain', in B. Hobson (ed.), *Making Men into Fathers: Men, Masculinities, and the Social Politics of Fatherhood* (Cambridge: Cambridge University Press).

Liebling, A. (1999) 'Doing Research in Prison: Breaking the Silence?', *Theoretical Criminology* 3(2): 147–73.

——, (2004) *Prisons and Their Moral Performance: A Study of Values, Quality, and Prison Life* (Oxford: Oxford University Press).

——, (2011) 'Moral Performance, Inhuman and Degrading Treatment and Prison Pain', *Punishment and Society* 13(5): 530–51.

——, Arnold, H., and Straub, C. (2012) *An Exploration of Staff-Prisoner Relationships at HMP Whitemoor: Twelve Years On* (London: MOJ).

Lloyd, C. (2010) *2008–09 Citizenship Survey Community Cohesion Topic Report* (London: DCLG).

Lofland, J. and Lofland, L.H. (1995) *Analysing Social Settings: A Guide to Qualitative Observation and Analysis* (3rd edn) (Belmont, CA: Wadsworth).

Loftus, B. (2008) 'Dominant Culture Interrupted: Recognition, Resentment and the Politics of Change in an English Police Force', *British Journal of Criminology* 48 (6): 756–77.

Lutze, F.E. and Murphy, D.W. (1999) 'Ultramasculine Prison Environments and Inmates' Adjustment: It's Time to Move beyond the Boys Will Be Boys Paradigm', *Justice Quarterly* 16(4): 709–33.

Macdonald, I. (1989) *Murder in the Playground: Report of the Macdonald Inquiry into Racism and Racial Violence in Manchester Schools* (London: New Beacon Books).

Macey, M. and Carling, A.H. (2011) *Ethnic, Racial and Religious Inequalities: The Perils of Subjectivity* (Basingstoke: Palgrave).

Macpherson, W. (1999) *The Stephen Lawrence Inquiry, Report of an Inquiry by Sir William Macpherson of Cluny*, Cm 4262–1 (London: Home Office).

Majors, R. and Mancini Billson, J. (1992) *Cool Pose: The Dilemmas of Black Manhood in America* (New York, NY: Lexington Books).

Mann, R. and Fenton, S. (2009) 'The Personal Contexts of National Sentiments', *Journal of Ethnic and Migration Studies* 35(4): 517–34.

Mares, D. (2001) 'Gangsta or Lager Louts? Working Class Street Gangs in Manchester', in M.W. Klein, H.-J. Kerner, C.L. Maxson and E.G.M. Weitekamp (eds), *The Eurogang Paradox: Street Gangs and Youth Groups in the U.S. and Europe* (Dordrecht: Kluwer Academic Publishers).

Marion Young, I. (1990) *Justice and the Politics of Difference* (Princeton, NJ: Princeton University Press).

Marsh, P. (1982) 'Rhetorics of Violence', in P. Marsh and A. Cambell (eds), *Aggression and Violence* (Oxford: Basil Blackwell).

Martel, J. and Brassard, R. (2008) 'Painting the Prison "Red": Constructing and Experiencing Aboriginal Identities in Prison', *British Journal of Social Work* 38(2): 340–61.

Maruna, S., Wilson, L., and Curran, K. (2006) 'Why God Is Often Found behind Bars: Prison Conversions and the Crisis of Self-Narrative', *Research in Human Development* 3(2/3): 161–84.

Mason, D. (2000) *Race and Ethnicity in Modern Britain* (Oxford: Oxford University Press).

Massey, D. (1985) 'Ethnic Residential Segregation: A Theoretical Synthesis and Empirical Review', *Sociology and Social Research* 69(3): 315–50.

Mauer, M. and King, R.S. (2007) *Uneven Justice: State Rates of Incarceration by Race and Ethnicity* (Washington, DC: The Sentencing Project).

McDermott, K. (1990) 'We Have No Problem: The Experience of Racism in Prison', *New Community* 16(2): 213–28.

McDowell, L. (2002) 'Masculine Discourses and Dissonances: Strutting "Lads", Protest Masculinity, and Domestic Responsibility', *Environment and Planning D: Society and Space* 20(1): 97–119.

McGhee, D. (2003) 'Moving to "Our" Common Ground—a Critical Examination of Community Cohesion Discourse in Twenty-First Century Britain', *The Sociological Review* 51(3): 376–404.

McGowen, R. (1995) 'The Well-Ordered Prison: England, 1780–1865', in N. Morris and D. Rothman, J. (eds), *The Oxford History of the Prison: The Practice of Punishment in Western Society* (Oxford: Oxford University Press).

Meeks, R. (2007) 'The Parenting Possible Selves of Young Fathers in Prison', *Psychology, Crime and Law* 13(4): 371–82.

Meeks, R. (2011) 'The Possible Selves of Young Fathers in Prison', *Journal of Adolescence* 34(5): 941–9.

Melossi, D., Pavarini, M., and Cousin, T.B.G. (1977) *The Prison and the Factory: Origins of the Penitentiary System* (London: Macmillan).

Meltzer, B.N. and Musolf, G.R. (2002) 'Resentment and Ressentiment', *Sociological Inquiry* 72(2): 240–55.

Mendieta, E. (2007) 'Penalized Spaces: The Ghetto as Prison and the Prison as Ghetto', *City* 11(3): 384–9.

Mercer, K. (1994) *Welcome to the Jungle: New Positions in Black Cultural Studies* (London: Routledge).

Messerschmidt, J.W. (1993) *Masculinities and Crime: Critique and Reconceptualisation of Theory* (Oxford: Rowan & Littlefield).

——, (2005) 'Men, Masculinities, and Crime', in M. Kimmel, S.J. Hearn, and R. Connell (eds), *Handbook of Studies on Men and Masculinities* (London: Sage).

Ministry of Justice (2009) *Children of Offenders Review* (London: MOJ).

——, (2011a) *Statistics on Race and the Criminal Justice System 2010* (London: Ministry of Justice).

——, (2011b) *Equalities Annual Report 2010–11* (London: MOJ).

Minton, R.J. (1971) *Inside Prison American* Style (New York, NY: Random House).

Moolman, B. (2011) 'Permeable Boundaries: Incarcerated, Sex Offender Masculinities in South Africa' (University of California: Unpublished PhD Thesis).

Moore, J.W. (1978) *Homeboys: Gangs, Drugs, and Prison in the Barrios of Los Angeles* (Philadelphia, PA: Temple University Press).

NACRO (2000) *Race: A Snapshot Survey* (London: NACRO).

Nandi, M. (2005/2002) 'Re/Constructing Black Masculinity in Prison', in D.M. Britton (ed.), *Gender and Prisons* (Aldershot: Ashgate).

Narey, M. (2001) 'Foreword' in Her Majesty's Prison Service *Annual Report & Accounts April 2000 to March* 2001. HC 29 (London: TSO).

Nayak, A. (2003) *Race, Place and Globalization: Youth Cultures in a Changing World* (Oxford: Berg).

——, (2005) 'White Lives', in K. Murji and J. Solomos (eds), *Racialization: Studies in Theory and Practice* (Oxford: Oxford University Press).

——, (2006) 'Displaced Masculinities: Chavs, Youth and Class in the Post-Industrial City', *Sociology* 40(5): 813–31.

Nelken, D. (2010) 'Denouncing the Penal State', *Criminology and Criminal Justice* 10(4): 331–40.

Newburn, T. (2010) 'Diffusion, Differentiation and Resistance in Comparative Penality', *Criminology and Criminal Justice* 10(4): 341–52.

Newton, C. (1994) 'Gender Theory and Prison Sociology: Using Theories of Masculinities to Interpret the Sociology of Prisons for Men', *Howard Journal of Criminal Justice* 33(3): 193–202.

NOMS (2008) *Race Review 2008: Implementing Race Equality in Prisons—Five Years On* (London: NOMS).

O'Donnell, I. (2007) 'Prison Rape in Context', *British Journal of Criminology* 44(2): 241–55.

——, M. and Sharpe, S. (2000) *Uncertain Masculinities: Youth, Ethnicity and Class in Contemporary Britain* (London: Routledge).

ONS (2009) *ONS Mid-2007 Ethnic Group Population Estimates. GLA Demography Update 11–2009* (London: GLA).

——, (2011a) *Integrated Household Survey April 2010 to March 2011: Experimental Statistics*, accessed 27 December 2012 <http://www.ons.gov.uk/ons/rel/integrated-household-survey/integrated-household-survey/april-2010-to-march-2011/stb-integrated-household-survey-april-2010-to-march-2011.html#tab-Religion>

——, (2011b) *Population Estimates by Ethnic Group 2002–2009* (London: ONS).

——, (2012) *Labour Market Status for Young People by Ethnicity, March 2012*. Released: 12 March 2012 (London: ONS).

Pearson, G. (1993) 'Foreword: Talking a Good Fight: Authenticity and Distance in the Ethnographer's Craft', in D. Hobbs and T. May (eds), *Interpreting the Field: Accounts of Ethnography* (Oxford: Clarendon Press).

——, (2011) 'Perpetual Novelty: Youth, Modernity and Historical Amnesia', in B. Goldson (ed.), *Youth in Crisis? Gang's, Territoriality and Violence* (London: Routledge).

Phillips, A. (2007) *Multiculturalism without Culture* (Princeton, NJ: Princeton University Press).

Phillips, C. (2007) 'Ethnicity, Identity and Community Cohesion in Prison', in M. Wetherell, M. Lafleche, and R. Berkeley (eds), *Identity, Ethnic Diversity and Community Cohesion* (London: Sage).

——, (2008) 'Negotiating Identities: Ethnicity and Social Relations in a Young Offenders' Institution', *Theoretical Criminology* 12(3): 313–31.

——, (2011) 'Institutional Racism and Ethnic Inequalities: An Expanded Multilevel Framework', *Journal of Social Policy* 40(1): 173–92.

——, (2012) '"It Ain't Nothing Like America with the Bloods and the Crips": Gang Narratives inside Two English Prisons', *Punishment and Society* 14(1): 51–68.

——, and Bowling, B. (2012) 'Ethnicity, Racism, Crime and Criminal Justice', in M. Maguire, R. Morgan, and R. Reiner (eds), *The Oxford Handbook of Criminology* (5th edn) (Oxford: Oxford University Press).

Phillips, C. and Earle, R. (2010) 'Reading Difference Differently: Identity, Epistemology, and Prison Ethnography', *British Journal of Criminology* 50(2): 360–78.

Phillips, D. (2006) 'Parallel Lives? Challenging Discourses of British Muslim Self-Segregation', *Environment and Planning D: Society and Space* 24(1): 25–40.

Phillips, T. (2005) 'After 7/7: Sleepwalking to Segregation', Speech to the Manchester Council for Community Relations, 22 September 2005.

Phoenix, A. (1998) 'Multiculture, Multiracisms and Young People', *Soundings* 10 (Autumn): 86–96.

——, (2010) 'Ethnicities', in M. Wetherell and C.T. Mohanty (eds), *The Sage Handbook of Identities* (London: Sage).

Picca, L.H. and Feagin, J.R. (2007) *Two-Faced Racism: Whites in the Backstage and Frontstage* (New York, NY: Routledge).

Pilkington, H. and Johnson, R. (2003) 'Peripheral Youth: Relations of Identity and Power in Global/Local Context', *European Journal of Cultural Studies* 6(3): 259–83.

Pini, B. (2005) 'Interviewing Men: Gender and the Collection and Interpretation of Qualitative Data', *Journal of Sociology* 41(2): 201–16.

Plummer, K. (2005) 'Male Sexualities', in M. Kimmel, S.J. Hearn, and R. Connell (eds), *Handbook of Studies on Men and Masculinities* (Thousand Oaks, CA: Sage).

Poole, E.D. and Regoli, R.M. (1980) 'Race, Institutional Rule Breaking, and Disciplinary Response: A Study of Discretionary Decision Making in Prison', *Law and Society Review* 14(4): 931–46.

Prison Reform Trust (2007) *Bromley Briefings Prison Factfile* (London: PRT).

Ralphs, R., Medina, J., and Aldridge, J. (2009) 'Who Needs Enemies with Friends Like These? The Importance of Place for Young People Living in Known Gang Areas', *Journal of Youth Studies* 12(5): 483–500.

Rampton, B. and Harris, R. (2009) 'Ethnicity without Guarantees', in M. Wetherell (ed.), *Identity in the 21st Century: New Trends in Changing Times* (Basingstoke: Palgrave).

Rattansi, A. (2005) 'The Uses of Racialization: The Time-Spaces and Subject-Objects of the Raced Body', in K. Murji and J. Solomos (eds), *Racialization: Studies in Theory and Practice* (Oxford: Oxford University Press).

——, (2007) *Racism: A Very Short Introduction* (Oxford: Oxford University Press).

Ray, L., Smith, D.A., and Wastell, L. (2004) 'Shame, Rage and Racist Violence', *British Journal of Criminology* 44(3): 350–68.

Reiner, R. (1998) 'Copping a Plea', in S. Holdaway and P. Rock (eds), *Thinking about Criminology* (London: UCL Press).

——, (2007) *Law and Order: An Honest Citizen's Guide to Crime and Control* (Cambridge: Polity).

Reissman, C.K. (1993) *Narrative Analysis. Qualitative Research Methods Series 30* (London: Sage).

Reynolds, T. (2009) 'Exploring the Absent/Present Dilemma: Black Fathers, Family Relationships, and Social Capital in Britain', *The Annals of the American Academy of Political and Social Science* 624(1): 12–28.

Rhodes, J. (2010) 'White Backlash, "Unfairness" and Justifications of British National Party (BNP) Support', *Ethnicities* 10(1): 77–99.

Richards, M., McWilliams, B., Batten, N., Cameron, C., and Cutler, J. (1995) 'Foreign Nationals in English Prisons: I. Family Ties and Their Maintenance', *The Howard Journal* 34(2): 158–75.

Riis, J.A. (1902) *The Children of the Poor* (New York, NY: C. Scribner's Sons).

Rios, V.M. (2009) 'The Consequences of the Criminal Justice Pipeline on Black and Latino Masculinity', *Annals of the American Academy of Political and Social Science* 623(1): 150–62.

Robertson, J.E. (2008) 'Foreword: Separate but Equal in Prison: Johnson V. California and Common Sense Racism Supreme Court Review', *Journal of Criminal Law and Criminology* 96(3): 795–848.

Robins, D. and Cohen, P. (1978) *Knuckle Sandwich: Growing up in the Working-Class City* (Harmondsworth: Penguin).

Rogaly, B. and Taylor, B. (2009) '"I Don't Wanted to Be Classed, but We Are All Classed": Making Liveable Lives across Generations', in M. Wetherell (ed.), *Identity in the 21st Century: New Trends in Changing Times* (Basingstoke: Palgrave).

Rusche, G. and Kirchheimer, O. (1939) *Punishment and Social Structure* (New York, NY: Columbia University Press).

Rutter, J. and Lattore, M. (2009) 'Migration, Migrants and Inequality', in J. Hills, T. Sefton, and K. Stewart (eds), *Towards a More Equal Society? New Labour, Poverty, Inequality and Exclusion* (Bristol: Policy Press).

Sabo, D. (2001) 'Doing Time, Doing Masculinity: Sports and Prison', in D. Sabo, T.A. Kupers, and W. London (eds), *Prison Masculinities* (Philadelphia, PA: Temple University Press).

Sabol, W.J., West, H.C., and Cooper, M. (2009) *Correctional Populations in the United States, 2008* (Washington, DC: US Department of Justice).

Sainsbury, D. (2006) 'Immigrants' Social Rights in Comparative Perspective: Welfare Regimes, Forms in Immigration and Immigration Policy Regimes', *Journal of European Social Policy* 16(3): 229–44.

Sallee, M.W. and Harris III, F. (2011) 'Gender Performance in Qualitative Studies of Masculinities', *Qualitative Inquiry* 11(4): 409–29.

Salter, M. and Tomsen, S. (2012) 'Violence and Carceral Masculinities in Felony Fights', *British Journal of Criminology* 52(2): 309–23.

Scarman, L. (1981) *The Scarman Report. The Brixton Disorders, 10–12 April 1981* (London: HMSO).

Scheler, M. (1913/1994) *Ressentiment* (translated by Lewis B. Coser and William W. Holdheim) (Milwaukee, WI: Marquette University Press).

Schmid, T. and Jones, R. (1991) 'Suspended Identity: Identity Transformation in a Maximum Security Prison', *Symbolic Interaction* 14(4): 415–32.

Schwaebe, C. (2005) 'Learning to Pass: Sex Offenders' Strategies for Establishing a Viable Identity in the Prison General Population', *International Journal of Offender Therapy and Comparative Criminology* 49(6): 614–25.

Schwalbe, M. and Wolkomir, M. (2001) 'The Masculine Self as Problem and Resource in Interview Studies of Men', *Men and Masculinities* 4(1): 90–103.

Seaton, G. (2007) 'Toward a Theoretical Understanding of Hypermasculine Coping among Urban Black Adolescent Males', *Journal of Human Behavior in the Social Environment* 15(2/3): 367–90.

Seidler, V.J. (2006) *Transforming Masculinities: Men, Culture, Bodies, Power, Sex and Love* (London: Routledge).

Sewell, T. (1997) *Black Masculinities and Schooling: How Black Boys Survive Modern Schooling* (London: Trentham Books).

Shabazz, R. (2009) 'So High You Can't Get over It, So Low You Can't Get under It: Carceral Spatiality and Black Masculinities in the United States and South Africa', *Souls* 11(3): 276–94.

Sharma, S., Hutnyk, J., and Sharma, A. (1996) *Dis-Orienting Rhythms: The Politics of the New Asian Dance Music* (London: Zed Books).

Sim, J. (1994) 'Tougher Than the Rest? Men in Prison', in T. Newburn and E. Stanko (eds), *Just Boys Doing Business?: Men, Masculinities and Crime* (London: Routledge).

Simon, J. (2000) 'The "Society of Captives" in the Era of Hyper-Incarceration', *Theoretical Criminology* 4(3): 285–308.

——, (2007) *Governing through Crime: How the War on Crime Transformed American Democracy and Created a Culture of Fear. Studies in Crime and Public Policy* (New York, NY: Oxford University Press).

Simpson, L. (2007) 'Ghettos of the Mind: The Empirical Behaviour of Indices of Segregation and Diversity', *Journal of the Royal Statistical Society* A170(2): 405–24.

Skeggs, B. (2004) *Class, Self, Culture* (London: Routledge).

Small, M.L. (2007) 'Is There Such a Thing as "the Ghetto"? The Perils of Assuming that the South Side of Chicago Represents Poor Black Neighbourhoods', *City* 11(3): 413–21.

Social Exclusion Unit (2002) *Reducing Re-Offending by Ex-Prisoners* (London: Social Exclusion Unit).

Solomos, J., Findlay, B., Jones, S., and Gilroy, P. (1982) 'The Organic Crisis of British Capitalism and Race: The Experience of the Seventies', in CCCS (ed.), *The Empire Strikes Back: Race and Racism in 70s Britain* (London: Hutchinson in association with the Centre for Contemporary Cultural Studies).

Spalek, B. and El-Hassan, S. (2007) 'Muslim Converts in Prison', *The Howard Journal* 46(2): 99–114.

Sparks, R., Bottoms, A., and Hay, W. (1996) *Prisons and the Problem of Order* (Oxford: Oxford University Press).

Spellers, R.E. and Moffitt, K.R. (2010) *Blackberries and Redbones: Critical Articulations in Black Hair/Body Politics in Africana Communities* (Cresskill, NJ: Hamton Press).

St Louis, B. (2009) 'On the Necessity and the "Impossibility" of Identities', *Cultural Studies* 23(4): 559–82.

Stampp, K.M. (1956) *The Peculiar Institution: Slavery in the Ante-Bellum South* (New York, NY: Alfred A Knopf).

Stewart, D. (2008) *The Problems and Needs of Newly Sentenced Prisoners: Results from a National Survey* (London: MOJ).

Swain, J. (2002) 'The Resources and Strategies Boys Use to Establish Status in a Junior School without Competitive Sport', *Discourse: Studies in the Cultural Politics of Education* 23(1): 1–17.

Sykes, G.M. (1958) *The Society of Captives: A Study of a Maximum Security Prison* (Princeton, NJ: Princeton University Press).

Sykes, G.M. and Messinger, S.L. (1960) 'The Inmate Social System', in R.A. Cloward, D.R. Cressey, G.H. Grosser, R. McCleery, S.L. Messinger, L.E. Ohlin, and G.M. Sykes (eds), *Theoretical Studies in the Social Organization of the Prison* (New York, NY: Social Science Research Council).

Taylor, C. (2003) 'The Politics of Recognition', in J. Stone and R. Dennis (eds), *Race and Ethnicity: Comparative and Theoretical Approaches* (Oxford: Blackwell).

Taylor, D. (2010) 'Structured Communications in Prison: A Project to Achieve More Consistent Performance and Fairer Outcomes for Staff and Prisoners', *Prison Service Journal* 191: 24–6.

Thomas, C.W., Petersen, D.M., and Zingraff, R.M. (1978) 'Structural and Social Psychological Correlates of Prisonization', *Criminology* 16(3): 383–93.

Thrasher, F. (1927) *The Gang* (Chicago, IL: University of Chicago Press).

Thurston, R. (1996) 'Are You Sitting Comfortably? Men's Storytelling, Masculinities, Prison Culture and Violence', in M. Mac An Ghaill (ed.), *Understanding Masculinities: Social Relations and Cultural Arenas* (Buckingham: Open University Press).

Toch, H. (1998) 'Hypermasculinity and Prison Violence. Masculinities and Violence', in L. Bowker (ed.), *Masculinities and Violence* (Thousand Oaks, CA: Sage).

Tolson, A. (1977) *The Limits of Masculinity* (London: Routledge).

Tonry, M. (1994) 'Racial Disproportion in US Prisons', *British Journal of Criminology* 34 (Special Issue): 97–115.

——, (1997) *Ethnicity, Crime and Immigration* (London: University of Chicago Press).

Trulson, C.R. and Marquart, J.W. (2002a) 'The Caged Melting Pot: Toward an Understanding of the Consequences of Desegregation in Prisons', *Law and Society Review* 36(4): 743–81.

——, and Marquart, J.W. (2002b) 'Inmate Racial Integration: Achieving Racial Integration in the Texas Prison System', *Prison Journal* 82(4): 498–525.

——, Marquart, J.W., Hemmens, C., and Carroll, L. (2008) 'Racial Desegregation in Prisons', *The Prison Journal* 88(2): 270–99.

Twine, F.W. (2000) 'Racial Ideologies and Racial Methodologies', in F.W. Twine and J.W. Warren (eds), *Racing Research, Researching Race: Methodological Dilemmas in Critical Race Studies* (New York, NY: New York University Press).

Tyler, T.R. (2010) '"Legitimacy in Corrections": Policy Implications', *Criminology and Public Policy* 9(1): 127–34.

Ugelvik, T. (2011) 'The Hidden Food: Mealtime Resistance and Identity Work in a Norwegian Prison', *Punishment and Society* 13(1): 47–63.

Uggen, C., Manza, J., and Behrens, A. (2004) '"Less Than the Average Citizen": Stigma, Role Transition and the Civic Reintegration of Convicted Felons', in S. Maruna (ed.), *After Crime and Punishment: Pathways to Offender Reintegration* (Cullompton: Willan Publishing).

US Census Bureau (2005) *Population Profile of the United States: Dynamic Version - Race and Hispanic Origin in 2005.* <http://www.census.gov/population/pop-profile/dynamic/RACEHO.pdf>

Wacquant, L. (1999) '"Suitable Enemies": Foreigners and Immigrants in the Prisons of Europe', *Punishment and Society* 1(2): 215–22.

——, (2001) 'Deadly Symbiosis: When Ghetto and Prison Meet and Mesh', in D. Garland (ed.), *Mass Imprisonment: Social Causes and Consequences* (London: Sage).

——, (2002) 'The Curious Eclipse of Prison Ethnography in the Age of Mass Incarceration', *Ethnography* 3(4): 371–97.

——, (2006) 'Penalization, Depoliticization, Racialization: On the over-Incarceration of Immigrants in the European Union', in S. Armstrong and L. McAra (eds), *Perspectives on Punishment: The Contours of Control* (Oxford: Oxford University Press).

——, (2008) *Urban Outcasts: A Comparative Sociology of Advanced Marginality* (Cambridge: Polity).

——, (2009a) *Punishing the Poor: The Neoliberal Government of Social Insecurity* (Durham, NC: Duke University Press).

——, (2009b) *Prisons of Poverty* (Minneapolis, MN: University of Minnesota Press).

Wahab, A. (2005) 'Consuming Narratives: Questioning Authority and the Politics of Representation in Social Science Research', in G. Dei, J. Sefa, and G.S. Johal (eds), *Critical Issues in Anti-Racist Research Methodologies* (New York, NY: Peter Lang Publishing).

Walker, S., Spohn, C., and DeLone, M. (2004) *The Color of Justice: Race, Ethnicity, and Crime in America* (2nd edn) (Belmont, CA: Wadsworth).

Ware, V. (2008) 'Towards a Sociology of Resentment: A Debate on Class and Whiteness', *Sociological Research Online* 13(5): <http://www.socresonline.org.uk/13/15/19.htm>.

Weber, L. and Bowling, B. (2004) 'Policing Migration: A Framework for Investigating the Regulation of Global Mobility', *Policing and Society* 14(3): 195–212.

West, C. and Zimmerman, D. (1987) 'Doing Gender', *Gender and Society* 1(2): 125–51.

Western, B. and Beckett, K. (1999) 'How Unregulated is the U.S. Labor Market? The Penal System as a Labor Market Institution', *The American Journal of Sociology* 104(4): 1030–60.

Wetherell, M. and Edley, N. (1999) 'Negotiating Hegemonic Masculinity: Imaginary Positions and Psycho-Discursive Practices', *Feminism and Psychology* 9(3): 335–56.

Wilson, D. (2003) '"Keeping Quiet" or "Going Nuts": Some Emerging Strategies Used by Young Black People in Custody at a Time of Childhood Being Re-Constructed', *Howard Journal of Criminal Justice* 42(5): 411–25.

Wilson, W.J. (1987) *The Truly Disadvantaged: The Inner City, the Underclass, and Public Policy* (Chicago, IL: The University of Chicago Press).

Wolff, N. and Shi, J. (2011) 'Patterns of Victimization and Feelings of Safety inside Prison: The Experience of Male and Female Inmates', *Crime and Delinquency* 57(1): 29–55.

Wood, M., Hales, J., Purdon, S., Sejersen, T., and Hayllar, O. (2009) *A Test for Racial Discrimination in Recruitment Practice in British Cities. Research Report No 607* (London: DWP).

Wright, K.N. (1989) 'Race and Economic Marginality in Explaining Prison Adjustment', *Journal of Research in Crime and Delinquency* 26(1): 67–89.

Young, J. (1999) *The Exclusive Society: Social Exclusion in Crime and Difference in Late Modernity* (London: Sage).

——, (2009) 'Moral Panic: Its Origins in Resistance, Ressentiment and the Translation of Fantasy into Reality', *British Journal of Criminology* 49(1): 4–16.

——, (2011) *The Criminological Imagination* (Cambridge: Polity).

Yuval-Davis, N. and Kaptani, E. (2009) 'Performing Identities: Participatory Theatre among Refugees', in M. Wetherell (ed.), *Theorizing Identities and Social Action* (Basingstoke: Palgrave).

Ziersch, A.M., Gallaher, G., Baum, F., and Bentley, M. (2011) 'Responding to Racism: Insights on How Racism Can Damage Health from an Urban Study of Australian Aboriginal People', *Social Science and Medicine* 73(7): 1045–53.

Index